TO FIGHT FOR MY COUNTRY, SIR!

MEMOIRS OF A 19 YEAR OLD B-17 NAVIGATOR SHOT DOWN IN NAZI GERMANY AND IMPRISONED IN THE WWII "GREAT "ESCAPE" PRISON CAMP

DONALD E. CASEY

ISBN: 1448669871
ISBN-13: 978-1448669875
Library of Congress Control Number: 2009940436

Cover Design Copyright ©2009 Donald E. Casey.
Graphic Design and Layout: Ellen Hartwell Alderman
Photo Selection: Tim Anderson

Public Relations/Publicity:
STERLING COOPER PUBLISHING DIVISION
Chicago, IL 60611
www.sterlingcooper.info

Order from: www.Amazon.com

Donald E. Casey email:

doncasey@mail2world.com

websites:

www.doncasey.info

www.tofightformycountrysir.info

DEDICATION

To: My late father and mother, J. Douglas Casey and
Virginia Smith Casey, and to my late Uncle Emmett M. Casey,
whose name I bear; to the members of the Lew Jolls and Steve
King B-17 air crews with whom I flew a total of 28 combat
missions in World War II over France, Germany and Poland
in 1944 with the 379th Bomb Group (Heavy); and to my
fellow prisoners of war of Room 5, Block 135 of Stalag Luft
III, Sagan, Poland and Stalag VII-A, Moosberg, Germany. To
Valleau Wilkie, sole surviving fellow-cellmate at Luft III. Also
in memory of Anne Hollis Casey and to our sons, Dr. Don, Jr.,
Brian D., Jerome D and Matthew J. Casey. Also, Ralph G. Scheu
who has celebrated author's first and only parachute jump on
the appointed date for many years. A special mention of Mrs.
Alice Rae Casey who energized (read "bullied") the author into
writing this book and to my two grandchildren, Hollis Anne
Casey and Keenan Casey. Finally, to Col. Steven King, USAF,
ret., aircraft commander of the B-17 "GI Jane" on its last flight
who blames the author for not giving him a better course to
avoid the German anti-aircraft guns (the author likewise blames
him for not zigzagging) and my good friend and fellow 379th
BG navigator, Jack Sinise, whose place I took on my disastrous
last mission and whose resulting debt to me for doing so is now
forgiven at long last.

Donald Emmett Casey, Sr. J.D. DFC

TABLE OF CONTENTS

ACKNOWLEDGMENTS

Peter Copeland, Managing Editor, Scripps-Howard News Services

The late Bruce Felknor, former editor of Encyclopedia Brittanica

Mary Grey Kay

Merriam Leeke and Neal Vanover

Michael Piontek, Esquire

SPECIAL MENTION:

Tim Anderson of Chicago, artist in charge of photo selections
and Ellen Hartwell Alderman, Graphic Design and Digital Imaging.

INTRODUCTION

It is true that wars must be fought by the young and adventurous as I was at 18 years of age. The truism is that to engage in a struggle with a deadly enemy, one has to feel invulnerable, be old enough to know better but be determined to prove his mettle. Combat is a deadly serious business but also the highest form of adventure - at least until it sinks in that the enemy is shooting back with real bullets.

There was a kind of a transformation for me on entering active duty with the United States Army. Yesterday I was a baby-faced, 18 year old kid and today I am a soldier.

A New York Times book reviewer in 1994 criticized books about war for failing to tell how it feels so the reader can better appreciate the experiences in the story. This became the goal in writing my story to try to bring the reader along with me starting with the day I volunteered to be an aviation cadet through basic training and 6 month's of aerial navigation instruction and finally in combat in a war the outcome of which was a matter of my country's national survival.

I wrote letters to the family throughout my Army service. My dear mother saved every one I wrote and they are offered as an integral part of this book. They expressed my youthful enthusiasm for what I was doing without dwelling on my mortality. I tried to tell my mother and father what was going on in my life while leaving out any negative thoughts. I did not want to worry them and therefore tempered my language with positive thoughts. I could not tell them how it felt to put my neck in the noose of mortal combat flying day after day. I was humorous when it was appropriate and told of spending "D-Day" in London on pass as a decoy while others were fighting and dying. I sent home contemporaneous British newspaper clippings about the air war which detailed our struggle. When I became "hors de combat" in the Great Escape Camp in Germany, it was up to the

Army and the International Red Cross to bring the bitter news of my going missing with the obvious overlay of my possible demise.

The naivete of my youth is apparent in the letters. The reader should keep in mind my very young age and lack of maturity for the heavy responsibility given to me. I was learning about death before I had any understanding about life. To young readers I offer my story as an example of the capability they have to reach for - as I did - and take on fully adult responsibilities that appear beyond their ken. I never sold myself short. Don't you do so, either.

My favorite (and only) grandson, Keenan G. Casey, age 13, once asked me if I had ever been shot at in the war. My reply was: "hundreds of times." In order that he not think this was an exaggeration, I explained that the targets we bombed had hundreds of cannons pointing up in the sky at our planes. These guns could be reloaded, re-sighted and fired again and again very quickly.

My Bombardier, Lt. Jack Ellenberger, and I sat in the nose compartment of the B-17 named "Hells Belle" and watched the enemy's flak shells exploding around us and in the air up ahead at very close range. We held our positions on our bomb runs as the plane flew a straight and level course until the bombs were dropped on the target . The average bomb run lasted about 8 minutes. If you will just look at your watch and see how long the second hand takes to get all the way around, you can get the feeling I had and how eight minutes (an average bomb run) would seem to take forever. This short a time could seem like a lifetime to us who were doing the flying on bombing missions. The longest bomb run I ever flew was 13 minutes. In that length of time the German gunners inevitably sharpened their aim. The cost in men and planes went up with each minute flying straight and level in range of those guns.

My story starts in the middle with the arrival of the dreaded telegram from the Army Air Force that I was missing in action and the effects it had on my loved ones at home. Friends and relatives sent condolences of hope for my survival. Families of crew members who were killed in action wrote heart breaking letters to my folks of hopes that were dashed and the agony of the delay in waiting end-lessly for the final word that their son had been died that day.

I tell of my father's older brother, the uncle I never knew, Emmett M. Casey, who was killed in action in France in World War One on August 8, 1918. I have included Emmett's final letters to his parents and an eye-witness' report on his last battle. This memory and the fateful telegram about my plight caused special anguish to my father. Later, joy replaced desperation with the news of my being a prisoner of war and kept hope alive for my safe return.

Following my capture, I was questioned by interrogators. My first prison was the now famous "Great Escape" camp, Stalag Luft III, in German occupied western Poland. ("Stalag" is an abbreviation for "Stammlager" or permanent camp. The word "Luft" denoted that the prisoners were Airmen. An offficers' prison camp was an "Oflag" and a naval camp was a "Marlag.") 10,000 American and British fly-ing officers were being held there in the little town of Sagan behind double barriers of barbed wire and under 24 hour armed guard with orders to shoot to kill any prisoner stepping over what I call the dead man's wire. The summer months of 1944 were hopeful and tolerable as long as we had food brought in by the International Red Cross. That state of things would change and worsen as fall and winter drew nigh.

POW morale ebbed and flowed depending on the news of the war on two fronts. At least we knew that the Invasion of Nor-mandy, France was successful. Our hopes for early liberation defi-nitely waned with the news of the Germany's last desperate effort in December 1944 to dislodge the Allied Forces and recapture the port of Antwerp, Belgium in the "Battle of the Bulge." Our rations at Sta-lag Luft III were cut in half in September. News of Russian Army advances was encouraging until January 27, 1945. Hitler personally ordered our evacuation to prevent us from being freed by Russian forces. We were to be held as hostages for a possible truce with the Allied leadership or shot. They marched 10,000 of us westward in a blizzard in temperatures well below zero to the sounds of Russian cannons less than 20 miles away.

The story of this terrible winter march has been told many times. It was reported to be the worst winter in 25 years. This kind of violence to our persons was clearly contrary to the Geneva Convention. We prisoners started out on a snow-packed road in a driving blizzard at temperatures of 10 to 15 below zero. Many men suffered permanent injury from frostbite over the course of 60 miles. Prisoners from other camps were made to walk much farther. From there, unmarked freight cars built for 40 passenger, held 50 of us squeezed into each car of our long train. We took turns sitting down for lack of room. It was a long and painful journey but we finally reached another POW camp named Stalag VII-A in Moosburg, Germany northeast of Munich, Germany. Our arrival raised the prison population to 110,000. That number later increased to 130,000.

Stalag VII-A had been designed originally for 40,000 captives. Living conditions were worse than anything any of us had experienced. and we began to starve on miserable rations of inedible vegetables of unknown origin. Red Cross food was next to nil. No matter how long one had been a prisoner behind the wire, the winter march and this camp was the very worst part of the entire imprisonment for American POW's. By their conscious neglect, our captors inflicted pain, suffering, starvation and flea-ridden misery on each one and every of us without lifting a finger. There were simply too many of us to be singled out for other kinds of physical abuse.

I also tell of my high school days and senior year in 1941-1942 when World War II broke out with the Japanese attack on Pearl Harbor, Hawaii of December 7, 1941. I was still 11 months short of the age of majority waiting to join up. After my 18th birthday in November 1942, I volunteered for the Aviation Cadet program offered by the Army Air Corps (there was no separate "Air Force" until after the war.) The call to active duty came in early February 1943.

I tell of basic training and then the short six month course for aerial navigators. My commission as a second lieutenant occurred two weeks before my 19th birthday on October 23, 1943.. I wasn't the youngest lieutenant ever but perhaps one of the youngest. I looked it, too.

After training in 4-motor B-17s, my new crew and I flew a new ship across the Atlantic Ocean to Great Britain putting all my navigation skills to the test for the first time for keeps . We were assigned to the 379th Bomb Group (Heavy) in Kimbolton, which was located in the Midlands north of London, England.

Heavy bombers of the 8th Air Force in 1944 were being escorted for longer and longer distances by the new, long-range American P-51 Mustang fighter. The previous May of 1943 when our Group first started flying, it did so without fighter escort. That year, losses of men and aircraft bordered on prohibitive. By the spring of 1944, the survival "rate" had improved considerably because of increases in planes and crews. Luck was still very much a factor.

Our combat leadership in Europe learned by late 1943 that the B-17's moniker, "Flying Fortress", was an opinion, not necessarily a fact. It's crew manned thirteen 50 caliber machine guns capable of firing in all directions around the c lock and up and down carrying up to a mile. 36 ships flying in tight formations were supposed to present an impenetrable wall of machine gun bullets that no fighter would challenge. Proof of the truth was in the flying and fighting.

In the late summer and fall of 1943, the vulnerability of B-17 and B-24 airplanes against swarms of fast enemy fighter planes was made manifest. On two unescorted raids by our bombers to Schweinfurt, Germany to destroy vital ball bearing factories there, losses were horrific and unacceptable. The first such mission in August cost the 8th Air Force 60 bombers and 600 airmen. The second Schweinfurt mission in October met the same level of resistance from the Germans and virtually the same number of planes and crew were lost.

A loss rate of 20% per sortie could not be sustained. Trips to targets beyond France were temporarily curtailed. Royal Air Force Spitfires which had won the "Battle of Britain" in 1940 could not fly much farther than the French Coast before turning back to be refueled. Detachable "belly" gas tanks were not yet available. The bitter conclusion was that the 8th Air Force could not conduct serious strategic bombing without an effective long range fighter escort.

Back in "the States" the resourceful North American Aviation Company was making preparations to launch what became known as the P-51 Mustang fighter. The airplane went through many design changes but finally was tested to fligh higher and faster than any known enemy fighter. Superchargers were required for high altitudes of up to 30,000 feet. The available engines lacked sufficient power. With the cooperation of the British, their liquid-cooled Rolls-Royce Merlin engine was selected as the power plant of choice enabling speeds of up to 350 miles per hour at top levels of bombing.

By February of 1944, my era, P 51's manned by experienced American pilots were available to escort our long range bombers over Germany and beyond. Sightings of the best fighter America made flying in substantial numbers in the vicinity of the capitol city of Berlin were admitted by Reich's Marshall Herman Goering, the Commander of the Luftwaffe to be the signal for Germany's defeat. He had promised the Fuhrer Adolph Hitler that no enemy plane would ever penetrate into German Air Space. The truth was to the contrary.

The British Royal Air Force had extensive experience against the Germans going back to 1939 and the Battle of Britain. Our allies tried their best to convince the Americans that daylight bombing was not feasible. They had already tried and failed at it while suffering horrendous losses of their obsolete planes. They switched to night bombing with their planes flying in train to targets already lighted up for them by fast, "pathfinder" Mosquito bombers dropping markers around the targets. The Luftwaffe countered that idea with well trained "Nacht Jaegd Flieger" pilots and procedures for directing them to the bomber streams. The enemy developed effective night fighter strength and the RAF made its bomber crews bring back photos of their targets to certify completion of each mission.

The independent-minded leaders of Germany's Werhmacht

(Army) and Luftwaffe (air force) finally were able to recognize that the war could not be won. Germany did not have the resources to keep up with America's overwhelming manufacturing capacity.

The Fuhrer, Adolph Hitler, had taken control of every aspect of the Armed Forces so that no one else had the power or the will to stand up against him. His amateurish, micro-management of all military tactics and strategy actually benefited the allies. His order to his troops to stand fast and never surrender at Stalingrad and in other battles with the Russians cost his nation of over a million troops, captured, wounded or killed. When Germany made the world's first jet fighter, the Messerschmitt #262, Hitler wanted these planes equipped for bombing for purposes of retaliation. A potentially winning weapon was thus diverted according to his whim and was available in only limited numbers. By the end of the war Allied Air Supremacy made it impossible for the enemy to fight back any longer or even take off to attack our forces.

Yet, the outcome of the war in Europe was never a given. The view in Europe by 1945 was that the allies were lucky in suppressing Germany's ability to fight..The Nazi's had scientists and technicians working overtime for its side, too. These brilliant men were charged with building "wonder weapons" such as short and medium range missiles carrying 2,000 pounds of explosives - the V1's and the V2's. (The "V" stood for "Vertailung" or revenge.) These weapons were fired at London and other large cities and installations in England. Germany's jet airplane in sufficient numbers could have defeated the 8th Air Force and all its bombers and fighter planes. The only way to beat them was with overwhelming fighter and bomber strength which the Allies finally had by 1945.

Luftwaffe Generals and "experten" flying aces were so taken with this super-weapon that they pleaded with Hitler to turn out as many jets as possible. But the Fuhrer had his mind focused on the morale of his people and already had set 1 million men and boys to manning thousands of powerful anti-aircraft guns defending Germany's bigger cities. Even without the Me-262, the Luftwaffe was shooting down too many Allied planes but the number of our bombers attacking day and night kept growing. The tally of planes we lost in 1944 was high but the percentage of planes shot down per mission was declining. Our bomber forces grew daily. By mid-1944 and 1945 over two thousand Heavies were available for bombing missions.

I remember my personal air war like it was a black and white movie. Perhaps that's why the 1949 movie "Twelve O'clock High", starring Gregory Peck is one of my personal favorites. In the mid 1960's, I met retired Air Force General Frank Armstrong whose storied career as commander of the 306th Bomb Group was depicted in that film, including his virtual mental breakdown. (In the picture, Peck's Group was called "the 918th" - 306 x 3.) I also met POW's from the 306th Bomb group who flew with Armstrong and had nothing good to say about him, there were too many second passes or "go-arounds" over some of the worst targets which got many of them shot down.

Hitler's grand strategy in 1939 is said to have been to conquer France, Belgium and the Netherlands and then conquer or make peace with England.. In 1941, Germany stood astride Western Europe and also occupied Norway and Denmark and North Africa. Germany had signed a 100 year mutual defense treaty with the Soviets but in no time Hitler launched a massive attack (Operation Barbarosa) against Russia. His Blitzkrieg-programmed Panzer (tank) Corps and fast moving armies cut through opposing defenses at will capturing hundreds of thousands of troops and huge areas of Western Russia covering all the way to the suburbs of Moscow. But Germany failed to plan for the terrible Russian winters and for staged withdrawals to prevent encirclements.

Under Joseph Stalin's absolute dictatorship beginning in the 1920's, the country's intelligentsia and most of the experienced military leaders were executed or imprisoned. In addition, the Communist economy could not sustain the necessary preparations for a war with Germany. What Soviet armed forces the Russians had were ill trained and lacked the structure, machinery and organization to defend the nation. Their air force consisted of bi-planes and similar antiques of aviation. The result was a slaughter. The top German air ace on the Eastern Front, Eric Hartmann, personally shot down 352 planes, a virtual air force, in the course of 1500+ missions. (German pilots flew until they couldn't fly any more, meaning until they died. America had many times more planes and pilots who were equally skilled and courageous.)

Russia was well on its way to defeat until America stepped up and became its arsenal of war materials including airplanes, trucks and tanks. Without America's help and its vital supplies, Stalin could have lost that war. So why did Hitler ever attack Russia in the first place? The Soviet Communist regime was failing, obviously. On the other hand, it is reasonable to speculate that unless the Fuhrer kept the war and foreign conquests going he might well have been overthrown. His decisive land victories in the West and the surrender of France and the Netherlands belied Germany's weaknesses such as the lack of resources in such basic materials as oil and rubber Add to that, his ignorance of military tactics and strategy would eventually cost the nation whole armies including a Field Marshall in the battle of Stalingrad defending monstrously extended battle lines. Hitler had never read military history and therefore made no plans for the sensible withdrawal of troops when realities of war dictated.

The Allied invasion of France on "D-Day" June 6, 1944 sealed Germany's defeat at the cost of millions of lives. Fascism was a structural failure just as is communism. The only real difference between the two infamous systems was that Hitler's version of fascism purported to allow the people their right to private property and the private sector. The word "private" is used advisedly. In the end the Nazi's had total control of everything the nation possessed including the people all the way down to the country's youth who were forced into the fighting toward the end and lost their lives in battles they could not win. Still, today, fascism is deemed more of a bete' noire than communism as though there ever was anything good about either system. Both regimes can be credited with tyranny and human slaughter on a scale never before seen or imagined in world history. May a curse be on both their houses.

My book ends as I am graduating from college to take my place in the world of business and ultimately the professional life of a trial lawyer for over 50 years.

Looking forward from 2009 it is apparent that America is going to have to continue to keep its guard up at all times and be prepared to engage and repel enemies of liberty and freedom wherever they are around the world.

CHAPTER 1:

THE TELEGRAM

A telegram dated June 28, 1944 came addressed to my mother, Mrs. Virginia Casey, 100 West Monroe St. Chicago, Illinois. It said:

> **"The secretary of war desires me to express his deep regret   that your son Second Lt. Donald E. Casey has been reported missing in action since Eighteenth June over Germany. If further details or other information are received, you will be promptly notified."**

> **It was signed: "Ulio, the Adjutant General."**

My younger brother Dick, age 15, was staying with my mother's sister, Aunt Babe, for the summer in Maywood, IL because dad had rented out our house in nearby River Forest while he was in the service. About that time the folks were just arriving home from Florida where dad was stationed in the U. S. Army Air Force Training Command. As Dick tells the story, aunt Babe, received the telegram in Mother's absence. When the folks arrived back in Chicago, they were staying in a suite at the Morrison Hotel at Madison and Clark Street downtown adjoining the old First National Bank Building. She wanted to get word to them about me and Dick was going to take the telegram downtown in a taxicab because he was too young to drive.

Babe decided to drive into Chicago with Dick to see Mother. When they arrived at the hotel, Dad was in the living room. They handed him the telegram and Dick said that for a moment he saw dad almost lose control of himself. But he gathered himself up and called Mother into the room. She looked at their faces and immediately recognized that there was something terribly wrong. They told her the bad news and she collapsed. Everything had been looking so good, and then.... My brother John, then age nine, relates that he was taken down to see mother the next day and that he was expecting to have her greet him as usual with love and attention after several weeks absence, but that all that she could do was sit in a chair in her hotel room with her head down crying. He did not know exactly what to make of it at the time.

They were shocked at the news. Brother John remembers mother crying inconsolably. Dick said it was the worst day of his life. My father fought back the tears, regretting the encouragement he had given me to join the Army Air Force in the first place. Their friends sent letters trying to console them with the hope that I would turn up alive after all. My folks received a letter from the Bomb Group chaplain, Father Sullivan, shortly after the telegram to say that while no parachutes were observed from our burning plane, it was still possible I got out alive. Looking back on the letter, it might have been better if he had said nothing at all except for his comment that I had helped him at mass a few times and was a regular communicant before missions.

My brother Jim's fiancee', Helen Jackson, told how hard everyone at home was taking the news. Jim had just been given two weeks leave and was driving home from Florida to Chicago. A celebration had been planned for them because he had been on continuous active duty for the previous two years. My father was in the car with them and they stopped just outside of town to call Dad's office. It was then that they first learned that I was missing in action and possibly dead.

The fear and anxiety over the awful news was unbearable. Helen said that they tried to go on with the plans for a celebration with Jim but it just wasn't possible to even put a smile on their faces. At dinnertime, they hung their heads and sat in silence at the table unable to participate in the goings on. One night they had tickets to a hit musical show but had nothing to say to each other all night. There was no way to hold any other thought in their minds except to hope for my survival. This went on for the next two weeks without letup.

My dear aunt Kathleen Casey Talbot, my father's sister, was keeping a diary at the time and wrote the following touching memorial:

> **"July 15, 1944. Haven't had the heart, the time or the courage to put into words what has happened since the last time I wrote in this book. Don is missing since June 18th. We are all sunk. Doug and Virginia** (my parents) **are taking it beautifully and we are all very hopeful, but the waiting period is terrific. I do hope we hear soon. There have been so many missing boys whose cases go through the Red Cross and it seems that they always turn up if they are Air Corps boys. At least the percentage is very good."**

CHAPTER 2:

THE GREAT TRAGEDY OF WORLD WAR II

People who have not read history would have no idea what World War Two was all about. It started in 1939 when Germany invaded its neighbor Poland on a pretext that Poland had attacked Germany first. France and Great Britain had treaties for mutual defense with Poland and deemed the attack a declaration of war against them also. Land, sea and air battles ensued all over the world for the next six years between the "Axis" powers consisting of Germany, Japan and Italy and the "Allies," Great Britain, America, Russia, India and China as well as the nations of Southeast Asia, French and Polish forces that escaped to England, and Canada and Australia supplied additional forces to the Allies and in their own defense. South America, Spain, Sweden and Switzerland, remained neutral throughout.

Around the world, millions of people died. The death toll of American armed forces was estimated at 400,000. The number of wounded was three or four times more than those killed in action. The "Holocaust" alone caused six million dead. Russia's losses were upwards of 10 million of its armed forces and another 20 million civilians. In France, 30,000 were executed by firing squads. Germany lost 3 million dead, Poland 6 million, Japan 1.15 million and China 1.3 million.

June 18, 1944 was the day I began an entirely new way of life which I had never anticipated, never imagined and had never lived before. I had come to a fork in my road but with only one choice. That was to leave my high perch aboard a burning B-17 four-motored bomber at twenty four thousand feet in the air over Hamburg, Germany or die. I had to go, I could not stay. The airplane had taken two heavy hits from German anti-aircraft guns and was on fire in the right wing by the gas tank. The aircraft commander had given the bail-out order over the intercom.

I was about to end my status as a free soul in the uniform of my country in war-time and become a caged beast - a prisoner of war of Nazi Germany. What awaited me below I had no idea. The Air Force had told us absolutely nothing about what to expect in that situation. I had a parachute on but had never been trained for what I was about to do.

The B-17 had been dubbed "The Flying Fortress," America's finest four motored bomber. On the fuselage under the pilot's window was painted a name: "GI JANE."I had volunteered for this duty as soon as I turned eighteen in November 1942. I wanted to fly. By February 1944 I was nineteen years old, a 2d Lieutenant and an aerial navigator in the U.S. Army 8th Air Force stationed in England, with the 379th Bombardment Group.

By June 18, 1944 my combat experience consisted of 27 bombing missions over enemy territory. I was Deputy Lead Navigator that day, an important assignment which had us flying next to the Lead Ship in a formation of 30 B-17's over Hamburg. We dropped our bombs on the synthetic oil refineries just before being hit.

I delayed opening my parachute and let myself fall into the open air as ordered by the pilot, a twenty-one year old veteran, a 1st Lieutenant named Steve King. Whatever was going to be was now totally out of my hands. I prayed desperately to God and to the Blessed Virgin Mary, mother of Jesus, to save me. In seconds, my airplane exploded into fragments of aluminum, steel and Plexiglas. One crewman would die in that instant. Three others were doomed as well. I was not one of them.

CHAPTER 3:

MY SCHOOL BOY YEARS

In June 1942, I was a 17 year old American youth of no particular accomplishment graduating from Campion Jesuit High School, a boarding school in southwestern Wisconsin. My older brother Jim was with me for my first two years, 1938-40. He was an athlete and played all sports, I was a chubby little kid and quite short - about 5 feet eight inches. Jim always looked out for me and it was comforting being with him in my second year. Freshmen ate, slept and studied together. The bigger boys teased me a lot but I showed them. I was a top student and I made the golf team where muscles weren't that essential. I yearned to grow up quickly and become a man. My experiences would help me later on but it was something one had to go through.

I had no idea back then of what I might become or of ever writing a book about myself. Yet, here I am doing just that. Perhaps it is an ego trip. It is important to tell your heirs what life was like in another era and perhaps give them courage in their own lives to do things beyond what they think they can do. It might seem to be a form of boasting but everybody is entitled to some of that if they have done something worth while. There is the urge not to let the story be lost forever, so the writing of it enables one to leave behind a record from which others can learn something.

The Jesuits at Campion indoctrinated us in Catholic doctrine under the most rigid standards of behavior. There was conduct that was "right" and conduct that was "wrong" and by senior year, you had better know the difference. Most of us did. We were watched at all times by the "Novices" who were soon to be priests and were, in a sense, completing their own education teaching the boys under their charge. We studied hard, and the class work was rigorous. By senior year I had my own room in Marquette Hall next to the chapel where we spent a lot of time.

Campion offered a regimented existence, even for seniors. It was up every morning for 7:00 a.m. mass at chapel where they heaped on the daily dollop of guilt. Then, directly across campus to the "refectory" about 150 yards where we were served a minimal fare. We did have enough to eat, however, even by my standards. Breakfast was unremarkable, most of the time. Meatless Fridays were unbelievable: Cheese sandwiches, cream puffs, a banana and Jell-O - no vegetables.

Classes were small. The total student body numbered 400. They started me out in freshman year with Latin, English, Math and Religion. I did fairly well with grades in the high 80's to the low 90's; they classified me as an "Honors" student. This served me well at home, too, because older brother Jim was a varsity athlete first and a scholar second. He wasn't at all slow, just less interested. Our father reminded us repeatedly in our younger years that he abhorred lazy people, and he got on Jim to work harder. Jim was not in the honors program. Therefore, if I excelled in grades it made me look better in comparison. (Jim also was an example for me to follow during my early years to stay out of trouble at home. In other words, if he did something resulting in a reprimand, I learned to avoid doing that. On the other hand, I was impelled to do other things that Jim did not do and to "push the envelope" - in the modern vernacular - like lighting cigarettes left lying around the house the morning after the grownups had had a party. This was a detail, however, and what I liked to do most was please and impress my father because he reacted well to that.)

Jim was a lot bigger and stronger than I ever was. He played varsity football and I played on the golf team. He had matured faster than I did and loved athletics. Not that I didn't like sports, I just was either too small or too slow, or too weak to make any of the major sport teams. My contemporaries were mostly bigger and stronger, too. So that left golf, where size didn't much matter.

Being short, slow and pudgy as freshman didn't keep me from wanting to be first at something. Academics were within my reach regardless of my size and agility. It wasn't easy being one of the littler kids because young boys are not the least bit sympathetic with their less able peers.

One day my freshmen class had an outing which consisted of a short boat ride on the nearby Mississippi River and a treasure hunt in the hills some distance away. The craft was fairly good sized, big enough to hold about one hundred passengers. At the end of the day, we returned to the dock to disembark. The boat was being maneuvered to be tied up but was not yet touching the pier. I couldn't wait, for some reason, and I decided to make a leap for the dock in order to be the first one back on dry land. Well, I missed and fell in the river. Just then the boat started to swing in and it was my good fortune that the biggest and strongest of the scholastics, Reverend Mr. McKinney was right there and able to reach down, grab me by the collar and haul me back on board, albeit soaking wet.

Another memory I have of Campion was skating on the Mississippi River in the winter time. The river would freeze over when there was a long enough stretch of really cold weather and one of the scholastics who loved to skate would take a bunch of us out. I had a pair of racing blade skates which facilitated more gliding distance per stride than say the shorter hockey skate and they just suited this type of skating. We would go for a mile or two near the shore where the water was shallower and therefore more firmly frozen. I knew how to skate from learning as a child, but I was no champion racer, for sure. However, it gave me the experience of braving the bitter cold climate and enjoying it which would stand me in good stead later on. Then we would turn around and head back. With luck, the down home leg was with the wind.

Beside the campus (to which we were restricted under pain of punishment) we had the gymnasium, the library and our studies. The library was named for the dead poet, Joyce Kilmer, who wrote the beautiful poem, "Trees". He was killed in World War I not long after writing the poem. I spent a fair amount of time in there and learned to enjoy reading.

I wouldn't want to leave the impression that I was having fun, even though showing up Brother Jim was some of that. After he graduated, I was more homesick. By my junior year I had my own friends, of course. Let's say, I coped. It would be a while later that I began to appreciate the benefits of the discipline on my character, self-reliance and intestinal fortitude.

Most of the time at Campion it was late fall, winter or early spring. (Post war, it was sold and turned into a prison. All it needed was stronger fences.) We spent a lot of time in church praying. On Wednesdays and Saturdays we were marching because we had an ROTC unit there. Our Commanding Officer was a retired army major. ROTC started with sophomore year. We were drilled just like the Army in military formations and even had a class in Military Science which was not all that stimulating. And, we had parades every weekend. By my senior year, I was promoted to Color Sergeant. As such I got to carry the American flag in a special holster which sat on my groin and was in charge of the Color Guard of four (two with flags and two with rifles) and gave the commands for marching. When we stood at attention as the priest passed by with the Blessed Sacrament, everyone doffed his hat or cap except the Color Guard.

The school afforded the opportunity for a fine classical education - four years of Latin and three years of Greek. Of my teachers I remember best, one was Mr. (later "Father") William Dooley, Bill to his friends, no doubt. He was a scholar's scholar in my eyes. He taught us second year Greek and some English, too. He was strict and intellectually imposing. I can still remember his shock in grading one of my English papers when I manufactured a new word: "lugubrified". I had ingeniously (or ingenuously) taken the good word "lugubrious" and made it into a new adjective. Notwithstanding this failed invention, I was a better than average writer, and wrote for the school newspaper, "The Campionette", mostly feature stories about life on campus. I loved to write letters - because I loved to receive them. Writing was never a chore for me, but rather a pleasure.

Father Nebricht was our senior Latin and Greek teacher. He was in his seventies, really old to us then, and he had a serious snuff habit. It was terribly distracting to sit a few feet away at our desks and watch as the snuff induced mucous began to ooze from his nostrils. He would wait until the last minute as a moist tobacco-stained droplet was poised and ready to fall on his desk before reaching for his kerchief and wiping away the brownish mess. I should be the last one to put the knock on good old Father Nebricht, because he gave me the best grades in his classes in senior year - no less than a 98 in Latin and a 99 in Greek. With those high marks, I achieved "second honors", missing "first honors" by no more than a point.

I don't want to forget Father Schuette, who was in his middle seventies at the time. He taught us religion in such a boring way that my lack of interest resulted in a large, embarrassing "D". I felt bad when Father S. died. They held a funeral mass for him as he lay in the chapel in his simple wooden coffin covered with black cloth and a crucifix on top.

CHAPTER 4:

PEARL HARBOR CHANGES THE LIVES OF EVERY AMERICAN

Then it was December 7, 1941 of my senior year. War was declared after The Japanese bombed Pearl Harbor, Hawaii. We students huddled around the radio in the recreation building and smoking area of old Campion Hall. We could only guess what effect the war would have on us at that time. Most of us were destined to be involved and too many would not survive. Still, it was exciting to think about it.

All I knew about war had been gleaned from reading my father's four volume pictorial work on the American side of World War 1. I also enjoyed the paper pulp magazines about the First War and the great "G-8 and his Battle Aces" who flew in the wooden, fabric covered flying machines. Flying was just aborning. "G-8" and his pals "Nippy" and "Bull" fought with the hated "Boche" (Germans) in the skies over the battle front in France.

My dad was an aerial observer in the Great War for a few months in 1918 in France. He never would talk about his experiences but he did buy a set of books which had many pictures of the dead soldiers on both sides and one horrendous photo of an American soldier, naked from the waist up, with a very large, silver-dollar-sized bullet hole below his right shoulder which you could actually see through. Photos of the Germans riding in box cars included one of a soldier holding sign that said: "Ich hat einen Kameraden" (I had a comrade). I remembered that phrase when I was a passenger myself under guard on one of those very same railroad cars together with my American comrades.

I learned a lot at Campion. I didn't realize how much until a couple of years later in service. The Jesuits taught me (or forced me to learn) self reliance, toughness of inner-self, obedience, studiousness and belief in God. In later years, I also came to realize that I had received a fine education, equal to beginning college level in many respects. Maturity came later, as did physical development. By senior year I was still only 5 feet 8 inches tall.

When graduation time came around in June 1942, two members of the faculty came to visit me in my room. They had sized me up as a likely candidate for the Holy Orders of the priesthood: poverty, chastity and obedience for life. I was impressed to be asked for this honor but took only seconds to give my answer which was in the negative.

That summer my younger brothers Dick and John and I went with our mother down south to Biloxi, Mississippi where my father was stationed in the Army Training Command. We visited the post several times and watched the soldiers being put through their paces in Basic Training.

In the fall of 1942, my folks being preoccupied by dad's new career just let me go on my own to Purdue University in West Lafayette, Indiana. A neighbor boy who was already a student there recruited me. It wasn't a good idea, but what did I know? I just was swept along with the tide. (Campion high school had only four hundred students, Purdue had perhaps twelve thousand.) I had never imagined what was involved in registration for classes and picking my curriculum. What the heck, at Campion, there were no electives at all.

At Purdue, you were assumed to know what to do and no one was there to guide me as an entering freshman. As a result, my first semester consisted of Advanced Algebra, Calculus, Chemistry, Mechanical Drawing, Heat-Treating and Welding. The latter course started me out with an electrical torch with which I welded two pieces of scrap metal to my work table. I was too late to sign up for something relevant like an English course.

When I finally talked to a student counselor he told me that my aptitude tests indicated that I was marginally qualified for advanced algebra and calculus. So why not set yourself up for failure by trying to keep up from the bottom of the class instead of at the top? The result was that I failed both math courses, made a B in chemistry and slept through the terribly boring early morning and late evening sessions. Due to my ignorance and naiveté the drawing and the welding classes were held at 7:00 a.m. and 7:00 p.m. respectively.

To make matters worse for myself, I was recruited into a fraternity where we were subjected to juvenile hazing with paddles and a lot of other nonsense which detracted from my study time. By the time I realized what a hole I had dug for myself academically, it appeared to be marginal whether I would survive. Did I care? Not really, because the war was going full tilt by the winter of 1942-43 and my fraternity brothers were leaving in droves to join up or be drafted. It was a chance to escape disgrace with honor.

My father had no good reason for going into the service in 1942 except that during the war there was virtually no investment banking business going on. Every spare dollar was dedicated to defense spending. He had been a teen-age second lieutenant - just as I was destined to be - in World War I in the "Air Service." His older brother Emmett (whose name I bore) had joined the Army Engineers in 1917 because of his experience with his father working on railroad construction jobs in his early teens. Dad figured out from his previous war experience that being an enlisted man in the Army was no place to be if you could avoid it. He had received a good basic education at Proviso Township High School in Maywood, Illinois and was an above average student as well as an athlete - he played on the Varsity baseball team with my mother's brother, Vernon Smith.

When the opportunity came along for dad to get some College training and have a chance to become an officer in the then very romantic flying corps, he took it willingly. His combat time was short as an aerial observer because the Americans were very late getting into flying against the Germans in France. Whatever his experiences, he never spoke about them, which is sad to say for I never learned enough about it except out of the set of books he brought home.

My father had come from absolutely nothing as a boy on a farm in northern Indiana and had made a real success of himself in the investment banking business after World War I. He started out as a messenger for a fine local Chicago firm, A. C. Allyn & Co. He was a wonderful salesman and he made friends wherever he went, leading to the development of a "syndicate" of colleagues in the business with different firms around the country upon whom he could call when necessary to raise money for the underwriting of new stock and bond issues to sell to the investing public. He embodied a potent combination of talent and a commanding personality. Furthermore, he loved to have a good time with his spare time. He enjoyed the Chicago nightlife which was always plentiful. So why go into the service, then?

Dad was a patriot. He was also an adventurous sort as his business career exemplified. The investment business had become quiescent after Japan bombed Pearl Harbor. No one was starting up any new businesses, unless they had to do with the war. He was 43 years old and he saw a chance to secure a commission in the Army Air Corps and get into the thick of things. And so he did. Once he was in the service, his personality, knowledge and experience in dealing with people enabled him to rise out of the pack and he wound up in the Army Air Corps Training Command where he soon was promoted from Major to Lieutenant Colonel, a fairly high rank for a non-professional soldier. He also developed a circle of friends in important positions in the Training Command who stood him in good stead when dealing with the stolid types of professional senior officers who had never had any other experience.

CHAPTER 5:

TIME FOR ME TO JOIN UP OR BE DRAFTED

When I wrote to Dad that I had a choice of joining the ROTC which was devoted to artillery, or being drafted, he warned me not to let myself be relegated to enlisted status. He knew from experience that life as a "dog-faced" soldier was not to be sought after. "Become an officer, if at all possible" was his advice. Being on the loose as a pink-cheeked 18 year old with judgment and inexperience to match, I fended for myself and volunteered for the Army Air Corps' aviation cadet program and waited to be called up. At least I did not have to worry about being drafted after that. Nobody could be forced to fly against his will. But, no one had to talk me into anything, this was what I wanted to do and the risks be damned.

It did not take long. When my orders came in late January 1943, considering my doubtful academic standing and the alternative of being drafted, it was a relief. I celebrated by buying beer for the entire fraternity house and foolishly tried to drink most of it myself, downing a full pitcher on my way to oblivion for the night. Next stop, Columbus, Ohio.

On my way to report for duty I went home to Chicago, but there was no one there anymore. The folks were in Atlantic City or Texas in the Air Training Command. Jim was an Aviation Cadet at a college in Pennsylvania. Dick was at Campion High in Wisconsin and Johnny was with the folks. Aunt Alice Casey, Dad's spinster sister, met my train. I only had a short time to visit and then I was off to the war.

My father gave me some instruction in how to deal with all the strangers I was about to meet. He said simply, but wisely, not to be in a hurry to tell everybody your life story. Let the other guy tell you his first and then you would be in a better position to decide whether to tell him yours.

With high hopes. I boarded the train in Chicago to Columbus, Ohio. I was in for a real shock on arrival there. Thousands of raw recruits were pouring off the trains coming from all directions each day. We were processed quickly, which meant standing around in the altogether with hundreds of others and being poked and looked up and down and in the mouth. The doctors moved us along on a fast assembly line because we were presumed to be in good health. That done, we next boarded a troop train for San Antonio, Texas. The journey lasted almost two days and a night. We ate and slept in our seats and breakfasted out of individual dry cereal boxes which we opened along perforated seams and poured in milk and sugar. The other meals were generally awful.

Then we were in San Antonio at the SAACC (as in "sack") - the camp's official acronym for the "San Antonio Aviation Cadet Center." We were given our first uniforms consisting of everything we would need from head to toe. No more civilian clothes. They were shipped home because we wouldn't be needing them for the foreseeable future. I was a soldier in the U.S. Army Air Corps now and under orders to dress like a soldier at all times.

I can still remember the smell and the texture of the new woolen clothes. I had a feeling of anticipation and enjoyment at putting them on for the first time. It was like Christmas and receiving a whole new wardrobe. We were herded through the massive supply center and were given our olive drab -"OD" - shirts and trousers, a blouse, and a fore and aft "overseas" hat which fit the head snugly. Each of us was given a dress cap adorned with the aviation cadet symbol of the wings and propeller. They gave us overcoats and ankle high boots which took a shine well and were very comfortable with the rounded toe and thick sole and heel. The material from which our equipment was made was first rate. This was really the Army where every need was provided for according to regulations. Our tan web belt had a brass buckle which was to be kept shiny at all times with what was called a "blitz cloth". Later, as the weather warmed, we were given summer gear consisting of heavy cotton khaki shirts, trousers and a summer overseas cap.

There wasn't time to be homesick and, besides, I had just come from boarding at school where I had learned how to cope with loneliness a long time ago. They moved us into barracks which were the standard two-story army model used all over the country. Each man had a single bunk and the bunks were in two rows separated by about an eight foot aisle. There was a separate room for the sergeant and his assistant and the inevitable latrine which was kept spic and span. At inspection, usually on Saturdays, we lined up in front of our bunks with everything laid out according to the rule book.

The reason we were there was for "classification" - for assignment to aviation skill courses. They gave us a battery of tests on everything from physical coordination to intelligence. Then we met with the counselors who probed for a decision as to which type of training to assign us. We all were volunteers and brighter than average or we wouldn't have been there. I can still remember the interviewer I talked to telling me that I qualified for all 3 types of air training, pilot, bombardier and navigator but that I was especially suited for aerial navigation - and they needed navigators, badly. Furthermore navigation school was my best opportunity for an accelerated route to a commission, with the least chance of failure. Student pilots had a notoriously high "wash-out" rate and if you washed-out of pilot training, you were doomed, or worse - grounded with little or no chance to be an officer. People on "ground duty only " ("GDO" for short) were referred to disparagingly as "ground-grippers" and "paddle-feet."

There was a song we sang about ground duty which was set to the tune of "Alouette" and included the phrase: "open post (being allowed off the base on pass), caught the Clapp (a well known social disease), GDO (ground duty only), OOOOHHHH, Alouette," etc.

John Steinbeck, in his jingoistic book entitled "Bombs Away", published in 1941, wrote about Army Air Corps recruiting as follows:

> **"The Army Air Force is recruiting thousands of young men and they must be a very special kind of young men. They must, in fact, be the best physical and mental specimens the country produces. .... It is better if the boy has gone two years to college, but it is not essential. Graduation from High School is sufficient."**

> **"If the young man in school has been interested in physics and mathematics and in general science, it will be easier for him. .... The applicant should be capable of individual judgment, for the Air Force is not an organization of commander and dull followers. It cannot be. Every member ... must make thousands of personal and individual decisions constantly. ... His manual coordination must be above the average. The discipline of limb and muscle must be perfect, and, while he need not be finely trained, he must have a physical system which will respond to the rigid training ... to emerge a toughened, disciplined soldier. A young man having these qualities should make application to join ... He should not specify that he wants to be a pilot or a navigator or a bombardier or a gunner, a radio operator or an engineer. The Air Force will give him tests which will prove definitely which position he is most capable of filling, for a man who is capable of being a good pilot need not at all be a good navigator, while a good navigator need not be a good bombardier. Each one has special qualities and careful Army psychological and physical tests will prove which qualities the applicant has. Lastly, the young man wishing to enter the Air Force should not for a moment get the idea that he is going into something**

easy. There is neither time nor room for softness or lazi-
ness in the Air Force. The cadet will work harder and
longer than he thought he could. He will study harder
than he has ever studied in school. He will play violently
and eat enormously and he will emerge tough, competent and sure. He will be a crew mate in the hardest-
hitting, most competent team this country has ever
produced. This is really the Big League in the toughest
game we have ever been up against, with the pennant,
the survival and future of the whole nation."

"If the training of a bomber crew is hard, it is hard for a
purpose. For great responsibilities are put in the hands
of these young men: the simple responsibility for the expense and   intricate machine that is the bombing
plane, responsibility for the secrecy of the bomb sight,
and beyond these the greatest responsibility of all, for
to a large extent the bomber team will be responsible for
the safety and survival of the nation."

Being the opportunist that I now realize that I was and still
very susceptible to suggestions, I bit on the counselor's recommen-
dation, just as I was expected to. I said I wanted to go to navigation school. I felt I had the math background. I wanted to get there
(wherever "there" was) in a hurry. Another one of my traits - "pa-
tience."

It was early March, 1943 by then. The first thing they did
was cut our hair down close to the scalp. The barbers had a mass
production setup so that before you realized it your hair was gone
and they were giving you an involuntary shampoo. Being nobody's
fool, when the barber did that to me, I complained that I had not
ordered a shampoo - but there I was with the stuff dripping off
my head. With what little I had left in hair, a wash cloth would
have done very nicely. The barber took a towel and mopped up the
extra moisture and turned me out of the chair annoyed that I had
deprived him of the extra dollar he was expecting to get. I rushed

back to the barracks and finished the job in the sink with the dollar still in my pocket. Hey, we were only getting $21 per month as a cadet on ground duty.

Again: John Steinbeck on "the Navigator".

> "The purpose of a long-range bomber is to fly to a given target and to drop its bombs. That is the simple statement of it and its complication arises in the technique of getting the bomber to the target and getting it home again. The bombardier is there to drop the bombs on the Target. The pilot will guide and control the ship. The crew chief will see to the engines. The gunner(s) protect the plane from attack and the radio operator keeps up communication with the ground and other planes. But bombers, given a pin point on a map to fly to, must have navigators to tell them how to get there. A plane cannot fly by sight over seas and deserts or at night or in clouds and arrive at its destination any more than a ship can."

> "The aerial navigator is a very necessary member of a bomber crew. The word 'navigation', referring as it does to the sea, is misused, but apparently it is going to continue to be misused. Aerial navigation is not much different from marine navigation except that things happen more quickly. The basic instruments are the same, the compass to tell the direction in which you are going and the sextant and chronometer to tell you where you are. Other instruments - airspeed indicators drift meters, etc. - are more recent inventions and their use is limited to airplanes. The basic instruments are very ancient. The compass has only changed in accuracy since early Chinese seamen placed a little lodestone bar on a chip of wood and floated the chip in a saucer."

> "The modern compass is a marvel of accuracy, but its principal is that of the lodestone on the chip... The modern radio time signal is the completely accurate grand-

child of the ... chronometer, and the aerial navigator is the child of the sea captain who shot sun and star from his quarterdeck and brought his ship over the curve of the earth to an unseen port. The aerial navigator, of all members of a bomber crew, except possibly the gunner, practices an ancient profession, and of all of the members of the crew the navigator needs more technical education and training. The ideal candidate for commission as aerial navigator ... will have some background in mathematics and in astronomy. Engineers make good navigators because, in addition to the basic knowledge, they have acquired the method of thinking and studying which is required..."

"The navigator enters the Air Force in the same way as do the bombardier and pilot. He makes application and is sent to an induction center where he is tested physically and mentally... The Navigator candidate will have a different temperament from (the) pilot and bombardier. He is rather more studious and more a perfectionist in his work. There is no 'fairly close' in navigation. The point indicated must be found exactly. For example, a squadron of bombers rarely takes off from the same place. Individual planes may leave from different stations with orders to rendezvous at a given place and at a given time. In each plane it will be the navigator's job to get his ship to that place in the sky at a given moment. His work must be exact; else his ship will not be in its place in the flight."

"When the navigation cadet has passed the physical and mental tests, the manual aptitude tests, and so forth, he will be assigned to a school. The school and the course will be described as follows: Its objective is to qualify students as navigator members of the combat crew. Its scope - qualification as a precision, dead reckoning, and celestial navigators and qualification as junior officer members of the combat crew. The duration of the course is 15 weeks. The course is divided into two parts, flying training and ground school, and in this particular there will be more ground work than flying work for the navigator has a great deal to learn."

"In ground school he will learn dead-reckoning navigation. He will learn instruments, maps and charts, radio navigation. In celestial navigation he will learn the general theory, time and hour angle, instruments, star identification, and astronomical triangles. In meteorology he will learn the theory and principles of weather analysis, the interpretation of weather maps, the discussion of forecasts. He will learn the meteorology of the ocean, of thunderstorms, tornadoes, and icing conditions, and on top of all of it, as in every other Air Force school, he will have constant athletic and military training."

I wrote to my folks on March 15, 1943 as follows:

"My tests are over and I'm waiting to be shipped to navigator's preflight. The tests were all aptitude and the board decided that I would be best as a navigator, so that's what I'm going to be. It's a six month course and it's a lot more important than the average civilian would make it out to be. I applied for pilot, but, honestly, I'm not too disappointed."

"The decision was based upon a group psychological test which is a written aptitude test and finds out just what a person's mental abilities are. Next, there is the psycho-motor test in which physical aptitude and coordination are tested. Then there is the physical which is supposedly tougher than that of West Point."

"The Group psychological includes definitions of words,

tables, and one's speed in reading them; math problems in speed such as approximations of large multiplications, word problems, algebra, formulae and their use, addition and subtraction speed, locating points on maps with pictures of these points taken from the air; mechanical knowledge; dial and meter readings for speed. The psychomotor calls for extreme coordination to score highly and includes lining up one trio of lights with another by means of air plane controls; turning square pegs half way around for speed; turning off switches according to signals, for speed. All the other tests were similar in testing for steadiness, coordination and quick reaction."

"On top of all this, there is a very important interview with a psychologist who asks you why you joined the Air Corps, why you want to fly, medical history and countless personal questions from which they pass judgment on you."

"Life here is tough, but only physically. In the morning, we rise at 5:30 a.m. and go to chow; then physical training at 7:55 a.m. where we do various limbering-up exercises and then we run a mile. Back we go at 9:15 a.m. to change clothes for drill, which lasts from 1 1/2 to 2 hours. After chow, we exercise some more, then drill, and finally parade about 4:00 p.m. After evening chow, we are free until lights out at 9:30 p.m."

"There are also KP and Guard duties which one incurs once in a while. At the present, I am scheduled for KP tomorrow, which means that I go on duty at 5:00 a.m. and go off duty 3:30 p.m. the next day. KP's rise at 4:00 a.m. I'll be able to tell you more about it in a couple of days."

"The weather is warm and occasionally hot, like today. It would be just my luck to be assigned to a special de-

tail for raking the parade ground. Boy is I burned, and I do mean sun."

"But I'm happy, and especially because I'm five months ahead of Jim. His training involves 15 long months while mine takes six when it starts. Come what may, I'll be directing my bomber to the enemy almost soon enough to suit me, and I will be the best navigator any pilot ever had. In the meantime, I'll go on making my bed and sweeping and mopping my bay every day."

The KP and Guard duty I mentioned in my letter were two traditional experiences of basic training. "KP", was short for kitchen police or dishwashing. Being on guard duty for an entire day was probably the worst. We had to carry the heavy old Springfield rifle, which was not loaded. We were marched to our post to relieve some other poor sap and then we were obliged to march up and down, back and forth, ad nauseam, for hours and hours. Each tour was two hours. Then you were relieved for a four hour rest. Then back out again, and so forth. Fortunately, there were enough of us that I did not have to do it again while in Basic Training.

KP was another matter. Eating was a three times a day matter and the troops were always hungry. But, when you are on KP duty, you get up in the middle of the night and start to get ready for the breakfast rush. Naturally, my first assignment, "pots and pans", was the most rigorous job of all. At breakfast time, I sat around waiting. Then the dirty pots and pans started coming, fast and furiously. I actually liked the work. There is some strange quirk I seemed to have about dishes and getting them cleaned. In no time, I had those utensils looking first rate again. By that time, however, breakfast was over and the lunch preparations were already underway. And, what do you know; the dirty pots and pans started rolling in again, with a vengeance. Let me tell you, that was hard work.

My second KP assignment was some days later - peeling potatoes. This outfit was fully mechanized and we had an electric potato peeler, plus paring knives. There were three of us on the peeling crew and it didn't take us long to figure out a way to make the machine do most of the work. The trick was not to take the potatoes out of the peeler too soon - as you were supposed to do and cut out the eyes. We found that if we waited long enough, the machine would also remove the potato eyes, albeit along with a lot of good potato, as well. So what! They never caught us at it.

My third and final KP assignment was mopping floors in the mess hall. I found that the best place to mop was right outside the walk-in refrigerator because that is where all the fresh produce was. I could mop a few strokes, rest, and when no one was looking, pop into the fridge (that's not what we called it at the time), I could feed my face with all kinds of wholesome things to eat. But no matter how much I ate, I did not gain weight. Unperceived by me, I was still growing, and with all of the exercise we were getting I needed nourishment, frequently. In that regard, when I left Campion High School in June of 1942, some nine months earlier, I was 5 feet 8 inches tall and weighed about 160 - still pudgy but at least still growing taller while maintaining my weight.

The Army was big on scrubbing the barracks floors and calisthenics. I was a golfer, remember, I had no muscles to speak of. We did push-ups, leg-raises, running, climbing a 12 foot wall, an obstacle course, and so forth. I never did complete scaling the wall nor the mile run all the way. But somehow I did get myself into better shape physically than I ever had been before.

In a letter to my father on April 5th, I wrote about my first time off the base for Open Post - come and go as you please for two days. The first thing I did was to go over to nearby Randolph Field for an experimental ride in a pressure chamber. I wrote further that on my way back through San Antonio I called Dad's friend and colleague in the investment business, Mr. Hal Dewar, who took me out for dinner at his country club. "He treated me like a king", I said. "He even called my commanding officer at the SAAC who told him that there was no power short of the White

House that could change my assignment from Navigation school to Pilot training." I told Dad, "I still don't mind because I want to fly".

I wrote again:

> **"Our squadron is full of new men now - mostly draftees from every branch and lots of aerial gunners. They are excused from the regular routine of athletics and drill, and also KP and Guard duty, so it's up to the remaining old men (who me?) to do their work. So you see, I have been slaving for the last week. I expect to move soon - probably to Ellington Field, Houston, Texas - and I hope it's very soon. This waiting is very tiresome. I'm still wearing 'OD' and will not be able to wear Khaki until the 18th of this month. The weather is warm enough for swimming, but this is the Army."**

Pretty soon, we were ready for navigation pre-flight training at Ellington Field. On April 9, 1943, I wrote to my mother about waiting for "pre-flight" school:

> **"There is still no definite news about moving as yet, but there are tons of Army rumors as can be expected - to which I try to keep my ears closed. Nothing new ever happens around here, so that's all I have to say for now."**

Again on April 10th, I wrote to Dad complaining about the delay:

> **"I'm sorry I don't write longer letters but there just doesn't seem to be anything happening around here that rates talking about. I have told you the general routine and that's about all there is to the SAACC. As I told you, the last time I saw Mr. Dewar, he said that nothing**

could be done about my classification. I personally think that I would make a much better navigator than pilot, anyway. Nevertheless, I'm dying to get into a plane."

"I'm still waiting on needles and pins for my orders of departure, but I remain here till the happy day comes along."

It was boring when you had the time to sit down and think about it. The other guys were mostly kids as I was and full of vinegar, etc.

Then the orders came and I wrote a completely different letter to Mother on April 24th from Ellington Field, Pre-Flight School:

"Consider this your first letter from your wandering son during the beginning of his training toward the accomplishment of his high mission. Personally, I'm very pleased with everything."

"I had been told that Ellington had the finest food of any Army post in the country, but never did I imagine it being as it is. We are served countless varieties of frozen vegetables and fruits and the best of meats and other foods. This morning, for example, we had fresh raspberries, and this noon, sweet corn. On top of all this, we are not limited to any amount of this."

"Classes have started and our curriculum is math, physics, army ground forces, naval and aircraft identification. Major Thurston Richardson (Dad and Mother's friend from River Forest and the investment business) **stopped by yesterday with son Dana and talked to me. He assures me that I won't have any trouble nor will I be delayed after I finish. He also says that Houston is the best army town in the country. I really consider myself lucky."**

A little while later, Mother received a letter from Mrs. Richardson about seeing me. She wrote:

> **"Your second son having just left, I am hastening to write and tell you how grand he looks and how good it was to see him. Thurston and Dana drove out to the Field and picked him up around noontime and then brought him back here for dinner."**

> **"I hope he did not mind it that I put my arms around him and kissed him when he walked in. I could not resist it. This was the first time he has been off the Post since arriving here. He was on duty yesterday as Corporal of the Guard. Thurston said to tell you that after talking with Don, he certainly knows the score."**

The Richardsons had another function to go to after dinner, so, at my request, they dropped me off at the USO (United Services Organization) in town.

The next day, Mrs. Richardson wrote a longer letter to Mother to say that the Major is deliberately staying out of my way to avoid any hint of favoritism or embarrassment to me. She did note that I was already a "flight sergeant" when we got together, so perhaps I earned that on my own without any help.

On May 26th, I wrote again to Dad. In unbelievable style, I went on:

> **"After I've had a few Japs in my sights long enough to pull the trigger, I may think about the ATC** (Air Transport Command), **but until then I don't think so. I'm afraid I didn't join the Air Corps to see the world."**

> **"School here is fine and very interesting. Our instructors habitually make it a point to say that our very life and the lives of others depend on our diligence in class."**

> **"I was promoted from flight sergeant to cadet lieutenant. I'm really becoming a man and a soldier now for I**

give orders to men of twenty-five and six and have more responsibility than I have ever had before in my life. You probably wouldn't know me anymore so I wish you could come down while there's still a chance. But this is the Army."

On June 10th with only two weeks to go of preflight, I wrote Mother about being anxious to move.

"I've finished all my school work and I'm taking first aid, code and chemical warfare - and, of course, drill and PT. Chemical warfare just about makes you sick to listen when they talk about these gasses and the havoc they play with the body. I'm glad I'm going to be up in the air."

"I wouldn't think about coming down here if I were you. God only knows where I'm going, but it will probably be Texas; and besides, I will be entirely busy at advanced (flying school) to make your visit worth while. I'm getting along fine and there's no need to worry."

"Have my trunk painted O.D. and have my name and serial no. painted on like this: 'DONALD E. CASEY AAF 15342875.' Just hold onto it until I get settled again."

Then on June 16th I wrote to Dad:

"One more week to go and then to San Marcos, Texas and Advanced school. Sunday is Father's day and you're in St. Jo' (Mo.) all by yourself. I want you to know that the navigation branch of the family is with you in spirit, anyway. Texas is a great state to be out of in the summer time. Not only does the air cling to you, but it slaps you in the face. I spend a lot of money on laundry."

My recollection about pre-flight school was that it was very hot and we marched everywhere and sat in those steamy class rooms and tried to concentrate as if our lives depended on it. I "lucked out" (not a phrase we knew in 1943) at Ellington Field because Major Richardson, our family's friend from home, was one of the commanding officers. I suspected that he fixed it so that I was appointed platoon leader. But, actually, I was better qualified than most based on my three years of ROTC training at Campion High.

It got hotter and hotter every day at Houston. When we had "Open Post" we were allowed to leave the Field and we went in town - and got drunk, on rum and cokes, mostly - and that coke would make you really sick if you drank enough of it. One by one we rolled into our shared hotel room and headed quickly for the room with the big white bowl that flushes. I already knew by then that if you felt like throwing up, you were much better off the next day getting rid of whatever it was you had on your stomach now. There was no problem buying liquor even at age 18. What the hell, we were men on our way to war, death and destruction. Why not let the kids grow up in every way?

Finally came flight training at San Marcos Army Air Base in San Marcos, Texas, just south of Austin. This was positively thrilling to an 18 year old. At last we were airborne. We flew the AT-7 Beech Craft twin engine plane with a pilot, a navigation instructor and room for three navigators, each with his own desk.

Figure 1. Flight of three Beachcraft AT-7 Navigation training planes each carrying a pilot, a navigation instructor and 3 student navigators San Marcos, Texas, 1943.

Figure 2. Author (Rt.) and fellow aviation cadets at Advanced Navigation School.

We practiced "dead reckoning" defined as starting from a known point of departure heading for another known point of arrival and charting the course on the Mercator map which is made by projecting the surface of the earth on to a paper cylinder. It was a very accurate map when you were flying from west to east or from South to North and adapted well to the compass. However, the farther north or south you were from the Equator, the less accurate it was. Obviously, the shortest distance between two points on a globe is a curved line. A compromise had to be made to transpose a sphere shape onto a flat surface. It was first invented in the 16th century by a man named: "Mercator."

"Celestial navigation" is something altogether different from "Dead Reckoning." For one thing, it is commonly a night time exercise. As described in our Navigation school ("yearbook") to do celestial navigation, the navigator needs a sextant, a Mercator chart, a Weems plotter, an E6B computer, a pair of dividers, an air almanac, a book of tables (showing star positions or sub-stellar points), scrap paper (not me), log book and pencil."

Our Advanced Navigation graduation book quoted General Brant, the commanding officer, as saying "The world's most exacting scientists are the Army Air Forces' navigators". (He never saw me in uniform and in operation, or my picture in the graduation book at age 18.)

The book went on: "And because of the exact science of aerial navigation that Air Forces' navigation students are learning at San Marcos Army Air Field, and with San Marcos trained navigators finding the way, the Axis partners are going to find plenty of things to regret."

A lot of our celestial training was done on the ground, identifying the stars we wanted to shoot with our Octants (like a sextant but with a bubble level to replicate the horizon for aerial use), sighting them and then marking the angle of each shot on a small wax disc recording for purposes of computations. It was very easy on the ground. I remember my favorite star, "Antares", the red star in the notch of "Scorpio" (the sign of the scorpion) was always right over the fire house. What I overlooked was that there would be no fire house in the air. Pretty soon we were flying and navigating from the air. This was it, the real thing. We flew day missions and night missions. In finding the stars, you had to know where to look in the sky. That was part of our training. In daylight, we learned how to shoot "sun lines."

On one trip, we flew from San Marcos to Oklahoma City, Oklahoma City to Tulsa, Tulsa to Pueblo, Colorado, and then back to San Marcos. We shot those stars to our hearts content and plotted our course and were graded on our final instruction to the pilot based on the accuracy of our computations of the direction, and arrival time at our planned destination. They never told us our grades but my final report showed me passing celestial with a grade of 80. Nobody ever got 100 so I was close enough to earn my wings.

Shooting the stars and translating the information into accurate spotting of our plane as to course, speed and direction still amazes me. Magellan did the same thing from the deck of his ship a hundreds of years before. The system works because of the precise plotting of the course of the star every second over the face of the earth. At any given moment, each star has a designated "substellar" point on earth.

The navigator in "shooting" the star levels his octant with a lighted bubble level, centers the star in the center of the circle and presses a button which causes a stylus to leave a mark on a waxed disc. The angle he has measured between the horizon (as determined by the leveled bubble) and the star is translated into a curved line on our maps. The waxed disc permitted several shots at a time from which we averaged the angle by looking by the markings. The tables showed us that at the time of the particular shot, and knowing the sub-stellar point of the star, a line could be drawn on the map based on the angle of the shot. The airplane was somewhere along this line.

We then selected another star at approximately right angles

to the previous star and draw another line the map. If both shots were perfect, the crossing point of the two lines was your exact location at the particular moment. To check further, still another star would be shot and a third line drawn. If you were really off on one of the shots, you wound up with a triangle with a lot of space in the center. If you were doing it right, you had a tight triangle the center of which closely approximated your location. By repeating the process over and over, a navigator could chart his course, speed and arrival time and make accurate estimations of the airplane's course and expected travel time.

Sixty years later, such navigation is done by pushing buttons on the airborne computer and, using satellites in space, to get the aircraft's precise location in the blink of an eye. But what does one of these space age navigators do if there is no power to run his machine? Little did we know in training school how seldom we would actually get to use celestial navigation. In fact, in actual operations, it was used only once by me. But when I needed to do it, I performed as I was trained. What an experience! The training worked. We got where we were going.

Training meant flying and flying included risks. The navigation class ahead of mine flew a practice mission one night that summer into a thunderstorm and every single plane either crashed or made a forced landing. Many were killed. It was so hushed up it was years later before the story leaked out. I was there at the time but never heard anything about it.

It wasn't all work at San Marcos. We had girls in Austin at Texas, University. They were a little old for me (20+), but fun. (What choices did they have?) Also, in the heat of summer, we went to a town nearby called "New Braunfels" where they had the greatest little man-made falls created by damming up the river. It was a German settlement as the name probably tells you. Even the Catholic churches used German in preaching to the parishioners. I should have taken the time to listen better and learn about where I was going to wind up.

Another fun exercise in advanced navigation school was "swinging the compass." As hard as they try, when installing a compass in an air plane, there is always some error which, no matter how slight, could cause a navigator to miss his destination by miles over a long enough course. The technique we used was to measure deviations in the compass was to find a set of railroad tracks the exact and true direction of which could be determined, unfailingly. With this information, we simply flew back and forth over the tracks from every possible direction noting as we did the angle so made in our drift meter and comparing it with the compass reading. (The "drift meter" was an optical device standing about 30 inches high on the airplane floor through which one sighted the ground and observed the angle -the drift - of the plane's direction over the earth.) Any error in the compass reading could thereby be determined and noted on an attached card. This was the one mission on which all the student navigators became air-sick because of the way the plane was constantly being banked and turned. To prove my mettle, I brought along some cigars to smoke during the trip. Everyone got sick, but me. I was fine and proud of it.

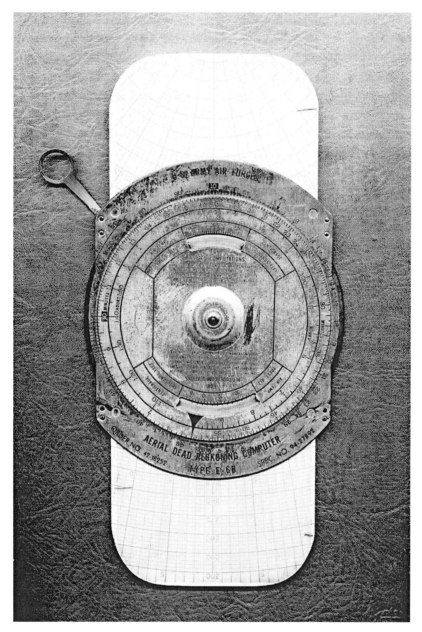

Figure 3. 1943 – Latest Model Navigator's "Slide Rule" – labeled "Aerial Dead Reckoning Computer, model E-6B. No navigator would take off without this invaluable tool.

A letter I wrote to the folks on July 22, 1943 reminds me that they came and visited me at San Marcos AAFB and brought along brothers Dick and Johnny.

> **"I must confess you made me homesick when you left. I'm over it though because I just haven't time to be that way. Dick and Johnny really surprised me with their change, especially, John. I give odds that he will be another pudgy just as I was and still partly am."**

> **"I flew my first 'dead reckoning mission - all by instruments without so much as one look out the window. I did just fair, missing my destination by 4 miles and 3 minutes (late, but not too lost). It was still an above average job for the first time as I was given to understand, but not the best."**

On August 16th I wrote to my Mother:

> **"Life goes on normally here and nothing has happened since I last saw you. I'm still learning navigation and how! They are really throwing it to us - but fast! I think I'll make it though so don't worry."**

On August 26th I wrote:

> **"Well I have finally finished my daytime flying and from now on it's all at night, with the exception of the day-night flights on which we fly to some field at night and back the next day. I may get as far as Kansas or Mississippi".**

On September 8th I wrote to Brother Dick at Campion:

> **"If you think you're having a tough time, just let me tell you my story. The food here is about Campion standard and the work makes your job look like duck's soup. Yesterday, for instance, I went to school from eight in the morning until twelve that night. Of course we had three**

hours off - two for meals and one for P.T.”

In a letter to Mother dated the same day, discussing the news that Jim had been accepted for pilot training, I wrote:

> **“I'm glad I'm in navigation because it would hurt me to wash out. The (failure) rate in pilot training is sixty to seventy-five percent. If Jim makes the grade, he'll be a hot pilot.”**

On September 16th I sent a post card from Tulsa to Dick addressed simply: “Richard Casey, Campion, Prairie du Chien Wis.” (There were no “Zip Codes” in those days.)

> **“Dear Dick, No, I haven't moved but I'm just on a three or four day tour of the country by air - navigating by the sun in the daylight and the stars at night. If the weather forces us, we may hit Chicago. See you in October.”**

A postcard to my cousin Joyce Holland in Chicago, who was my best liaison to my folks who were on the move constantly, contained the message that I was in Pueblo, Colorado on my way to California. Actually, because of weather, we turned back to Tulsa and then returned to San Marcos.

On September 26th, about one month before graduation, I wrote again to Dick:

> **“Things are going along fine here, although I wouldn't lay my fortune on graduation because we still have plenty of flights left and it is easy to mess up. I've done all right so far and I'm sure that they can't cook up anything I can't take care of well enough to get by. You can expect to see me around the Feast of Christ the King. I'll see if I can't get home for a couple days.**

At last a letter came from Dad in Fort Worth dated September 27th assuring me he would be at my graduation on October

23rd. (A ticket Mother preserved for me states it was on a Saturday at 9:30 a.m. I weighed 155 pounds and was 5' 9". My new officer's serial number was 0-696058. But first, I had to be discharged from the Army cadet corps, which I was.

A favorite cartoon from <u>Yank Magazine,</u> the weekly army newspaper, fit me to a tee at the time. Picture a very young, baby-faced officer sitting at a desk before whom stands a veteran, balding and pot-bellied PFC. The soldier says to his young leader: "I'd like a little fatherly advice, Sir!"

My favorite aunt on the Casey side, Aunt Kathleen Talbot, wrote to me on October 19th to say that I should show her letter to the Commanding Officer and press him for a leave and give the girls a treat once more.

On October 17th, I wrote my Mother:

"I still don't know whether or not I'm going to be a lieutenant, but I will graduate and have ten days to spend as I choose. From then on, God only knows where I will be. I will graduate Saturday morning and get my orders then."

Graduation day came and Dad was there in person. He pinned on my wings and I gave my first salute as a second lieutenant to an opportunistic enlisted man who stood nearby for the very purpose of making me pay him the traditional $1. Dad was a Lieutenant Colonel at the time and he had great credentials from training command headquarters. He found out that I was being assigned to medium bombers, probably B-26's which were regarded as bad airplanes - very fast and hot to land, but with too short a wing-span for the weight. Not being the least bit indecisive, I told Dad I wanted the heavies, the B-17, because that is where the navigator gets to do his stuff at long range. None of those low-flying short hops for me, no sir.

Dad arranged with the base C.O. to transfer me to B-17s as I had asked. (Later, it came out that he deeply regretted intervening as he had done.) He and I went out on the town that night and he bought me a pint of "Black Gold" bourbon whiskey which was my eighteen year old choice. We ate, drank and enjoyed ourselves, but I never knew for sure how he felt about what I was getting into. It all seemed very glamorous at the time and I was very proud of myself.

An item in a student publication about my navigation school class, "43-15-1", read as follows:

> **"The approaching completion of the navigation course at SMAAF** (San Marcos Army Air Force base) **brings a shiver of anticipation to some -- just a shiver to others. The most acute loss probably will not be felt until the old gang has drifted to the various combat outfits."**

> **"Somewhat poignantly we'll always remember Mike Cornelison (our cadet squadron leader) bellowing 'Fall out', and everyone chorusing 'blow it out'... The gang around Bill Blackwell's bed when one of those 'bundles from Blackwell' arrived ... 'Bantam Braje sparring with (big) Herb Conyers... Leo Carzoli; 'But Pete, only a 98?' Bill Callam's reports on that bit of lush he met in New Braunfels, is such a thing possible in N.B.... Bob Bricker cussing the Yankees and we don't mean the ball club... Ted Allen stoutly insisting that Texas A&M has no domestic science course.' Leo Carzoli was very Italian and amused us at length with stories of his early exploits with the girls. He would end by holding up his forefinger and middle finger together saying: 'dese are da two'."**

Figure 4. Author in first officer's uniform as a lieutenant, still age 18 by two weeks.

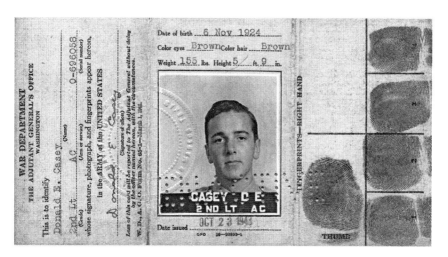

Figure 5. Eighteen year old Author's AGO identification card upon graduation from Navigation School, Class 43-15. 10/23/43.

Now it was time to get into those officer's uniforms we coveted for so long. The tailors were all over hustling us to buy their clothes. I fell for the first one without hesitation because he promised fast delivery. He conned me into buying the tunic without all of the seams because it looked "smoother". What he didn't tell me was all the money he was saving by eliminating the extra sewing. Whatever it cost, it was not a whole lot and I got better clothes later on. When I got back to Chicago, briefly, mother bought a "short-coat" for me at Marshall Fields. This was an overcoat cut off below the hip and looked very smart in camel hair fabric.

It was moving time again. I went through Chicago, as I said, for a few days. On my way to combat training, I remember flying from Chicago to Dallas. In Dallas I had to take a Greyhound bus to Pyote (not Peyote), Texas which was way out west, not too far from El Paso. Twelve hours later, after numerous stops, we arrived and I entered combat training at the Rattle Snake Army Air Base.

I wrote to Mother on November 5th:

"Well, I'm afraid I made it safely but not very soundly. I arrived in Dallas at 4:00 p.m., Wednesday, and found that the only way I could get to Pyote was by bus. So, I took the bus at 7:00 p.m. and rode all night to Big Springs, Texas, where I got a room and slept for about four hours. Then I took the next bus to Pyote which made a nice three hour trip. I have made up my mind about one thing, and that is never to travel by bus again."

"My new home has the name of 'Rattlesnake Bomber Base' which fits it perfectly. Why in God's name they ever took it away from the rattlesnakes is more than I can understand."

"I don't think I'll be flying for at least a week, so don't worry! They have more navigators than they can use for a long time and they are short on pilots. Right now I'm attached to the 19th but not assigned."

Another letter on November 9th:

"Well, yesterday, the ball started rolling and they assigned me to a crew. I've only been with them a few hours but I'm sure that they will be a lot of fun. I'm finally going to fly tomorrow and I'll know more about things when that's over."

"November 6th (1943, my 19th birthday) has come and gone but not without a celebration. Some of the boys and myself scoured the nearest large trading post and found some rum and then went to the dance hall and had a terrific steak and then woofed and hoofed away the evening with everybody else's girls. We shared the rum with eight other people who stopped by the table and never went home."

My Christmas list at that time included a bottle of bourbon with the reason being that "This is war, Ma." It never arrived but we had our sources. My new address was Sect. I, Flt. C, HBCTD - AAB, Pyote, Texas.

We fellow officers were so excited that we immediately accepted and liked each other very much. The pilot was Lew Jolls, a Michigan boy, about 21 years old. Before joining up, he was the projectionist in a movie theater. The co-pilot was Milton Miller, 20, from Pennsylvania who looked and acted the part, cool with a neat mustache. The bombardier was a 19 year old commercial artist, Jack Ellenberger from Texas. I was the pink-cheeked kid from Chicago, but I was cocky. We were all good looking, too. I was the last one to join the crew. Lew, Milt and Jack had been assigned at Ardmore, Oklahoma before coming to Pyote.

Figure 6. Author's first B-17 air crew officers, L-R Lew Jolls, pilot, Jack Ellenberger, bombardier, Milt Miller, copilot, author, navigator

Figure 7. Another shot of new crew, L-R Miller, Ellenberger, Author and Aircraft Commander Lew Jolls taken at /Rattle-Snake Army Air Base, Pyote, Texas 1943.

The enlisted crews were Staff Sergeant Bill McMillian - Flight Engineer and top gunner, Staff Sergeant Carnot Carlson - radio operator, Sergeant Neal Reed - ball turret, Sergeant Gus Hattenbach - right waist gunner, Sergeant Ken Harnack - left waist gunner, and Sergeant Charlie Taylor - tail gunner. I regret now that I had to let being an officer get between me and knowing these guys better. We just didn't fraternize on the ground. It wasn't done for reasons of military discipline.

Then we saw our training plane. It was a wreck of a B-17, but it was still flying - when it flew. The navigator's compartment, which was also shared with the bombardier, was a conical space about 7-8 feet wide at the base which came to a point at the front end. There was room for a desk on the left side and a chair for me to sit in and navigate. On each side of the nose there was a slot for a fifty-caliber machine gun. The bombardier had a semi-circular platform which fit right into the nose of Plexiglas and on which he sat facing front-ward. On his left was a panel for the bomb switches and up against the glass in front was a mount on the deck at his knees for the top-secret Norden bombsight.

In the B-17 model F, which was what we had, there was a 50 caliber machine gun mount through the Plexiglas for the bombardier's 50 caliber machine gun consisting of a hole in the center of the glass nose in a rubber grommet. In the later model B-17G there was a machine gun turret under the nose with two 50's and electric controls inside with which the bombardier could aim and operate the guns. The 50 Caliber gun was a potent weapon. The cartridge, including the casing, was almost six inches long. The bullet was about two inches long. No airplane could withstand the impact of a few of these shells in the right place.

The vital statistics of the B-17 were: Wing span - 109 feet, 9 inches; length - 74 feet 4 inches; height - 19 feet, one inch; weight - empty, 36,135 pounds, maximum load 72,000 pounds. It had four nine cylinder air-cooled radial engines, 1200 horse-power each. The plane could take 2,900 gallons of gasoline which were carried in the wings and what were called "Tokyo tanks" and had a stated maximum range of 4,400 miles. Maximum ceiling was 35,600 feet.

The book at the time on the B-17 said that it had a maximum continuous speed of 263 mph at 25,000 feet and a rate of climb of 37 minutes to 20,000 feet. This was pure propaganda because with a full load of gas, bombs and crew, we cruised at 150 mph and only got up to 170 mph when letting down empty of bombs and fuel from altitude. The maximum bomb load was 4,800 pounds (we usually carried 4,000.) It was supposed to carry a crew of 10. And, there were thirteen 50 caliber machine guns - two for the bombardier, two for the navigator (one on either side of the nose compartment) two in the top turret, two in the ball turret, two waist guns, one for the ventral position and two tail guns. The nose and waist guns were mounted through the hull and with their heavy butt ends suspended by wire cables attached to springs which helped balance off the heavy weight of the guns.

The B-17 first flew in 1937 and was billed as the new 300 mph bomber. It was supposed to cruise at 200 mph, but never did while I was in one. The plane's design was developed over the years into a remarkably sturdy aircraft. Its most prominent feature was the tall vertical stabilizer which made the craft very steady, such that it would keep itself on a straight course even if you took your hands off the controls. The landing gear consisted of a single wheel under each wing with a small tail wheel - a three-point landing plane in the traditional sense. It was painted olive drab to make it harder to see from above - but easy to spot from the ground. Later in the war, the new planes had a beautiful, unpainted silver aluminum skin except for the required markings. The paint, it was learned, only added unnecessary weight. The ship and equipment cost around $300,000.

A lot of time was spent at Pyote waiting for the ground crew to get our plane airworthy. We flew some training missions consisting of triangular courses which tested all our skills. The flight engineer was a stocky, bright eyed sergeant named McMillian. The others were kids like I was. We were getting acclimated to the airplane and enjoying every minute of it. In between flying, we went to the nearest big city of Midland, Texas. I celebrated my 19th birthday at the "Ace of Clubs." We had plenty to drink out of the bottles we were allowed to bring in with us.

I wrote to Mother on November 14th.

"Well, I finally got to fly in a B-17, and what a ride! The pilot was shooting landings and on the second one he felt the wheels giving way as we turned off the runway so he stopped the plane and all of a sudden it just collapsed and there we were flat on our belly. The unretractable ball turret just crushed like an egg. It was so unusual it was funny. My first ride cost the government about $200,000 because the wings cracked when the

prop blades didn't bend under." [Actually, it was the co-pilot who inadvertently flipped the switch to retract the wheels that caused the plane to collapse to the ground.]

"I'm leading a soft life these days but a dull one. We never go more than 50 miles away during this first phase so I just sleep. Today, however, I had my hands on the wheel and I made a few turns under the careful supervision of the pilot. He says he wants me to learn how to land and all the rest, just in case."

A week later, I wrote again to my Mother:

"Things are picking up now and we're flying all the time. It's a pretty sure fact that they're moving us out soon to another base, possibly outside Texas. Just the thought of leaving this god-forsaken state has me all 'hyped' up."

"We've been out on the gunnery range the last two flights and what a time that was. All I know about the fifty caliber (machine gun) is how to load and fire it, but I have a lot of fun anyway. We fly along at about 500 feet and just let fly at targets as they come into view. We try to correct our aim by watching where the shots kick up the dust."

"I'm enclosing some pictures of the crew and I'm going to have a big one made of the best one. I hope you like them."

Figure 8. Author's first B -17 crew: Jolls (partially obscured), author, copilot Milton Miller and bombardier Jack Ellenberger taken at Pyote, Texas Rattlesnake Army Air Base, November, 1943.

I wrote also to my brother Dick:

"Things are really popping at Pyote AAB and I'll soon be moving out. We're flying every day at about five hours per and I haven't done a lick of navigation as yet. We're limited to a fifty mile radius so there's not much use for it. All we do is shoot off the fifties and drop bombs, but its loads of fun. The guns don't kick too much but they are heavy as hell."

"Pyote AAB is called Rattlesnake Bomber Base. It's nothing but desert and sagebrush. In Biloxi, it was mildew, but here its dust. It's a standing tradition that the first man awake in the morning goes around and dusts off his crewmates. The 17's are swell, but they don't fly. They lumber across the sky. My pilot and crew are a bunch of swell fellows and I'm having a big time with them."

Figure 9. Model B-17-G in which we flew in combat training while still in the U.S.

A letter the same day to Dad:

"I've got the best crew they ever put out and I wouldn't trade for the world. My pilot is a Michigan farm boy and when it comes to his boys, he's consideration plus. He's quiet and nerveless and just a hell of a flyer at all times. The copilot is from Pittsburgh, Pa., but he's not a direct opposite from the pilot as you might think. He's not quiet and not loud and he knows his B-17 and also that it's not a P-38 and is not to be treated as such. The bombardier (Jack Ellenberger) is the wild one. If you ask him if he's from Texas, he'll loudly answer: 'Hell no, I'm from Dallas.' He has a girl at every airbase town but he says there is really only one in Boise where he is going to move after the war. He raises the roof every place he goes but when it comes to bombing, he's a different person and can really ring that bell in the pickle

barrel."

"So far we haven't done anything except instrument flying, gunnery and bombing. I can't seem to get enough of
firing that fifty to satisfy my desires. Gunnery is so dras-
tically important that it's terrible. When those German
fighters are diving at you with all guns blazing, its get
him before he gets you and that means precision shooting. From now on, its kill or be killed, so I'm going to
be the hottest gunner ever seen or I'll know the reason
why. I hope you don't mind my sounding off like this,
but you might as well know how I feel about it if you
hadn't guessed before. We're moving to a new base soon
and hope it's out of Texas just for a change in scenery.
It will be nice to look out and see something beside sand
and cactus. They should give Texas back to the rattlesnakes where it belongs. Write soon and let me know
what's cooking."

Figure 10. Author and his totally outranked older brother, Aviation Cadet James D. Casey, Jr.,

Figure 11. Author with his mother Virginia Smith Casey, brother James, December 1943, Miami Beach, Florida.

I got a short leave and visited the folks in Miami Beach. Brother Jim came down, too. He was still a cadet and terribly outranked by his second lieutenant kid brother. This didn't stop him from greeting me with a wrestling take-down to the floor of the house just to show that was the biggest. Dad had been promoted to Lieutenant Colonel and the newspaper said he had been a second lieutenant with the 163rd Bomber Squadron as a combat observer in France in 1918. He joined up again in 1942, the article said, and served with the Army Air Forces Training command headquarters at Fort Worth, Texas after being a group leader at Kesler Field, Mississippi. He had been a wing commander and a personnel officer in Atlantic City, N.J. and with the Transport Command in Brownsville, Texas.

Figure 12. Author (right) with brother Jim Casey, Jr. and father, Lt. Col. J. Douglas Casey wearing WWI Overseas Stripe.

A short time later, we shipped out of Pyote and headed for Dyersburg, Tennessee, about 50 miles north of Memphis. We spent more time flying and getting combat advice, but again, the planes were in bad shape. I remember one day, we were taxiing and ran off the runway into the sticky mud and had to get a "tug" to pull us out. The officer in charge raised holy hell. That was minor compared to the accident at Pyote. Operations was screaming about the $300,000 airplane which might have been ruined. They were right and we were wrong.

I wrote Dad on December 1st.

"This is my second base as an officer in the second Air Force and I have had just about enough. I'm speaking for the entire group of combat people when I say that this Air Force is a scrambled mess. At Pyote, they treated us like a bunch of kids, even threatening to make up for being tardy by punishment tours on the ramp. Half the time they didn't even know who was supposed to be there. Then they shipped us here by troop train to replace a group that had not had as complete training as we had who were going some place else for more advanced training."

"We arrived here and they marched us to our barracks which are hutments with coal stoves and no glass windows. The next day we went to the dispensary for a medical check and instead of going right down a line as one might normally do, we had to shift for ourselves and find out individually what was to be done. Well, when you have two hundred doing that, it becomes a mad turmoil. Instead of organizing things, the head medic ran up and down cursing us and shouting and not accomplishing anything."

"That's typical Second Air Force activities! Anyone that ranks above a 2d Lt. treats us like cadets. One Major at Pyote chewed about a hundred of us out in the briefing

room because we didn't come to attention the second he entered the room. Then he said that another demonstration of that kind and we would all walk punishment tours. What I want to know is just why did they give us commissions anyway?"

"If you think San Marcos is in a bad state, you ought to see the Second Air Force. Honestly, dad it's lousy and something should be done. When a field knows that you're coming and doesn't make any preparations, then something should be done. As for myself, I would like to talk to you about that. I think we might have made a mistake back at San Marcos."

This letter was followed a few days by another complaining missive about the Second Air Force.

"They don't even honor our AGO passes here, so they issue a special pass which must be turned in at their wish which is whenever they feel like it, usually all the time except for official off-days. Some afternoons we have nothing to do and could be in town, but no, they don't see it that way. We're just a bunch of glorified cadets."

"I think you're wrong about Germany and me. I'm afraid they have made up their minds to stick out this war to the last German. Another thing, about me; the training is all aimed towards the European theater right down to the English air traffic procedure. In Aircraft identification, they are stressing planes like: the Me-110, the Me-109 F&G, JU-88, P-47, P-51, Spitfire, Beaufort, Hurricane and two others which I don't remember at present. In other words, they want us to be able to distinguish between our escort and the German pursuit ships. They are stressing formation flying, gunnery,

landmark navigation and aircraft identification."

**"I doubt if I can get off for Christmas and I'm begin-
ning to doubt about that pre-overseas leave you promised. We'll know for sure in a couple of months, so I
guess I'll have to sweat it out."**

On December 9th, I wrote again to my Mother:

**"Tennessee is muddy, rainy and foggy, so I'm not too
happy here. Still, there is always Memphis, which com-
pensates in spite of the** (50 mile) **distance. I've only
flown four hours in two weeks, so you can imagine the
Air Corps isn't too happy about things either."**

In Memphis, we found things to do. We usually stayed at
the famous Peabody Hotel. One Saturday night, after the usual
drinking and carousing, Jack Ellenberger and I retired to our room
for a night's sleep. Sometime after midnight there came a rap on
the door. It was a friend from another crew with whom we had
been close all the way. He was "three sheets to the wind", as the
expression went, and he had a woman with him, also very drunk.
Instead of closing the door in his face, we let them in. They needed
a bed so one of us had to do the gentlemanly thing and allow the
needy couple to get their rest. After a lot of moaning and groan-
ing, the woman said: "Hey, you're not Joe," and finally they both
passed out. The next morning, he said, after the woman had left,
"You should have come over and pushed me out and helped yourselves. She wouldn't have known the difference." The thought
never crossed my mind, but it surely would have been rape under
the circumstances.

My father wrote a lot of letters to me but I didn't or
couldn't save them. I wish now that I had. My letter to him just
before Christmas from Dyersburg, expressed my surprise and pleasure:

"Last weekend I went to Chicago with the officers of my crew and took them to the Athletic Club at your expense. They were impressed no end by what they saw and heard and, I'm afraid now that they think you're a millionaire. One instance especially: They heard some gentlemen mention that he had lost some $2,000 in a little game, and another fellow said somewhat jokingly, 'too bad.' They almost hit the ceiling. We went swimming, had lunch and that's about all. Before I came back, however, I stopped by the Club and picked up your Christmas presents to me. It was swell of you. Would you like to know what they were? OK, just a fifth of Lord Calvert and one of Three Feathers. I'm doling it out like liquid gold, one ounce at a time."

"It's colder than the devil up here, so you and Mother can forget about mentioning that sunshine and swimming. I also haven't been flying much lately, so I really have nothing to go into detail about. I still haven't had a navigation mission, but I have done a lot of riding in circles within fifty miles or less of home base. Oh, but that is exciting at times when things go wrong in the cockpit. More than once, I've been more frightened than in that little car accident we had in Wisconsin."

"Before I finish with a resounding cheer, I want to know how sure you are about that overseas leave. I'm not getting worried or anything. I just want to have the straight dope. I wish you all a very merry Christmas without me."

On Christmas Eve, I wrote Mother again.

"It's only another work day for us. I realize how nice it would have been to be with the family again, but then it's out of my reach. You know I haven't gotten one gift

for anybody. I've got the money, but no opportunities to buy. I hope you don't mind my sending you some to spend on yourself."

I saw my first 'porno' movie at the base, of all places. Very enlightening to one who had never heard of pornography and whose closest brush with it was a few nude photos in Popular Photography Magazine which I subscribed to at Campion High. I didn't even know the words yet to describe everything they were doing on screen.

From Dyersburg on January 18th, I wrote again to my Mother:

"We went through overseas processing today and got all our shortages filled and a few new things such as blankets, canteens and leggings added. They checked my teeth and pronounced them perfect. When I said that I hadn't had any dental work for a year and a half, they said that I could thank my dentist for that.

"We're flying every day and most of the time at 20,000 feet. Boy, is it cold. We went down to Baton Rouge last week and this week we're going to Gulfport. I don't think I'll get lost down there."

On February 6th, I telegraphed cryptically to the folks that we were leaving the next day, but did not say where we were going. It turned out to be Kearney, Nebraska where we picked up a brand new B-17 for an overseas trip.

I wrote home on February 13th:

"Enclosed is a money order for $100. Please purchase a $100 war bond and start my savings account with the

remainder. I have a $100 bond coming out of my pay and a $50 allotment and both are being sent to you in care of Dad's office in Chicago. We're on our way to some place, and besides that there's not much else I can say. I'll write when I reach my destination"

Kearney was not the place to be in February, to say the least. It was colder than anywhere else I had been before. The snow was deep and the wind blew unrelentingly and hard across the vast openness of the treeless plains. We were assigned our airplane, a brand shiny new silver B-17 with all the latest equipment. On February 12th we flew a two hour mission to calibrate all the instruments, especially air speed and the compass. Other than that we spent the time eating frequently and heartily and waited. However, we were not allowed off the base. It was all a secret, of course, but we were off for the British Isles. It had been a relief to depart Dyersburg because of the depressing atmosphere of the Tennessee weather in January and the tired airplanes they made us fly.

On February 19th, I wrote my Mother again from Kearney on a piece of stationery which had a picture at the top of a man falling through the air in an unopened parachute reading a book. The balloon to the left said: "I'll be down to where I can write you more often".

In the letter I wrote: "Well, we finally left Kearney, but where we are now, I can't tell. I'm all right and so is everything else, and besides that, there's nothing else to say so I'll say 'so long' and write soon." We had been there a little over a week.

Leaving Kearney was the start of an exciting trip. We knew that this was it, we were headed overseas for operational flying. We took off from Kearney in the morning and flew non-stop to our destination. It was fun at the time cruising past Chicago and over New York City. We had good weather and the navigation was quite simple. We all thought we would have a chance to "buzz" our homes en route but the timing of the flight prevented this from working out. It took almost eight hours to get to our next stop, Grenier Field, Manchester, New Hampshire.

Arriving there, we dallied a day or so receiving briefings on arctic and water survival techniques. They issued us more equipment and heated flying suits. We prepared to take off for England. Everything looked great until we tried to start the engines. The rest of the ships had gone and there we were, still on the ground waiting for the mechanics to fix the problem. Time ticked away and still we remained in place. Finally, after what seemed hours, we too were in the air and on our way. In no time at all, we were over nothing but woods and snow covered wilderness. But the navigation was good and we landed after dark at Goose Bay, Labrador.

There was no welcoming committee waiting for us. The message was terse and to the point. "Get what rest you can because you're taking off for Iceland at midnight" which by that time was less than two hours away. Lew Jolls stayed with the airplane during refueling futilely trying to test his electric suit for which there was no power with the motors off. We ate whatever it was they had prepared for us without enthusiasm. The tension was great, though, and I for one could not sleep, even for a few minutes. They briefed us navigators by giving us the meteorological forecast and our maps. We were to fly in darkness using the heading dictated by the meteorologically predicted wind speed and direction. I had my celestial navigation equipment, my Octant and star position books, ready and waiting.

The rest of the crew was in good spirits. What the heck, they could nap in the back of the plane to their hearts content with confidence that the unerring kid navigator would bring them in safely. If the pilot was concerned, he didn't show it. We took off and headed east. I hadn't slept since the previous night, but I had plenty of nervous energy and a full load of responsibility for my crew and the airplane.

It is well to remember that the B-17 was not a fast airplane. We cruised at 150 mph which was a slow crawl even then. Aloft, we soon found ourselves between two layers of clouds, low and high. The pilot was ordered to maintain a given altitude in order to avoid colliding with other airplanes along the way. We were stuck there at 9,000 feet. I waited and watched for a break in the clouds so that I could get some shots of the stars. They were not to be seen through the upper layer of clouds under which we flew. There were no landmarks over the ocean, either.

Briefly, we broke into the clear and I was able to sight just one star, the North Star, the sub-stellar point of which is always the North Pole. I worked as fast as I could and got just that one star. Not enough for a fix. The line I drew on my map based on that one sighting ran east to west and told me only one thing. But it was a very important bit of information - if my calculations were correct. I concluded that we were still on the assigned course as the meteorologist had predicted we would be if we followed his forecast of the winds aloft. What I didn't know was *where* on the course we were. But if the wind direction was correct, there was a good chance that the wind speed was also right, leaving me with an educated guess as to our position. Meanwhile, the crew slept on. Even the pilot managed a nap while relieved by the co-pilot.

I stayed at my post, on my knees. And I must have dozed off, momentarily, because I immediately startled myself awake; but there was no time for sleep. Still, I had no way to accurately report my position, except by deduction based on the estimated wind speed and direction and the steady 150 mph of airspeed maintained by the pilot. When we passed Greenland, I got a reading on the radio compass from what was called "BW1" which gave us a longitudinal line which tended to further confirm the accuracy of the "meetro" winds as forecasted.

It was not all that comforting because we had been warned that German submarines could be stationed in the area and were wont to send out fake radio signals as if they were air force transmitters. Every great once in a while, somebody fell for this and wound up off course and out of fuel over the ocean, a tragic casualty of war. Whether they were working on us that day, I will never know, but I picked up the signal of our radio station at Reykjavík, Iceland from the direction it was supposed to be and we homed in the rest of the way, arriving around mid-morning. We heard later that one of our ships was lost en route, although the cause was never made clear.

Lew Jolls reminded me long after the war that on that flight to Iceland we developed icing on the wings which could have easily finished us off, causing our ship to crash into the ocean never to be seen again. Lew was up on this situation and was able to correct the problem. This was fairly common that night, it turned out.

As Lew tells it, "We had wing ice which we were able to break off with the deicer boots, but we were losing airspeed. I correctly assumed that we also had propeller ice and remembered that cycling the prop pitch up and down was the recommended procedure." When it broke loose, it was a preview of what flak fragments hitting the fuselage would sound like. Lew made it seem so routine at the time that we all quickly forgot about it. Our flying time to Iceland was a grueling nine hours and fifteen minutes and we landed with the sun shining.

Iceland was quite forgettable. There were absolutely no trees, anywhere. We were not allowed off the base, but we did get to visit the Officers Club and refresh ourselves. I still can remember shooting some pool at the Club because the table was at the end of the Nissen Hut, a semicircle of corrugated steel commonly used for overseas stations, and they handed us a two foot pool cue for use in the corners where the regular cue wouldn't fit.

I met a lovely Red Cross Lady who was acting as a hostess at the Club and she was so gracious to us. What a personal sacrifice she was making just to be there. She remarked about my name and told me that there had been another flier named "Casey" who had

been through there not too long before. She said he claimed that he
was going to be the hottest pilot in the 8th Air Force over Europe
and maybe I would run into him. How strange life is, for I did actually meet him and came to know him personally in Germany, eventually.

The next day we were on our way to Scotland. We had no
real view of Ireland because we flew to the north and landed at
Prestwick, Scotland, a little shorter flight of six and a half hours.
We were completely unaware at the time that this quaint city
was in fact the cradle of golf. We came in smartly and unloaded
our personal belongings and said goodbye to our plane forever. I
didn't even have time to dwell on my own personal accomplishment - navigating in a brand new government airplane with nine
passengers (seven of whom hadn't a clue as to the struggle they
survived together with me and with my brand new, previously un-
tested skill) across the vast Atlantic ocean, apparently flawlessly
at my ripe young age of 19 years. No one of my crew said a single
word of congratulations and I gave it no thought at the time myself. I had been trained for the job in 15 short weeks, my graduation had been acknowledged with a commission and silver wings,
and I performed the task assigned. The fact is that I was still growing and I hadn't even begun to shave yet. What I did have was too
much self-confidence for my own good. They had trained us well,
though, and this proved it.

We spent the night in a Scottish castle which Lew Jolls told
us was rumored to be haunted. We were too tired and too keyed
up, however, to dwell on it. The next day we boarded trucks and
trains and headed south to central England to "Stoke on Trent," the
replacement depot for aircrews. The city was a famous pottery center where they made such precious dinnerware as "Wedgewood"
china. Another less famous place where we were billeted after that
was "Stone". It was a small town in Staffordshire in the Midlands
and was famous for its brewery, which we never were afforded
the chance to visit. The winter climate there, indoors and out, was

appropriate for the name and the place, "stone cold." Now I knew why the movies I had seen about the olden days of England depicted the people as dressed in heavy robes at all times, even while indoors. Our winter clothes definitely did not do the job and we were miserable at all times.

Stone was another place new crews were warehoused while waiting for requisitions from combat bomb groups for replacements to replenish their losses. It was also where you were sent when you completed your tour before leaving for home, but we were never allowed to meet or mingle with any of these people. Perhaps it was for the best that new crews did not get to talk to the veterans, after all. We were full of anticipation for what lay ahead and did not need any one to deflate our balloons.

All I told the folks at home was written in a letter to my Mother's sister, my Aunt Babe Holland:

> **"Our new address is APO 1201 - AA 102, c/o Postmaster, NY, NY."** I related that I was very cold and asked that nobody said to expect a pleasant trip to Europe. I wrote that it was February and Stone had all the warmth one would expect of such substance in the middle of winter with no central heating and other sources of warmth that Henry VIII may have had on his personal drawing board. We were now in process of what might be called pre-flight combat training. And we were miserable at all times. But we had a surfeit of enthusiasm for the job that lay ahead. We just didn't care as long as we were moving in the direction we had hoped for.

In a previous letter to my mother dated February 26th I said:

> **"I am in the United Kingdom and feeling fine, but I miss the States already, especially Miami and that wonderful sunshine. I have traveled more this month than I probably ever will again in my life and when I return I will**

tell you all about it. I bought a lot of candy when I left but it is practically all gone, so send me some Hershey's. This is a request and you must show it to the postmaster in order to send it. Also, buy me a tonette (a sort of pocket flute made out of "Bakelite" - the 40's version of modern day plastic) **which I didn't get as you advised while I had the chance. I have plenty of cigarettes."**

Our next stop was Bovingdon airfield on the outskirts of London. We did aircraft-recon (recognition) but not much else that I can recall now. While there we witnessed a German Luftwaffe raid on London. We could see the arc lights in the sky and could hear the airplanes and bombs and anti-aircraft guns. Quoting Lew Jolls, "We stood outside in a very light snowfall and realized that there really was a war going on which we would soon be a part of."

We did get a little time off and I wrote to the folks that I was now authorized to wear the European Theater of Operations (ETO) ribbon. Of course none of us put this one on. **"Everybody here knows where I am, and besides, there are so many other fellows with more valuable ribbons that I would look foolish."**

Letters home were now sent via "V-mail". The V was for victory, we hoped. The letter was censored and then micro-filmed and shipped back home in rolls for reprocessing on 3 1/2 by 5 photographic print paper on arrival.

"I have been visiting the local towns and find them quite interesting and quaint. All one can buy to drink is beer and an occasional gin and orange, so I'm lonesome for the States. The girls wander around the streets or stand in front of the hotels waiting for the date that always when you ask them is late already. Any date over five minutes qualifies you to kiss them goodnight and they feel hurt if you don't. I hope you can get that candy because we only get one bar a week and a roll of English Toffee. I'm hungry all the time as you can easily imagine.

When I think of that roast beef at the country club it makes my mouth water a gallon."

On March 8th I wrote again to the folks:

"Well, I'm getting that schooling I told you about and for me it's all about getting to the target and getting away. We are also learning radar and aircraft recognition and the latter is really being pressed. From school we go to our combat base and I don't know how soon that will be. We have a black-out every night, but we usually go to bed early so it doesn't bother us too much."

"All our gunners are now at gunnery school and I only hope they get all the possible good out of it they can. I'm sure they're worried enough about their skins that they will be really eager to learn. The new shiny airplane we had was taken away, so I don't know what kind of ship we will get now. That sure was a swell plane. I'm constantly cold in the feet and have all but given up being warm again until I get home. All I want is a nice roaring fireplace and I'll be happy. I'm no longer hard to please as you can see."

"The food is plain but nourishing and I'm so hungry that I eat anything they give me, regardless of taste or smell. You can send me candy, fruit juice and stationery. They are all very hard to get. Coat hangars cost $2.50, so I'm glad I brought some along. Write soon and often."

Then I wrote the letter I had been waiting to send. March 16th, address 526 Sqd. 379th Bomb Group, Kimbolton.

"England is cold, this base is cold, I'm cold, I have a cold, and so on into the night. Words fail me when it

comes time to praise merry old England. I am not on operational status but this is my permanent station, and after a little more school and some practice missions, we'll be ready. This is supposed to be a very good squadron and group, but I suppose any squadron will be as good as its members make it."

"The 379th Bomb Group was located in the town of Kimbolton in south central England, near Bedford. Kimbolton had a castle which during Henry the VIII's reign housed his first wife, Katherine of Aragon. Unfortunately for her, she wound up dying there, too. The air base was only a couple of miles out of town, a short bicycle ride and it had the usual metal clad buildings, barracks, operations room and tower. The land had been used primarily for farming prior to the war."

"They moved our crew into a corrugated steel Nissen hut barracks building which could best described as a sixteen foot in diameter and fifty foot long tin can cut in half lengthwise and plunked down on a wooden deck. There were two rows of single bunks, eight to a side, with about a four foot aisle down the middle. In the center of the hut was a real, honest-to-goodness pot-bellied coal burning stove which was our only source of heat. Beside each bunk was a rack hanging from the ceiling for the clothes. The foot locker each of us had served as a bureau for the non-hanging clothing, such as underwear, shirts and socks.

On March 20th I wrote:

"My health is fine and everything is OK, seeing as I'm still noncombatant"

March 24th: **"I'm still a home front boy, but at last on the**

operational list. I will send you clippings of all my exploits and I want you to make a scrapbook."

What we had been doing mostly was flying practice missions to get the feel of the close formation flying we would be called on to do as well as the airplane and the surroundings. The experienced crews were going out on combat missions but we were not really aware yet of what was going on or what we had to look forward to.

On the same piece of paper under March 25, 1944 I wrote:

"Well, our first raid was for us a trip to London and back. One engine went out and we couldn't keep up with the formation. We turned around and at least I made the boys feel a little better by splitting the field. I got five letters today, 3 from mother and 2 from dad. Just keep writing and everything will be OK."

"The food here is the best in the ETO. I'm sure, so don't worry about me on that account. I'm even putting on weight. We haven't got a ship that's really our own, meaning that somebody else has already named it, but we tacked on our own name: 'Hells Belle'. Our bombardier is an ex-commercial artist and we have a real work of art on the backs of our A-2 jackets. I'm fine, else I wouldn't be flying. England is the damndest, dampest country I've ever seen, but I'm getting used to it day by day."

"My love to all and get Jim on the ball if you want him to hear from his big brother."

On April 2nd, I sent several newspaper clippings. One headline read:

"FORTS GIVEN BITTER BATTLE BY LUFTWAFFE".
In the text the writer said **"The Luftwaffe struck desper-**

**ately at Flying Fortresses yesterday as the American
heavies penetrated to central Germany and bombed
military targets in the Brunswick area through almost
solid clouds. German fighter pilots in formations of up to
150 slashed at the bombers and their American escorts in
brief but fierce battles over the heart of the Reich". The
Germans were reported to have lost 39 planes in the air
and more on the ground while we lost nine bombers and
nine fighters."**

**"All bombers attacked their targets - which were un-
specified in the official announcement - with the 'through
the clouds' technique. The German raid-warning system
began to function shortly after noon with 'Achtung' announcements going on the air to report formations approaching northwestern Germany. The announcements
soon afterward put the bombers over central Germany
and radio broadcasts began to refer to 'giant air battles'
over the Reich."**

Our personal version of the first complete mission was just
as exciting for us. We flew to Dijon, France and saw no German
fighters at all. That is not to say that we hadn't been scared out of
our socks, starting with the wake-up call that day. We got out of
bed and hustled into our clothes. Breakfast and then on to the briefing. The navigators picked up their maps all marked out as to the
route and checked their watches and "hacked" the second hand so
that it read exactly what the master clock said. There was a short
recess while we met the Chaplain and took communion - sort of
like the last rites, if you will. For some it would be and for the rest
of us it could be. Stomachs were churning all the way and there
was always a serious bathroom call or two to empty out while we
could. The bladders and bowels needed no urging, I remember for
sure.

We picked up our flight gear which consisted of the heavy
fleece jackets and trousers. Most of the crews had electric suits

which we got eventually. The heated jacket and trousers were dark green and made of a fabric called barathea wired like an electric blanket. When plugged in, the suit was cozy and warm even at 50 degrees below zero. We wore the heavy fleece lined flying boots and felt slippers with more wiring which plugged into the trousers' cuffs.

I was the one with the bright orangish-tan leather brief case holding the maps and the radio signals of the day encased in plastic holders (each day the signals and the locations of the "splasher beacons" were different and always top secret.)They hauled us out in canvas covered trucks to the "hard stand" where our ship, fueled and armed by the ground crew, was ready to go.

The "hard stand" was a circular concrete pad on which the plane rested between missions, connected to the taxi strip by a concrete stem. Each plane had its own place scattered away from the others so that in the event of an attack by air, one bomb could not damage or destroy all of us at once. The ground crew members had a tent they worked from and where they stored all of their tools for repairing the airplane. They regarded us with some awe, maybe a bit of jealousy, but they didn't have to care what happened because they could always get another airplane. Personally, I can't remember one of them who stood out as a cheerleader for our efforts or who kissed our feet on returning. Perhaps they had learned from experience that it was better not to get to close in case we didn't come back one day.

On arrival at the hard stand, we worked off some of our nervous energy pulling the props through to pump some gas into the cylinders. The pilots, navigator, bombardier and Crew Chief entered the plane from the front through the nose emergency hatch. (A B-17 sits on the ground in a three-point attitude - two big tires in front and a small tail-wheel in back.) I would throw my bulky bag of flying gear - parachute and brief case into the open nose hatch. Then I would jump up to grasp the top side of the hatch and swing my legs up about six and a half feet off the ground into the catwalk.

Figure 13. Nose compartment of B-17-G showing "chin" turret, top turret, navigator's port machine gun and the door of the nose hatch.

Pictures following on the next two pages were taken in 1990 at Meigs Field, Chicago.

Figure 14. Above: author beside the Nose Hatch, 3 feet away from his navigator's desk in the nose compartment. This was the opening out of which author parachuted to safety during the shoot down of his plane.

Below: Navigator's desk sans flight instruments: altimeter, airspeed indicator, compass, and the RAF "Gee Box" navigation aid.

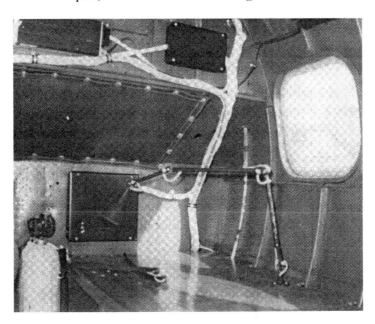

Once on board, I crawled to my position about 3 feet away, checked my equipment and laid out my maps on the small navigator's desk. My two 50 caliber machine guns were loaded but on safety. The question on my mind was would they work when I needed them? Then pre-flight procedures commenced.

Figure 15. Waist cabin with machine guns for two gunners, ball turret (amidship) forward view shows radio room and bomb bay. Tail gunner's position to the rear.

Check the intercom, check in from each position on the plane, and check this and that in a long list of things that needed to work for us to make it where we were going and back. Then it was time to start engines. The ground crew signaled to us to begin taxiing to the runway.

Figure 16. Outside view of ball turret in which sat the gunner with his knees up under his chin. Turret had full 360 degree horizontal rotation and 180 degree vertical position.

Figure 17. Tail gunner's position at the rear of the plane with 180 degree horizontal panorama. The gunner usually assumed a kneeling position to fire his guns. This position on the lead ship was often manned by an officer to monitor the positions of other planes following in the formation.

It seemed to take forever for the planes to line up. Once at the edge of the runway, each engine was separately "run up" to check its "mags" or magnetos. The sound was deafening but as long as there were no backfires, the engines sounded good enough to do the job. When we centered ourselves on the runway for take off, the co-pilot confirmed "tail wheel locked, light on, light out," which meant the ship was now ready to go.

The tension continued to mount. The planes took off one by one. We were anxious to get going but thoroughly scared of the unknown that lay ahead. We waited our turn. Taking off was always an adventure, particularly when the wind direction required us to use the shortest runway. Nevertheless, the bombardier and I both stayed right there in the nose compartment oblivious to the prospect that we would be right there in front in case the plane were to nose-dive in. We did that to show our disdain (a shorter word for foolhardiness) for the dangers involved in just getting off the ground. The ground crew, as a joke, rigged my navigator's chair, a swivel secretary-type chair on wheels, with a seat belt. Once secured in that chair, one could be assured that whatever bouncing around one did in the nose compartment, it stayed glued to one's bottom. (Of course, I never fastened the belt.)

After becoming airborne just after 11:00 a.m., we slowly climbed to altitude. The airplane was fully loaded with fuel, bombs and ammunition and nine men. Its rate of climb was not all that fast even when empty. Once we were out of the clouds, which so often hung over the field, we assembled as the Group leader circled slowly to the left on the climb. We knew the departure time but not the strict order of the day as far as leaving for the enemy coast. We flew in a somewhat loose formation which would tighten up when once we were over the Continent and even more-so if any German fighters were sighted. Our ship crept up and out of England. The coastline gave me a ready reference to do some "pilotage" which means essentially identifying reference points on the ground so as to fix our position.

When we could see the French coast not all that far away, our anticipation continued to build. I knew where we were at all times by keeping track of the effects of the "winds aloft" and the time between checkpoints.

No enemy fighters were in sight and none of ours either - our usual escorts - as we bore on toward the target which was Dijon, France. It was over forty degrees below zero at 19,000 feet altitude. We donned our flak vests and steel helmets and breathed heavily into our oxygen masks without which one was certain to pass out and die in minutes from anoxia. The B-17 was not pressurized as planes are today. We watched and waited.

Not knowing really what to expect the first time out, we were probably not as nervous as we should have been. When the mission proved uneventful, we were exuberant with unjustifiable confidence in our ability to meet the enemy, which we hadn't that time, at least. Our target was a German fighter base and our load was incendiaries. We unloaded at about 2:45 p.m. It was reported that for all our efforts we destroyed 3 German planes and several hangars and workshops. The Flak was light, but a couple of the planes sustained minor damage. Our ship was undamaged and I had the feeling that if all the missions could be like this one, it would not be all that bad. We were back on the ground after a total flying time of seven hours.

COMBAT AIRCREWS AT THE TIP OF THE SPEAR WERE TOTALLY DEPENDENT ON THE SKILLS OF THE GROUND CREWS TO KEEP THEM FLYING

General James H. Doolittle of the famed Tokyo raiders was made commanding general of the 8th Air Force shortly after the Jolls crew began flying with the 379th Bomb Group. One of his first morale-building steps was to order the preparation of an official Army publication explaining and praising the work of our ground crews and staff in keeping us flying. The following is a paraphrasing of his report in the Spring of 1944:

We fliers really had nothing to do with maintaining our airplane and its guns, bombs and equipment in good working order for each mission. Maintenance, armament and the all of the things required by each aircraft and its equipment were the job of many experts on the ground. There were 30 men involved for every bomber starting with those who fed and clothed the air crews, those that ran Operations and Intelligence, identified the targets, mapped the routes to avoid Flak. Highly trained bomb handlers carefully loaded the explosives we carried on board the planes two at a time fully realizing that any projectile can blow up, fuse or no fuse, if dropped from as low as four feet.

The armorers would head for the tent just as the oxygen truck arrived. Our planes were already filled with gas when they landed after the mission the day before. Each plane's crew chief knew that at least 100 gallons of gas would be used in just taxiing and take-off. The Oxygen pressure for each crew position had to be checked in the bottles on board. Above 10,000 feet, all air crewmen wore oxygen masks lest they pass out and die of anoxia at higher altitudes. Also attending the planes were 6 instrument specialists who repaired and maintained the electrical wiring on board.

The crew chief methodically checked and double checked the preflight list. Armament specialists (3) then arrived to see that the solenoids are properly adjusted. The bombsight man installed the Norden bombsight and the autopilot expert gave the equipment its last ground check. Each machine gun was put on safety position and it's supply of bullets topped up.

In the briefing room, the curtain would be pulled back revealing the mission and routing to the target. The anxious crews cheered or moaned depending on the target of the day. The weather officer announced weather conditions expected on the way to the target, visibility for bombing and the forecast on returning to base several hours later. The navigators were alerted that straying from the appointed route could mean flying over flak areas the exact routing would avoid. Once the aircrews were on board, the Control Tower took over. Two flares burst in the air signaling to start taxiing in train into takeoff positions.

Once -the planes were gone, the ground crews would return to their barracks to catch up on their sleep. Whatever happened after that was out of their control but not their minds - until the time of the Group's return some hours later when the ground crews would get back to work getting ready for the next mission.

A March 29th British newspaper article was headlined:

"LUFTWAFFE NESTS HIT AFTER 'INVASION SPIES RANGE OVER BRITAIN. 2100 Enemy planes KOd in 8 weeks, Gen. Doolittle Says."

The article went on: **"As the German press sounded fresh warnings that an Allied invasion was imminent the Luftwaffe sent over Britain a comparatively strong force of planes, apparently for reconnaissance. American heavy bombers struck their third successive blow yesterday at the bases in northern France from which the Luftwaffe defends Europe."**

"The Luftwaffe seemed to be leaving the defense to thinly scattered batteries of anti-aircraft guns. Despite the clear weather, the attacking forces met no enemy fighter position and bombed 'with good results'. This work ... had been done by 'an invading force' of some 170,000 U.S. airmen."

This was the news story of the Jolls' crew's second mission which took us to Brunswick, Germany, about 100 miles southeast of Hamburg and the same distance west of Berlin. The target was clouded over so we bombed through the clouds. At the time

I couldn't help remarking that the flak bursts were way off to our right. When we got back, we learned in the debriefing that the flak bursts were where the target actually was and we had bombed a "Brussel Sprout patch" without suffering a scratch. So much for the highly-skilled and experienced lead navigator. I was doing my job of keeping track of where we were, trusting the lead ship to get us to the target. Again, we saw no enemy fighters to speak of. We were back on the home ground around 5:00 p.m.

I wrote to the folks on April 3rd:

"Enclosed find a sketch done by my bombardier (of his painting on the side of our plane 'Hells Belle') which is self-explanatory. Put it with my clippings."

Dad had an army artist copy it in color and framed it and mounted it on the wall at home for me when I returned.

"Spring is here in England and in the dampest way. Thank God I have a roof over my head and sheets to crawl between. It just doesn't seem like we are in the war in body and somehow that fact doesn't disturb me in the least. However, one can sit down and think about it and then is when you realize what is going on."

"The only thing to do is not to think about it, hard as it sometimes may become. I read an article today about the evacuation of Miami (the folks had moved), **so I'm using the Chicago address. I hope dad doesn't want to go overseas because he would be much happier where he is. You remember 1917, don't you dad? Well it isn't half that bad, but you aren't that young, either."**

Again on April 8th, I wrote:

"I missed an opportunity to send some flowers for Mothers' day on purpose because I thought you would be moving out soon. I wish you a happy holiday and that's as far as I can go at this date. Also, I wish a big happy

birthday to Johnny and may he have many more as happy. I just returned from London and find it exciting and tiring. It's big and over-crowded, and can't compare in entertainment to any American city of fair size. I'm happy I'm here and not in Italy or India, or any other battle front. At least it's civilized."

"Well folks, it's getting late and we are alerted so I'd better close now and go to bed. There is work scheduled for tomorrow and I hope Hitler feels its full effects. Write soon."

The news on April 12th headlined:

"STREAMS OF U.S. SHIPS PAST FRANCE, REICH; 1,000 TON RAF RAID. Forts, Libs, B26's Hit Widespread Targets; You'll Soon Fly Dawn-to-Dusk in the Invasion, Eisenhower Tells Pilots."

"American bombers and fighters struck their heaviest pre-invasion blows yesterday as they smashed Nazi targets the width of Europe - from France to the Baltic Sea - in the wake of a 4,000-ton night assault by the RAF. An air fleet of nearly 2,000 U.S. warplanes thundered out from Britain just after dawn and dispatched task forces through bitter opposition to half a dozen points spread across Germany."

"With aircraft over the Channel and North Sea almost continuously from dawn to dark, the newest Allied air offensive passed 96 hours of sustained attack obviously designed to smash the enemy forces in the air and immobilize them on the ground. As the air fleet went out, Gen. Eisenhower told a group of American pilots (they never told the navigators anything) they soon would be flying from dawn to dusk in a great land-sea-air invasion of Western Europe which would crush the Germans and crush them properly. They would forego sleep and food

for weeks - but they would knock out the Nazis, he declared emphatically."

"German radio last night claimed that more than 100 American aircraft were destroyed during the day. Unofficial indications were that U.S. losses would be approximately half the Nazi claims."

"Returning crewmen reported heavy enemy fighter opposition but praised their own fighter escort.'The fighters made vicious attacks on some of the groups, but we got through OK', said 2d Lt. William Etheredge of Chicago, a navigator."

"Saturday, the USTAF (the T was for "tactical" or low level) **lost 14 bombers and 24 fighters while the bomber gunners destroyed 60 enemy craft and the fighters 88. Sunday, unescorted Fortress formations flew across the Baltic to Marienberg, Gdynia and Posen, fought through intense opposition and flak. Monday, airdromes and plane-repair depots in Belgium and France took a pounding as the Fortresses went in modest strength to the Junkers engine-repair station at Vilvorde, the Heinkel and Messerschmitt repair works at Ever and the airdrome at Melsbrock. The day's losses were three bombers and four fighters, with seven enemy planes destroyed by the bombers and eight in air combat by the fighters."** (An easy day if you weren't on one of the lost ships; and note that there was no mention of killed and wounded among the returnees. This also may have been the mission depicted in the movie made for home consumption entitled: "Target for Today.")

The newspapers also told about the mission of April 11th which took our group to Sorau, Germany to a Focke Wulf fighter assembly plant. (The Luftwaffe named this top notch fighter: "The Butcher Bird.")We flew over Holland and a place called "Dummer Lake" in the area of Hanover, Germany. There was plenty of Flak and over half our planes sustained some sort of damage. The German fighters were there, too, but passed us by for some reason. It was just after noon when we dropped our bombs and headed back west and home. We had just one loss, a plane which blew up accidentally before we even left England. The total elapsed time from take-off to landing was just around 11 hours. We had been lucky again.

On April 16th I wrote to the folks again thanking them for some pictures they sent. I reported that my little 35 mm Kodak Retina camera which dad had bought for me in 1937 for $50 was stolen. It was one of my treasured possessions and now it was gone for good. I asked them to send me a cheap box camera but it never arrived. I added:

"The C.O. of our group is Col. Preston, a West Pointer who seems to like to carry on the traditions of the Academy with his men. Class A uniform is compulsory at the evening meal and Saturday inspections of personnel and barracks are a regular routine. Yet, we have come through all these big raids with very small losses, quite a feather in the cap of the Colonel. I guess we can't have our cake and eat it too."

April 17th again I wrote:

"I have been operational for a couple or four weeks now and have tasted battle and wish I could get the taste out of my mouth. You can save the uniform if you want to, but don't send it over. The tailor service here makes it impractical. Please write by air mail from now on as that has proven to be the fastest. Besides, so much more can be said with it than V mail. You two are doing a swell job of writing and I am very grateful, even though I don't write too often myself. If dad gets a new post, I hope it's somewhere near home. I expect to be home in July or August and I would like to go back home for a change."

Figure 18. Heavily damaged B-17, Navigator and Bombardier presumed dead!

Our next mission fell on April 18th. This time we went to Oranienburg-Perelberg, Germany, just north of Berlin. We put up all our 38 ships this time and headed out of England to the northeast over the North Sea and stayed away from the Continent until time to head south to the target, another aircraft plant. Again we saw traces of rockets which were fired at us either from the ground or by Messerschmitt 110's, a twin-engine fighter-bomber, but no direct fighter attacks. In spite of the usual Flak, we all got back without a scratch.

Figure 19. Shattered B-17 still flying and able to return to base.

On April 19th, I wrote to my brother Dick:

"My first mission has come and gone, and also four more, so you see I'm sweating out my first Air-Medal. It only takes five missions to win it and it is awarded again for each succeeding five. By the time you get this letter, I will probably have a few more. If my luck holds, I will be home in July because the weather improves around here to the point where we can hit old Adolf everyday."

"I'm glad Jim is going to fighters because that branch of flying is the best, no matter how many engines a B-17 has. You see one fighter in a million get shot down by flak or enemy aircraft when he is trying to make himself scarce. In a B-17, you just sit there and take it if it comes your way. It's up to the lead navigator to steer you out of the danger areas. Just try pulling out of formation and you're a dead duck whether you come back home or not. You ought to see those fighters tease Jerry's Flak and then just rack it up and get the hell out faster than greased lightning. Our plane is a veteran of thirty missions, but we have promises of new ships, soon."

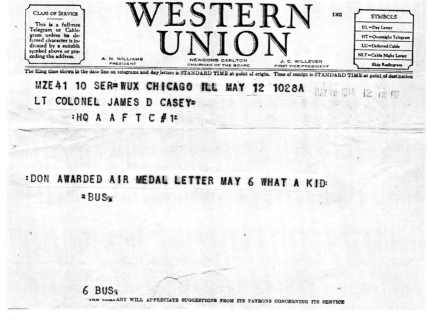

Figure 20. Telegram to author's father announcing son's award of first Air Medal for five combat missions flown.

The same day I wrote to the folks enclosing another clipping of one of our missions. I mentioned that I was awaiting the award of my first Air Medal and that the group commander was probably waiting for there to be enough awards to make it worth while holding a ceremony. The clipping was head-lined:

"HEAVIES HIT FROM CALAIS TO BERLIN; NAZIS DECLARE INVASION IMMINENT." The story said:

"American bombers and fighters - between 1,500 and 2,000 of them slugged their way across German skies to Berlin in daylight yesterday in a resumption of large-scale aerial assault which saw the Luftwaffe and Nazi targets hammered from the Pas de Calais to the heart of the Reich. Unofficial preliminary indications were that bomber losses would be almost fantastically light. The attack on Berlin was the Eighth Air Force's sixth and brought back to the ETO the major share of the three-way air pincer on Germany."

I also sent a column by the leading war correspondent of the day, Ernie Pyle writing from Italy about the Air Force which is excerpted here.

"In the past year I have written so much about the ground forces that they have become an obsession with me. They live and die so miserably and they do it with determined acceptance that your admiration for them blinds you to the rest of the war."

"To any individual the war is seldom any bigger than the space of a few hundred yards on each side of him. All the war in the world is concentrated down into his own personal fight. To me all the war of the world has seemed to be borne by a few thousand front-line soldiers here, destined merely by chance to suffer and die for the rest of us."

"All over the world other millions are fighting, too, many of them as wretchedly as our infantry in Italy. But it is easy to forget them in your intentness upon your own

hundred yards."

"You have to make some psychological adjustments when you switch from the infantry to the Air Forces. You approach death rather decently in the Air Forces. You die well-fed and clean-shaven, if that's any comfort. You're at the front only a few hours of the day, instead of day and night for months on end. In the evening you come back to something, a home and fireside. In the Air Forces you still have some semblance of an orderly life, even though you may be living in tents. But in the infantry you must become half beast in order to survive."

"I'm now with a dive-bomber squadron of the 12th Air Force. There are about 50 officers and 250 enlisted men. They all live in a big apartment house that the Italian government built to house war workers."

"Don't get the wrong impression. Their life is not luxurious. At home we wouldn't consider it adequate. It has the security of walls and doors, but it is a dog's life at that. It's tough getting up two hours before daylight for a dawn mission. The floors are cold. There are no rugs. Some of the windows are still blown out."

"And yet, as the airmen unblushingly admit, their life is paradise compared with the infantry."

Another news story dated April 19th screamed:

"8,500 TONS RAINED ON NAZIS IN 30 HOURS. Luftwaffe's Fields, Invasion Defenses Rent by U.S. Fleets. So light was the opposition encountered that it appeared evident that the Germans were holding their fighter strength for the day of the invasion. Losses in all operations were remarkably light. The RAF, sending it's biggest-ever force, lost only 14 bombers, less than 1.4 per cent."

April 19th had been our fifth mission, this time to Kassel, Germany. Again, we crossed Holland and headed for Northwestern Germany. The target was another fighter manufacturing plant. We bombed from 23,000 feet with incendiaries. This time we could clearly see the Flak bursts with their red hearts at the center. It was heavy, but we got through it intact and with no injuries. This time the mission lasted just over seven hours. It seemed a hell of lot longer. When you're on edge and your nerve endings are about worn raw, it is interminable. When you have been shot at and missed, it seems that it can be forgotten with some dinner and drinks.

No rest for the wicked. The next day, we were off again for "Sottevast- Mesnil au Val" (Valognes, France) on the Cherbourg peninsula. The target was the site of flying bomb launchers, referred to by the group executive officer as "fly-bomb sites", the famous V-1 (the "V" stood for "Vertailungs" or retaliation.) We sat around all morning waiting for the fog lift and finally took off at about 3:00 p.m. with a very low ceiling. This was a separate but necessary thrill climbing into the clouds in a set direction not knowing whether the way was clear or not. You had to be really young in mind and heart to do this because it was a damned-fool thing to do. It was no mean trick to climb out of those clouds into the clear and then hope that you could spot the rest of the group forming up for departure. The clouds were quite high that day, too. But again, we made it back without a loss, and only one wounded on another plane. This was a short one, just over four hours.

Finally, a day off and we fooled around in the rain on the ground. Some of us flew a practice mission, for whatever purpose. It went unrecorded by me.

Then, back at it again on April 22d. This time we were off to Hamm-Bonn, Germany to bomb the large railroad marshaling yards there where they split off to Holland and France. It was Saturday (there were no weekends off for us) and we took off late for us, well after lunch in the afternoon. This was no problem because we were on "Double British Summer Time" which meant two extra hours of daylight. It was the Group's 100th mission and there was to be a party when we got back - if we got back. Not a cheery invitation.

We dropped our bombs just around 7:30 p.m. and landed after 9:00 p.m. All planes returned safely. There wasn't a lot of Flak and we had no complaints about that. Other groups were not as lucky, losing 15 heavies. There were 10 more losses when the Germans followed a group of B-24's back to base and shot them down in the landing pattern - something we had never even heard of before. We thought we were safe when we got back over England, but far from it if the Germans were going to be daring enough to follow us home.

On April 23rd we were "stood down" so I wrote the folks a letter. I told them that our co-pilot (Milt Miller) **"now has his own crew because of his experience and qualifications. In his place we have a 23 mission boy who was made a permanent copilot for some reckless flying over here. He is a good flyer and has combat experience, which helps out a lot."** (Miller was later returned to co-pilot status and wound up temporarily on another crew. He was having problems, mostly in his head, about being first pilot. The story we heard was that he had broken down in flight momentarily and had put his ship into a dive. This scared hell out of his crew who removed him forcibly from his pilot's seat and then reported him to the management and he was reassigned. The truth of it is Milt should not have been flying at all after that episode. In the end, I think he died unnecessarily and should have been grounded for treatment or sent home.) Unfortunately for him, our Group Commander was of the same regular Army background and mind as Gen. Patton in viewing "combat fatigue" as a sign of cowardice.

In spite of the stigma of refusing to fly combat, some crew members actually did it. One of our own gunners told the Squadron Commander that he wanted out of his aircrew duties. We wished him well but heard later that the CO saw to it that he was thoroughly repudiated.

April 24th saw us going to Landsberg, just west of Munich. We were up at 4:30 a.m., more like our regular routine, and we were briefed an hour later about an aircraft manufacturing plant target. The Wing was being led that day by General Robert Travis, from another base. We took off around 9:00 a.m. and left England about 11:00. We passed Paris at 20,000 feet, made a fake pass at Munich and bombed Landsberg just at 2:00 p.m. Other groups again were subject to fighter attacks which we missed out on. Seven B-17's were observed going down in the process. We must have hit the target well because General Jimmy Doolittle, then in command of the whole 8th Air Force, commended the 379th for its effort and for "penetrating severe resistance" and bombing with "excellent results." (From the book: "The Screwball Express" by the late Kenneth Cassens.) All of the Flak had been over Munich which we had sneakily by-passed.

On our return that day, I wrote again to the folks and enclosed another newspaper article and a cartoon showing a comical looking downed American air crew, still in their flying togs, standing on a German city sidewalk just down the street from the building into which their plane had just crashed and was still protruding. The crew was attempting to hail a cab. A menacing Nazi stormtrooper eyed them closely and suspiciously with his arms folded across his chest.

The news article was headlined:

"USAAF OUT AFTER GIANT RAF BLOW. Nearly 30,000 Tons Smear Nazis From the Atlantic Wall to the Balkans. Heavy damage was done to the Hamm yards, photographs showed, with bombs striking all along a three-mile stretch of tracks and switching trains. Fires, possibly from tank cars, spread after the attack and the main station and repair shops also seemed to have been hit solidly... The day's box score showed 18 bombers and 13 fighters missing for the destruction of 20 German

planes by bomber gunners and another 34 in aerial combat with the fighters."

The Group went to Metz-Nancy, France on April 25th to bomb another airfield. I kept no notes on this flight which should not be assumed to be because it was a "milk run." As far as I was concerned, it was a milk run mission only if we got back safely without being necessarily frightened out of our wits by either enemy Flak or fighters. For whatever reason, we were "stood down" through the 27th and went to London on pass for some fun and relaxation.

On April 28th, I wrote to the folks again:

> **"We returned from another pass to London again today and a good time was had by all. We took in the theater and "Panama Hattie" with Bebe Daniels, who is getting along pretty well for her age. During intermission, they brought us a tray of tea and cakes, both in small amounts for small dining ware. As I remember, it was just four O'clock on the head. The play was very good."**

> **"We also took in Westminster Abbey and the House of Commons** (where we met Lord Fermoy who gave us his card and took us around being very courteous and hospitable as well). **The tonette arrived so all I'm waiting for is the newspaper picture unless there is something else."**

> **"I saw the Eiffel Tower the other day (referring to the Mission of April 24th to Landsberg, Germany) from a nice safe distance and the people below didn't seem to appreciate us because up came a few of those small black clouds with the metal fragments inside. Rude of them, don't you think?"**

Another contemporaneous news story was headlined:

"HEAVIES HIT IN RUMANIA AND REICH Coordinated Thrust One of War's Biggest; Nazis Tell of Fierce Battles"

"Between 750 and 1,000 Eighth Air Force Fortresses and Liberators, escorted by the same number of fighters, slugged their way more than 500 miles to hit airdromes near Munich and aircraft factories at Friedrichshafen. Most of the bomber formations, which split into task forces as they skirted the Swiss borders, found clear weather to pinpoint their targets as they carried their sixth operation in the last eight days. German radio stations described the progress of the bomber formations across Europe as they closed in from north and south, and claimed that 'gigantic air battles' were being fought by the Luftwaffe as it sought to preserve some of the battered factories which, it was revealed Sunday, even now are unable to replace current losses."

"One Fortress Division came back from Friedrichshafen to report not a single attack by enemy fighters, although a few were sighted in the distance, but a veteran B-17 division ran into one of the toughest battles of its career, with the Nazis hurling rocket firing interceptors and single and twin-engine planes into headlong flight at the bombers."

"The Forts and Libs went out to Europe early in the morning after the RAF had kept the offensive going with night blows on Bilvorde, a German communications depot near Brussels, in Belgium, and Mannheim, in Germany, for the loss of six aircraft. The Luftwaffe, for its part, showed it was still a fighting force to be reckoned with when it sent night bombers against southern and southwestern England, losing five planes in what may have been a reconnaissance in force to check British port activity."

Came April 29th, we were off to "Big B", Berlin. Ever mindful of the some 600 anti-aircraft guns there, we held our collective breaths as we flew into and through the blackening clouds of burst Flak. It was a slow crawl for us. The black remains of bursting shells seemed bigger than ever - about the size of a small car. One of these large shells would easily take down a B-17 if not cause it to explode on the spot. The Germans were using their bigger guns on us over their capitol. This might have been the mission referred to later on in a letter home about the B-17 being hit in the number two engine, which fell off the airplane, while the ship kept right on going on the remaining three engines.

Figure 21. Actual German Anti-Aircraft shell fragments courtesy of Alphanse (Al) Antonwitz, Chicago, IL, 379th Bomb Group ground crew member, 1944-45.

War movies depict Flak as being audible and causing the airplane to bob up and down. Nonsense! If it was that close, you were hit for sure. No, the leftover puffs of black smoke from Flak shells did not cause air turbulence. But an exploding shell could bring an airplane down from 5 miles up. Commonly in flight when I looked ahead and saw the exploding bursts, I could not hear them going off even from a short distance. Occasionally small shell fragments would fall on the hull of the ship sounding like hailstones on a tin roof but causing no damage. That I heard many times.

On some of our missions we dropped leaflets as we flew over Germany. Roughly translated, one of the papers I saved noted that the combined allied air forces had dropped "54,430 tons of bomben im Marz" (March) and this amounted to more tonnage on Germany and occupied territories than the Germans had dropped in the war so far.

In another letter on May 4th, I wrote:

"I have been writing more than twice a week, so I guess it is the postman you want to see. I think summer has gone already from the way the weather has been. Every night we build a fire no matter what the date is, and that is England for you. I wouldn't wish it on anybody."

"I have been getting some good stick time lately (in practice missions) **while my pilot did the navigation. We have a lot of fun that way and especially me when he gets lost we have to circle a field and call to find out where we are. I haven't noticed any complaints at all after that. England is a small country and is really packed, so there is a town and a half dozen air fields for about every ten miles. All the towns look alike and half the fields aren't on the map, so navigation is no snap."**

My letter of May 8th spoke of having visited "Big B" (Berlin).

"I found that I was much more frightened sitting on the

runway thinking about it than when actually there. The Luftwaffe was in the air-raid shelter, so it was pretty near a 'milk run'. As long as you don't hear the flak crunching against your ship, it's a milk run."

"When I return, I would like a few months rest with the ATC (Air transport command) before returning to combat. I know for sure that I will go back to war again, so I might as well have a vacation. I have ten missions now and the Air Medal for the first five. They have upped the Air Medal to six now, so I need one more for my first cluster."

"I'm surprised at you, Dad, saying that I'm too scrupulous about violating security measures. The chances are slim of the enemy reading this or that letter but why take those chances? The less they know about us, the better. Did you say was I busy? Busy, I am, trying to catch up on the 'rest'. One night we landed at 2200 (11:00 p.m.), retired at 0030 (12:30 a.m.) and rose again at 02:30 and went out again."

"Tell me Dad, what makes air combat appear so thrilling to the outsiders? I can't figure it out from here."

Figure 22. B-17-G With 379th Bomb Group insignia on vertical stabilizer - Triangle K for Kimbolton.

On May 12th, they sent us to Merseburg, Germany, a target protected by Flak as hot as Berlin, if not hotter. Our objective was a synthetic oil refinery and chemical plant. Finally our strategic planners had hit on the real German weak spot. Their sources of fuel were Rumania and their own synthetic plants, which were not unlimited. By hitting the energy processes, we could start pulling the plug on ships, tanks, aircraft and motor vehicles - everything that moved. The previous focus on railroad yards and airplane manufacturing had somehow missed this crucial target. (This is hindsight talking, because, at the time, we were too close to the war and combat tactics to be able to even think, however briefly, about what was strategically important to the war effort.)

This was one tough mission. Perhaps the Germans knew what we were after, but even so, the fighter opposition was intense. The third division lost 22 of 66 planes. Our Group, the 379th, saw one enemy fighter from a distance which did not take the dare to attack our closely massed formation. The Flak was something else.

One of our group's navigators was killed and a bombardier was wounded. Overall, the Eighth lost 42 heavies, but the Germans were reported to have lost 190 aircraft, of which 75 were shot down by our escort fighters and 115 by the bombers - an incredible number. We hit the target hard and the trip took nine hours. All but four of our planes sustained some sort of damage and we were one of the four.

Then on May 15th:

"**Your letters are pouring in and I feel like a heel the way I've been writing. I have been busy though and quite a few evenings I've had just enough strength to get undressed and go to bed. That picture of 'Hell's Belle'** (our airplane's nickname drawn by Bombardier Jack Ellenberger) **is swell, so the big one must be a whipper. I'll get the crew's signatures and send them on right away.**

"**Number thirteen has come and gone, but it was a thriller of thrillers for Hell's Belle. We sweated out Flak, fighters, going down in Germany, exploding and ditching in the North Sea. We were leaking gas like mad after a hell of a fighter attack, so we dropped our bombs, threw out ammo' after we had cleared enemy territory and got set for ditching. We dropped out of formation, still some three hundred miles from the friendly coast and picked up four beautiful P-38's for escort and from then on we all sweated me out. Our radar was in the groove so I fixed myself after about an hour and a half and whipped out a course and ETA that proved very successful, so we pulled in safely with no casualties but nine tired bodies and minds, and millions of strained nerves. Does that satisfy your inquisitive personalities? If it doesn't, you're out of luck, because that's all of it. We have a 48 hour rest starting tomorrow and I do need it. Keep writing.**"

What the folks must have thought on receiving this letter I do not know. However, this short version was not even the half of

it. First, this was the longest mission we had ever had and the worst so far in terms of potential for disaster. What I didn't tell them was that we flew all the way to Poland that day - over water most of the way, across Denmark to the northeast corner of Germany and then to the target at Stettin.

We rose at 4:00 a.m., breakfasted at 4:30, were briefed at 5:30 and took off just after 9:00 a.m. We were over the North Sea a good part of the time. Over water, we had no fear of flak, at least. We saw no fighters until we crossed the German coast near Stettin. Our fighters had been with us all the way until then. But this was just beyond their range and we bade them goodbye with real foreboding. We were cruising at 23,000 feet. Suddenly we saw them, the Germans, in a swarm or "Schwarm" as they referred to it. They flew a course parallel to ours at a safe distance out of range of our guns, about fifty of them. They looked like a swarm of bees to us, only bigger. The enemy's leader could well have been General Adolf Galland, one of their leading aces, who invented the Schwarm technique of attack on daylight bomber formations. In his book: "The First and the Last", he wrote that the Me 110 twin engine "destroyers" were becoming limited in their availability due to the escorting American fighters. "The destroyers could achieve satisfactory results only when they were lucky enough to find a heavy bomber formation whose fighter escort was momentarily busy elsewhere. On such an occasion (May, 1944) the ZG (his fighter group) was able to shoot down 15 bombers of a formation raiding the synthetic petrol plants at Stettin with a loss of only two of their own aircraft."

Our plight was being relayed on the radio by our leader to the nearest escort of P-51's of the US 4th Fighter Group of P-51's from Debden. Our "little friends," as we called them, were about a hundred miles to the West of us. They could hear us calling for their help and that we were without fighter support and under attack by enemy fighter planes but to no avail.

Figure 23. Author and crew in front of B-17 "Hell's Belle"

CHAPTER 6:

OUR FIGHTER ESCORT WAS OUT OF REACH

Our attackers flew FW-190's and Messerschmitt 109's we could see them clearly. They were flying parallel to our course out of range to the right looking us over. We were at our customary cruising speed of 150 miles per hour. The enemy could easily fly twice as fast and their wings were fluttering at such a slow rate. I manned my starboard machine gun just behind the bombardier's seat. Orders were given not to fire until the enemy was in range.

Our machine guns were loaded and ready. We waited nervously for them to make the next move. With well-practiced co-ordination, the fighters increased speed and flew on ahead of us. Then quickly, keeping their swarm positions, they wheeled to the left and came straight for us.

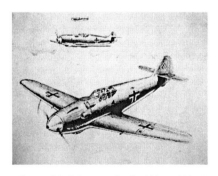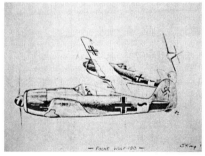

Figure 24. Messerschmitt 109 and Focke Wulf 190 fighters drawn by Steve King at Stalag Luft III.

Our group was arrayed in the standard high squadron, lead and low squadron formation. We were in the high squadron on the right side. The lead group was positioned to our left, below and slightly ahead. The low group was also behind the lead group and further to the left. In a moment, they were bearing in on us at a combined closing speed of 500 miles per hour. Their guns were blinking like flashing lights. It was no signal by any means. They had six 30 caliber machine guns mounted in the wings and 20 millimeter cannons as well, immense fire power for such small aircraft.

We didn't need any instructions or orders now. All guns that could be brought to bear were firing frantically. I remember that my gun jammed momentarily and I cleared the breach by pulling hard on the handle on the left side of the gun and resumed firing. It seemed an interminable period of seconds and then, in a flash, they were heading beneath us rolling over into a split-S maneuver showing us their armored bellies. The Focke-Wulf 190's also had an armored cowling and an oversized spinner that left only inches to shoot at from head-on.

It still amazes me how I was able to stand up straight behind my gun with nothing more than a quarter inch of solid Plexiglas, plus my flak-vest and steel helmet between me and the enemy's guns. Where was one to hide? That was the essence of aerial combat being out there in the open standing erect under enemy machine gun and cannon fire. If it wasn't fighters, it was "Flieger Abwehr Kanonen", otherwise known as FLAK.

We were in the wrong place at the wrong time because the head-on fighter attacks could be murderous. Another former 8th Air Force Navigator, Charles Mueller, of Chicago, told me how his group was attacked head on by German fighters on his last raid to Berlin. His ship was damaged and forced to drop out of formation. The enemy fighters came at their crippled ship head-on and, in their first pass, put a shell directly into the nose compartment killing his bombardier instantly and exploding his body all over the inside of the airplane. Charles survived that charge, but the next one immediately following wounded him so severely that he lost consciousness instantly and came to in a German hospital a few days later. His last recollection was seeing the flash of an oncoming gun barrel. The plane crashed with him in it and he somehow survived.

Our tail-gunner reported three B-17's going down in the low squadron. Someone called out over the intercom that we were hit somewhere in the right wing in the vicinity of the right inboard engine. The top-gunner shouted that there was fuel pouring out of the wing. I could see it for myself out my right window a few feet away. The gasoline was draining perilously close to the red hot supercharger on the number three engine. The pilot feathered number three (turning the propeller blades parallel to our line of flight so they no longer would windmill in the air- stream and slow down the ship) and we unloaded our bombs and turned back north.

With only three motors, we could not keep up with the group which was not about to wait for us. That's what they call "Group Integrity." They couldn't wait for us and we couldn't keep up without burning out our three good power plants. A panic began to set in. We were dead for sure, out there all by ourselves. We were as far away from home base as we had ever been before (500 air miles.) I watched as the formation pulled steadily away and we were alone. Our course had us heading north to the Baltic Sea. Once we reached the water I directed the pilot to turn to 270 degrees West toward Denmark.

We talked anxiously on the intercom about ditching in the sea or, perhaps, just continuing north to Sweden where we and our ship would be interned for the duration of the war.

I said to myself "God, help us." I was sure we were all dead now. We waited for the Germans to come back and kill us. A lone, crippled aircraft, limping along at 140 miles per hour or less, and losing altitude had no chance defending itself even against a single attacker. We were goners if the enemy saw us.

The German pilots loved just such a target because we were an easy shoot-down and making a kill on a four-motored bomber brought extra credit to their records. Hitler doted on the "Kampf-Flugzeuge Experten" (Luftwaffe super-aces) and they were doing unbelievably well at killing allied planes of all kinds. But where were they? Nowhere in sight, thank the Lord. Perhaps back on the ground being refueled to come for us later.

We stuck to our course. The gasoline stopped flowing out of the right wing and we were still well under control and able to make it back, if ... And it was a big if. We still had to cross Denmark and traverse the North Sea and we were still terribly exposed and visible. Just as we reached the North Sea, four small airplanes came up from the rear. At first, we couldn't tell what they were. The tail gunner soon identified them as American P-38's, those twin-engine, forked-tail beauties.

We heaved a sigh of relief. We now had a great chance to make it home. As first pilot Lew Jolls tells it: "The rendezvous was no accident because there were pre-selected points along our route which were given code names where we were to meet our 'little friends' in just such circumstances." They were life savers, without doubt.

The P-38's were from the 55th Fighter Group at Nuthampstead. Like dolphins, they flew ahead of our slow moving ship, dipping in and out of our path, giving us the friendly bump of their slipstreams. We loved them more than any best friend we ever had. Time dragged on anxiously. And then we felt we were in the clear. The P-38's waved at us and took off for home base.

P-38's first came to England in October 1943 as one of only six fighter groups at the time and were the only aircraft which had range sufficient to escort our bombers into Germany. It was a great ship under 20,000 feet but could not keep up with the German fighters at higher altitudes.

Over the North Sea, we were in range of the British radar

and the set I had aboard showed exactly where we were so that I could plot the course and give the pilot a precise arrival time. We crawled over the English coast and headed in, late but unhurt on the outside. Airplane and crew present and accounted for, sir. Time aloft: eleven hours plus, each succeeding hour more grueling than the previous one.

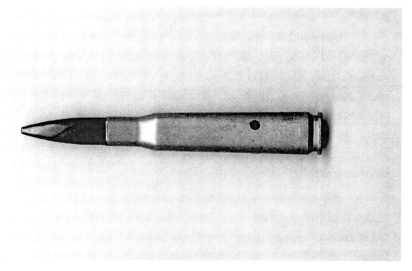

Figure 25. Disarmed 50 caliber machine gun bullet - range one mile. /actual size 5.5 inches long .75 inch base.

On landing, we inspected the damage in the right wing. The conclusion was that we had been hit by a single 50 caliber bullet fired by one of our own group members. The damage to the aircraft was easily fixed. Not so our former air of cocky confidence and invincibility.

I couldn't help but think what would have happened if we had gone to Sweden. It was our duty to keep going as we did, but what if we hadn't? Internment in Sweden was rumored to be a punishment that could have been considered paradise. All those Swedish women and we young men, quartered in a fine hotel with nothing but time and a semi-unlimited expense account - or so the stories went. Who knows? I could have met and married one of them, and then my kids would all have been half Swedish. (Colonel Preston, our CO, made it known that internees would be deemed deserters no matter what the circumstances.)

We were debriefed and told our story, a saga of doing our duty. The plane was saved and would be repaired. Debriefing was something I always looked forward to. First, it meant we had made it back in one piece. But more important, it meant each of us was given a shot of "Old Overholt" rye whiskey to settle us down. Some of the crew didn't take their whiskey ration, so I grabbed the leftovers as I usually did, sometimes downing three or four good sized portions. This day they had no effect on me. I couldn't seem to come down from altitude and get back to normal.

We were given 48 hours off in consideration of what we had gone through. Our crew went to London and enjoyed a steak of questionable origin at a Greek restaurant. This was the first fresh meat we had seen in quite a while and we enjoyed our feast until we were filled. We then strolled around Piccadilly Circus and encountered some "Piccadilly Commandos" (British prostitutes) waiting willingly there. Jack Ellenberger shooed them off by saying that he had "crabs", to which one of the girls replied: "Oh, you mean bugs in the bush." They left us alone after that.

The fighter experience was completely different from the bombers. As told by Eric Hammel in "Aces Against Germany",

"The bombers had to take off hours before any of the fighters. There were hundreds of them, and they had to form up into their combat boxes, combat wings and combat divisions. That took a long time. Also, the Germans had deployed a belt of 88mm and other flak guns along the Dutch and Belgian coasts where the bombers usually crossed in. The bombers liked to pass over the flak guns at least 20,000 feet, and that meant they had to circle higher and higher with their heavy bomb loads while the were still over England. Hundreds of bombers were circling long before it was time for us to get up. As usual,

I was awakened by the drone of their engines. Because the bombers were overhead, I knew the mission was on long before it was announced officially. I also knew that, unfortunately, their contrails were creating an overcast through which we would have to take off later."

"If it was clear, we only needed to follow the bomber stream out of England and overtake the leaders before they reached the target. In an effort to confuse the Germans - make them think they were somewhere else - the bombers were flying along a route that would have been too long for us to follow anyway."

"We were to sweep ahead of the bombers as they came in over the target, and then we were to hand the escort off to fresh groups, plus or minus 75 miles along the route home."

(At the target - Berlin) "There were German fighters stacked all the way from the level of the bombers to the upper cloud ceiling. They were just still specks when I saw them. They looked like a swarm of bees, maybe 7 to 10 miles distant. They were going flat out for the bombers. Thirty or forty twin-engine fighters were going in first to fire rockets in order to break up the bomber boxes. And coming up behind... were many-single engine fighters, Me-109's and FW 190's. Higher up was their top cover, thirty or forty Me-109's. Between all of them and the bombers was (our) group - thirty-three of us."

"We flew straight into the main German formation. We could have done more damage if there had been more of us, but we were able to break up their main attack. Within seconds, it was just a hell of a mess. Everything was going in all directions at once. Individual dogfights were breaking out all over the place."

Hammel went on to tell about following the Germans

over the target under the bombers just as they were releasing their bombs - which he described as looking "like a ladder going straight down." He dived his plane parallel to the falling bombs finally pulling out at only 500 feet and then climbed back up to altitude. The bombers would not really have been able to see this part of the fighter's action, but they were extremely grateful for their presence, so helpful in a time of severe need.

One of the guys came back to the base of a morning with a puppy. According to his story, he had paid a lovely lady five pounds sterling for an evening of delight and she threw in the dog as a bonus. Being the dog lover that I am and the new owner having no interest in him, I became its master. The name I gave him was "hemorrhoid", "Heemo" for short. He was the official mascot of Hells Belle. I liked to take him up on practice missions regularly ordered by the C.O. no matter how many missions you had had. Heemo loved it while the plane sat silently on the ground, but when we started the engines and took off, he quivered and shook the whole time. But, as soon as we were back on the ground with the engines shut off, he would stand in the nose of our ship and bark at the ground crew, his courage restored.

Drinking was a traditional sport at the base. We had very inexpensive drinks at the officers club and no one was asking if we were old enough. Like I said, if you're old enough to hang your rear-end out where the Germans can shoot it off, you certainly are entitled to a drink. One night at the club as were relaxing somebody suggested a foolish but funny - at the time - stunt. We ordered enough glasses of "gin and orange" so that the table top was almost filled with them. Then we started drinking toward the center. It could have been my idea because it was crazy enough, but everybody went along.

We were well into the game when along came one of the senior officers on the staff who said: "You guys better get to bed, we have a mission in the morning." Whether we finished all the drinks or not, I don't know. I do remember one of our gang, copilot

Olie Olson, telling the next day of his vomiting into his oxygen mask because of it. Not I, though.

You might get the impression that it was a lot of fun and games. What we were doing was trying to keep our sanity. We even had a phrase for being shot down. It was referred to as being "Scragged", probably a British-RAF saying. Perhaps it was not being completely honest with ourselves, but you just couldn't keep saying the exact truth of the matter which was that the plane had gone down in flames or simply exploded and counting how many were probably killed. Whichever it was, the crew did not return, so they were "scragged". But we kept our eye on tomorrow and never lost that assurance that it would not happen to us, the living. In other words, we were not morbid about the prospects for survival or the lack thereof. Fatalistic, maybe, but not morose.

The Luftwaffe had their own words of encouragement for the fliers about to set off on a sortie and defend the Vaterland.

"Hals und Beinbruch," they would say to one another which translated into English as "Break your neck and bones." (Kind of like the show business people saying to one another on opening night: "Break a Leg.")

Jack Sinise and I were fellow navigators who felt that we never got the respect to which we were entitled. He and I went looking for something to do on the base on a rainy day and wandered into the building where they kept the "Link Trainer." This was a fabulous piece of equipment designed to train pilots to fly on instruments at night. No one ever used it because the pilots were already trained in this technique.

The sergeant in charge told us to go ahead and help ourselves, so we did. The trainer itself was a stubby looking box with short, fake wings and a tail and a cockpit for one pilot which had a cover which was closed to keep the trainee in the dark and concentrating on the instruments. Jack and I would take turns flying it. A frantic call would come over the intercom to "pull up" when the thing was in an uncontrollable spin and headed down - according to the instruments, at least. If the guy inside didn't pull out of the spin, the ground man would say, "You are now 200 feet below ground level." We got the feel of flying an airplane but we never did learn how to work the thing, let alone use the instruments, and we were oblivious to the fact that lessons on this magnificent instrument would have cost $200 or more per hour back home. For us it was like a Christmas toy. It was an enjoyable distraction from our appointed jobs.

The May 13th mission to Poland took a serious toll on my psyche. There were other missions, too, but this one severely shook my confidence. Jack Ellenberger and I asked the crew chief to add more armor plate to the deck of the nose where we flew. Next, I abandoned the chest-pack parachute which was about the size of bulging brief case that snapped on to the front of your harness. It was comfortable and convenient. You could put the chute pack down wherever you were and put it on at your leisure. But what if you were in a situation where you had no leisure? What if the plane were to spin out or blow up and there you'd be with no chute, falling through the air?

It happened to a lot of guys. So, no more chest-pack for me. I went in and got myself a back pack which I wore at all times from then on. There were two kinds of back pack chutes, one was a large, bulging super-knapsack type which looked like it held a couple of footballs, and the other (which I chose) was of a soft, flat configuration about 4 inches thick and 24 inches wide which laid on your back from shoulder to bottom. I chose the latter. Another reason for wearing that style of backpack chute was that the flak vest easily fit right over it, which it didn't with the other types of parachutes.

Speaking of the Flak Vest, the damnable thing weighed about 25 lbs. We all had them on board on every mission. On my early missions I wore it religiously starting with the crossing of the enemy coast. Then there was a period of time when I eschewed the heavy thing and left it on the deck at my feet until we saw some Flak or fighters or we were approaching the target. Beginning in the last third of our tour I went back to my original idea of putting it on early and wearing it all the way in and all the way out of enemy territory. The same for my steel helmet which had cut-outs for our intercom headsets. It was the standard GI (Government Issue) helmet worn by the infantry and weighed about 3 pounds. With every available protection on, I was heavily loaded down, as was our nose compartment with armor plate, but I felt better that way, somehow.

My letters home were still upbeat. On May 18th, I wrote:

"We have a brand new airplane that's really a neat trick. All it needs is a bit of armor and she'll be ready to go, in our estimation. Headquarters, however, doesn't think that way, so we'll have to get on the ball in a hurry."

"I'm sorry to the extreme because I didn't send something for mother's day. I have been in a few of those raids you mentioned and we are really raising hell with 'Jerry' whenever the weather half-way permits. I don't know how they're taking it, but I don't imagine they care for it at all. I only wish we could finish him off from the air and save having to invade."

On May 19th, it was off to Berlin again to hit an aircraft component plant. We were airborne at 9:00 a.m. and stayed over water until we reached the Danish coast and headed southeast toward the target. We had to climb to just over 24,000 feet. There was no Flak to speak of as yet, for a change. Very often en route, we came close to Flak centers which tried to get at us if they could. Our courses were usually selected to avoid these nests.

Then we were over the target and the big guns were busy trying their best to stop us. The air was full of those huge black clouds, dark enough to obscure the sunlight, however briefly. We hit our target and got the hell out to the Northwest. On reaching the Baltic Sea, we headed West over Denmark again and beat it for home. We lost two ships and the majority suffered at least some damage due to Flak. The Eighth lost a total of 28 heavy bombers half of which were due to enemy fighters. In two weeks our Group had lost 63 men and 7 aircraft.

Then on May 20th I wrote:

> "They gave me an oak leaf cluster for my Air Medal to-day and two more are forthcoming when I finish twenty three missions."

> "We have another new co-pilot because the second one finished his tour. This fellow wears the Purple Heart and he's definitely trying to avoid a second award, so he's a valuable man. Every day I thank God that I'm in B-17's, especially since I saw one ship get an engine and nacelle blown right off of its left wing and keep right on going. 'Flying Fortress' is hardly enough (of an appellation). They ought to call it the flying spider the way it climbs up that blue wall and stays. That's it for now. I hope I'm being newsy enough."

Another news article dated May 20, 1944 trumpeted:

> "BERLIN BLASTED AS AIR OFFENSIVE RESUMES - BRUNSWICK ALSO HIT; HEAVY BATTLES WITH LUFTWAFFE INDICATED." And continuing: "Germans tell of fierce Aerial Fighting; Early Reports Hint U.S. Planes Took Big Toll of Nazis. Announcing violent battles over its 'Achtung' alarm system, German radio said that 'three separate forces of the USAAF and Luftwaffe were engaged in combat over Berlin at the same time. Returning crews reported intense Flak and fighter opposition in the Brunswick area."

Actually, on May 20th, we were flying to Orly, France to

hit another airdrome and Marquise/Mimoyecques in the Pas de Calais area on the 21st to hit the sources of the German V-1 flying bombs. The announcement at the briefing was that even though the Group had bombed this same place five days before, there were several targets at this location and the flying-bomb sites were small and hard to hit. Regardless, it was in the interests of the British civilian population for us to try our best with any means at our disposal to dampen the effort of the Germans to retaliate with this frightening weapon aimed at London and other cities.

We left the English coast at 1:45 p.m. at 20,000 feet and almost immediately started our bomb run to the target just 20 miles across the channel. We were over the target in minutes but it was covered with clouds so we had to bomb with the new through-the clouds technique called "Gee H". The Flak was inconsiderable but still did some damage but no injuries and no bombers lost. No enemy fighters, at least.

I enclosed the May 20th clipping with a letter home dated May 23rd in which I cautioned my father.

> **"I'm afraid that you're not reading between the lines enough in the newspaper, Dad, because I happen to know personally that it's not as much down hill as you would be led to believe. We have grand fighter support but we go in much farther now than they ever did in the Memphis Belle era. I'm still in good health but rather downcast by the new promotion order they have issued** (which was: 'none at this time') **and also by the rumor of an increase in missions."**

What was missing from my letters were the frightening details which I could not bring myself to mention. Just reading them, one might conclude that it was one routine mission after another. Nothing could be further from the truth. Each day we flew was filled with great anticipation, crisis and finally relief to be back on the ground once again. I also omitted describing how Berlin's 600 Flak guns could be brought to bear on our formations. Those guns were firing, reloading in a matter of seconds and firing again and again.

The German guns themselves were a combination of calibers ranging from the 88, and 105 up to the 128 and 150 millimeter shells. The biggest guns, some mounted in twin gun mounts, were manned by regular Luftwaffe units supported by non-regulars, some of whom were boys of 15 and 16. They were referred to as "Luftwaffenhelfers" (air force helpers), too young for combat but capable of doing many things and recruited to operate the smaller guns. One such youngster, an "Oberhelfer" of 17, was quoted about being in a typical battery "manned by 90 schoolboys, 36 regular Luftwaffe men in command positions and 20 Russian prisoners to perform menial cleaning and laboring tasks. "We were in an odd position, sometimes treated as soldiers and sometimes as schoolboys. ... We were expected to shoot down enemy planes with our 105 mm guns but we were not considered old enough to carry rifles when we went to round up enemy aircrew that came down by parachute". ("Target Berlin" by Jeffrey Ethel and Alfred Price).

The enemy's guns were positioned to shoot in unison for maximum effect on command from the radar operators. The smaller guns fired a 22 pound shell that exploded into 1500 fragments of shrapnel (we collected a few fragments that pierced our airplane on several occasions - some between 2 and 3 inches long and a half of an inch wide with jagged edges that could tear a big hole in you) and were capable of firing several rounds by a well trained crew in a matter of minutes, ("The Air War in Europe World War II", Time Life Books.)

There were stories of dud shells winding up inside of our planes, even in the gas tanks, unexploded because of deliberate sabotage by the slave laborers put to work by the Germans in the factories. One story I heard told of an unexploded 20mm shell that contained a handwritten greeting. The Germans maintained up to the end of the war that they could not have been defeated by air power alone without the invasion. German industry was being widely dispersed, underground and counter-measures kept a strong pace repairing the bombing damage.

Reich's Marshall Goering conceded at his Nurenburg War Crimes trial that **"Allied precision bombing had a greater effect on the defeat of Germany than area bombing, because destroyed cities could be evacuated, but destroyed industry was difficult to replace. Allied selection of targets was good, particularly in regard to oil. As soon as we started to repair an oil installation, you always bombed it again before we could produce one ton. If I had to design the Luftwaffe again, the first airplane I would develop would be the jet fighter -- then the jet bomber. Before D-Day, the allied attacks in Northern France hurt us because we were not able to rebuild in France as quickly as at home. The attacks on marshaling yards were most effective, next came low-level attacks on bridges. The low-flying planes had a terror effect and caused great damage to our communications."**

On board our planes waiting to take off, we would sit nervously anticipating the signal to start engines. We knew where we were going and we knew how to worry about the long trips we would take. But, we couldn't control it. Once the motors were running, our ships would creep slowly into position in a line of ships for take-off. The hours on the taxi-strips brought additional stress. Occasionally they had us on the shortest one of our three runways, which meant that we had to really rev' up the engines in order to get into the air fully loaded as we were. The tension mounted and then we were airborne and climbing ever so slowly into formation. Sometimes, after takeoff as our Group was assembling in mid-air, suddenly we would be in the clouds unable to see the planes around us. The pilots just gritted their teeth and held to their courses until we climbed out of the soup. There was nothing else we could do about it. (Perhaps it was an advantage to be age 19 and thinking positively most of the time.)

Crossing the English coast was another moment to reflect

on what we were about to get into. By this time we usually were approaching combat altitude and were breathing through our oxygen masks. Our planes were not heated so the electrically heated suits kept us from suffering frost-bite which was a very dangerous aspect of our jobs. I kept myself busy checking points on the ground below to compare with my maps and plan ahead for a possible "abort" (which meant dropping out and heading back to base.) Then we were crossing the coast of Holland or France - if we were not staying over water to the North as we often did. It was time to check your guts and start looking for German fighters.

Were we lucky? Enemy fighter attacks had fallen off of late because of the depredation by our fighters. One mission we would see swarms of them in the distance. We took some comfort from our well-practiced formation flying which seemed to deter them from attacking our group in preference to other formations not nearly as tightly bunched. A swarm of enemy fighters on one particular day flew right by us and attacked the group in the rear. As I recall, that was the time when our pilot, Lew Jolls was suffering an attack of diarrhea and came down into the nose compartment to deal with it. Other times we saw the tracer-type trails of German rockets being fired at us from behind by twin engine Me-110's and JU88's. It was not a very effective weapon against us but we didn't like the rockets one bit.

I credit our Group Commander, Col. Maurice (Mo') Preston with the 379th BG's success in recording the lowest combat losses of any Group in the 8th Air Force during the entire war. He was a bear of a man and a West Pointer who must have winced day by day at the idea of teenagers operating his airplanes and doing the job well, too. Kids like I was didn't deserve to be 2d Lieutenants - according to him - and he would show his disdain for us by holding back on promotions. It became a bitter point to us aircrew officers when we would learn what other Group C.O.'s were doing for their skill-position fliers. His disciplined style of formation flying was outstanding and it showed from the respect accorded us by the enemy.

Times had changed for the Eighth Air Force, no doubt. But in other groups, the luck was not as good. From his book, "A Wing and a Prayer", Harry Crosby, writing the only navigator's account of the air war over Europe, came up with analysis that of thirty-five crews who arrived at the 100th Bomb Group in May of 1943, the survival rate was only 14% and not one complete crew made it through intact. This exemplifies what an accomplishment it was at about the same time for the "Memphis Belle" to complete twenty-five missions unscathed. By the spring of 1944, chances were a lot better, but we were flying longer distances and racking up more combat air time. Still, luck played an awfully big part. In addition, the number of missions required for a tour was increased. As the number of American bombers increased, the loss percentages went down but there were still many casualties and men taken prisoner.

On a mission near Munich a Me-109 fighter came from below and flew straight up through our formation, right in front of our ship. This intrepid pilot was close enough to permit me to see his face and I often wondered what he was thinking of at the time - probably scared to death just as we were. It was surprising that no one on board had time to draw a bead on him in order to get off even a round or two.

A famous 8th Air Force General, Curtis LeMay (later made commander of the 20th Air Force in the Pacific bombing Japan), came up with the theory that the German Flak guns were less of a threat the less time you spent in their range. He took into account the time it took the Germans to reload and re-sight the guns. Therefore, instead of zigzagging as the RAF did at night - as one might expect would be a good thing to do - we flew straight and level from the initial point to the point of bombs-away and the Flak guns be damned. From a percentage standpoint, perhaps the odds were better this way but you couldn't convince combat crews of that. Le May's rationale was based on the purpose of our missions to destroy enemy targets as expeditiously as possible. Weaving B-17's might make air crews feel more comfortable but not if it meant they would have to go back to the same target two or three times for the same result.

One of my buddies of later acquaintance who flew with the inglorious "Twelve O'clock High" 306th Bomb Group (the 306th was renamed in the movie as the 918th) frequently cursed his commander, General Frank Armstrong - played by Gregory Peck - for making repeat passes over a target at the cost of several planes downed by Flak. In 1960, I met General Armstrong, then retired, in Florida. He was a member of the board of directors of a company our law firm was preparing a stock offering on. I don't knock his pioneering leadership with the 8th Air Force in 1943, but he couldn't touch Gregory Peck's screen version of him for dynamism, in my opinion.

The German Flak gunners were guided by radar and were better than given credit for. If it was so hard to hit the high flying bombers, why then did a flak crew have to shoot down five enemy airplanes to receive the coveted Flak gunner's badge? Thank the lord they weren't any better than they were or it would have been a slaughter of our men and planes. One of their techniques was the block barrage in which a group of guns threw up shells simultaneously hoping to hit whatever was within range of the barrage. We saw enough of our ships being hit to remind us that it could happen to us at any time, too.

Leaving target areas after dropping our bombs was a traditional time to heave a sigh of relief at having escaped the grim reaper one more time. There still remained the long trip home with eyes "peeled" looking for the opposing fighters. Once we were over the English Channel again at lower altitude and off oxygen, we were permitted to relax a little, light up a cigarette. If we hadn't already fired our machine guns, we were allowed to do so, briefly. On mission after mission, by test-firing my machine gun, I found my gun jammed after a round or two. This made me very anxious to find out why my gun wasn't working properly. Having stood by it interminably over enemy territory and counting on it to work if needed and then finding my gun jamming gave me a kind of sick feeling. Once on the ground, I let the ground crew have it for that, but I was never sure that they did anything to fix it.

On one mission to France, we were flying "spare" with orders to return home if no one dropped out of the group by the time it departed the coast of England. Pilot Lew Jolls, with encouragement from all of us (were we crazy or something?), decided to tack onto another group and fly the mission anyway. We had no idea where they were going or what kind of bombing they were prepared to do, but we went along for the ride with our load of bombs. The target turned out to be an airfield in France not too deep into enemy territory. We dropped our bombs along with the rest of the group and it was only then that we realized that the others were carrying incendiary bombs while we had eight 500 pounders. The tail gunner remarked that he could see our high explosive bombs going off amid the fireworks of the incendiaries. We hit a target, but what it was we didn't know.

Now we were heading back home and as we crossed the coast of France, I made a simple but serious mistake in my navigation. I could see the coast below and misread it to put us in position to fly North by Northwest to England. I gave the pilot a heading which began separating us from the group which continued to head ten degrees more to the north than I had calculated. The gap began to grow and my confidence began to wane quickly. I capitulated to the better judgment of following the leader whose first class equipment made it almost certain he had the right course to England and called to the pilot over the intercom' to rejoin the group reciting on the intercom the old saw: "Fifty Million Frenchmen can't be wrong."

Soon we were over England and again I thought I knew where we were and set a course separate from the group. On we flew but nothing looked familiar. I was lost again, somewhere in the South of England, so I took the last resort of directing the pilot to circle while I located a "splasher" radio signal which helped get us back on the right course to home. This had never happened to me before and I swore that it would not happen ever again. The crew knew what had happened but to a man said not even one discouraging or disparaging word to me. At least I knew enough to admit when I was wrong. Once on the ground and with a few quick shots of whiskey in me, it was soon forgotten. There would be more missions and, what the hell, we got back in one piece didn't we?

May 24th we were over "Big B" again to hit another aircraft component assembly plant. Our Intelligence had learned that the enemy worked out a scheme for dispersing the production of the major parts of its fighter planes to prevent any one raid from knocking out their entire work in progress. By this method, fighter manufacturing continued in spite of our bombing.

It was cloudy all the way and very cloudy over the target. We were off early and headed for the North Sea. We passed over the enemy coast around 10:00 a.m. just east of Hamburg heading for the target. We saw some rocket trails but no fighters. Our load was general purpose bombs and incendiaries. The mission report at the National Archives said that the bombs fell into "a well built-up area near the center of the city." It was still a legitimate military target according to our Intelligence.

We had been over Germany 2 1/2 hours by the time we crossed the coast again along the same route we came in on. The Flak had been deadly accurate and damaged 28 planes. Three ships were lost, two due to fighter action and one to a mid-air collision with a wounded plane.

On May 27th, our target was Mannheim-Speyerdorf, a steel and armament factory. It was a Saturday again. We crossed over the French coast about 11:00 a.m. and headed for Mannheim. We saw flocks of enemy fighters but our escorts kept them at a safe distance. They hit other groups, though and there were reports that the Germans were shooting at parachuting crews of stricken planes. The Flak was bad enough but only a few of our group's planes were hit and none were lost.

That same day (10 days before the invasion about which we knew nothing at the time) I wrote:

> **"The latest report says that 100% censorship of outgoing mail in the ETO caused the deletion or destruction of 21% of officer's mail and 6% of enlisted men's mail. One of those was undoubtedly mine because you don't seem to have received it. I told the whole story of one of our raids excepting the route and target, hoping to satisfy some of your requests for more information. I guess you'll just have to wait until I get home."**

> **"We don't fly at night, but we do get up in the wee hours of the morning so we can start out early. We have an hour to eat, an hour to brief and another hour and a half to get our equipment to the ship, another hour to dress and put our guns in, and then we're off. I must retire now and rest up because we have work to do such as no manual laborer has ever known."**

This letter was sent by "V-Mail". Instructions on the back of each page told how to keep the writing inside the borders and warned against writing too small (because of the miniaturizing microfilming process which reduced the page by about 60%). It went on to say that the mail is subject to censorship and that contraband messages would be blacked out. The censor indorsed his name and rank just above the words "Censors Stamp" and forwarded the letter within 24 hours.

There was a lot more to flying these missions than I knew or wrote about. In fact, the 8th Air Force Bomber Command located at High Wycombe, a former girls school north of London, made elaborate plans each day we flew which were designed to confuse and mislead the Luftwaffe defenses. In retrospect, I can now see that these efforts often worked quite well. The proof of the pudding was that we were not running into the German fighters in the numbers that they were putting up in 1943 and early 1944. Enemy fighters had only about 90 minutes of fuel. The Germans were shooting down the same number of our bombers as in previous years but as our numbers increased, the loss percentages declined.

From "Screaming Eagle" by Major General Dale O. Smith comes this example of 8th Air Force tactics:

"Our attacks on enemy fighter plants and airfields near Leipzig on February 20, 1944, presented a striking illustration of bomber deception. German controllers saw our first force, a diversion of three hundred bound for Poland, swing across the North Sea to Denmark. Believing this a threat to Berlin, the Luftwaffe not only kept their northern fighters in place but dispatched seventy fighters from southern displacements to intercept. Eighty minutes later, our main force of seven hundred bombers thrust at Holland on a direct route to the targets. I led the 41st Combat Wing of almost sixty Forts in this bomber stream. German radar stations reported our huge strength and before the seventy enemy fighters sent north could intercept our diversionary force, their controllers recalled them."

"Some ninety local defenders attacked our main force on the   penetration to Leipzig, but they had to break off and refuel about target time. The seventy fighters recalled from the north hardly got in the fight before running out of fuel. Expecting a reciprocal withdrawal, German controllers marshaled all the refueled fighters together with many others along our penetration ready to swarm upon us on our way out. But we didn't return that way. By the time they (caught on), we were well on our way. Only an insignificant number caught the tail of our bomber column as it withdrew to the Channel."

"On this occasion, it was technically feasible for the en-

emy   to attack us with a thousand fighters. Yet little more than a hundred made contact."

May 29th, we were on our way to Krzesinki-Schneidemuhl (Posen, Poland) again, another long distance raid. Up at 3:00 a.m. for a 4:30 briefing, we were off at 8:00. Our target was an aircraft plant where they made the Focke-Wulf 190 the type flown into us head-on on May 13th when last we were over Poland. This time our own fighter escorts stayed with us and the enemy fighters were scarce around us at least. There were reported attacks in other formations, however. This time we stayed with our Group and made it back intact. The whole Eighth Air Force lost 37 heavies to fighters. Another 8 made it to Sweden

Again, on May 31st (just 7 days before D-day) I wrote telling the folks that when I returned, I wanted to go into pilot training, or the air transport command as an alternative.

"I can understand why Jim doesn't want the ATC, it's because he's normal. He thinks combat might be exciting and, besides, look at the decorations to be received. Nobody who hasn't seen combat can ever imagine what it's like, and therefore has no fear of it. You would probably hurt him more by putting him in the ATC than by letting him alone, although it would be infinitely safer. I only wish he could see and appreciate combat in the movies, but such is not so. Lord knows, I don't want him over here, especially in B-24's, which he is sure to get."

I went on,

"We are really plastering the Jerries now and at a terrific pace. I don't know who's going to wear out first, me or Jerry. My biggest streak is now seven raids in ten days. Nine now stand between me and home, so I'll be home soon if that's where they send me. It looks like they will give no promotions this side of the ocean because it

is a Group policy of late, unless one is on a lead crew. Not being on a lead crew, I don't see it that way. You won't be disappointed in me if I turn down another thirty missions over here, will you? If you are, it's too bad."

Then on June 5th, still completely oblivious about the invasion which began the next day, I wrote:

"Well, only seven more to go and am I getting worried. I only hope they are easy ones. I am in good health, so don't worry about that. Just write as you are doing."

(This was a tell-tale admission for me to make.)

Then it was June sixth, 1944. The invasion of France was on. It was "D-Day." Supreme Allied Commander, General Dwight Eisenhower, predicted that if our troops from England saw any planes in the air, they were more likely to be ours than theirs. It was the largest assembly of armed forces in the history of the world attacking the supposedly impregnable German Atlantic Wall in Normandy, France. American aircrews aloft that day reported that the mass of navy ships of all kinds seemed so thick it looked like our troops could step from one craft to another without getting their feet wet. Well, not quite. Many B-17 crews flew two missions that day because of the short flight time. There were innumerable sacrifices in the days to follow.

Some notable soldiers stayed behind in England that morning, i.e. General George ("Old Blood and Guts") Patton and the Lew Jolls crew. Whatever Patton was doing, we didn't know, but we were in London on passes resting comfortably in a nice hotel. Perhaps the General was informed of the start of the invasion but we had no clue. The timing of the Invasion was top secret information and no one was permitted on or off the base once the word was received from Supreme Allied Headquarters. We were already in London so we knew nothing.

I like to say we were decoys in London to throw the German spies off the trail. If nobody else is claiming it, then that's what we were. We walked the streets that morning like gawking tourists and it was strictly "business as usual" with men and women bustling to work. Coming out of a stage show around 3:00 p.m., we were accosted by newsboys holding their papers with huge black headlines that screamed: **INVASION!** We grabbed our bags and caught the first train back to our airbase where we knew there was important work for us to do.

Here's what we missed. According to Steven E. Ambrose' **"D-Day June 6, 1944: The Climactic Battle of World War II"**, the largest air armada ever gathered was in the air on D-Day.

"Many pilots and bomber crews flew three missions that day, nearly every airman flew two". They held back no reserves."

"They had earned their victory in the air war and had paid a price for it, partly in equipment, mainly in human lives. It was the most hazardous service in the war. It was also the most glamorous."

"The foot soldiers envied and resented the airmen. To their eyes, the flyboys hung around the barracks doing nothing much of anything, then went out at night and got the girls, and had an excess of rank. What the foot soldiers did not see was the Army Air Force in action. From the flyboys' point of view, they were the veterans who had been at war since 1939 (RAF) or 1942 (US) while the respective armies sat around doing not much of anything."

"They lived a strange existence. On bad-weather days, which were a majority, they led quiet barracks lives. On pass, they had their pick of London. On their way to action, for endless hours they were cramped, cold, tense, fearful and bored. When they entered action they

entered hell. With German flak thick enough to walk on coming up from below and German fighters coming in from behind and above, the air crews went through an hour more of pure terror."

"They took heavy casualties. Statistically, bomber crews could not survive twenty-five missions. Catch-22 was not fiction. They persevered and triumphed. If how much they accomplished in trying to knock out German war production is a subject of continuing controversy, what they had accomplished in driving the Luftwaffe out of France, forcing it back into Germany and a defensive role, is not. They had gone past air superiority to achieve air supremacy."

According to Mr. Ambrose' book, the B-17 groups saw very little of the invasion itself and while many turned back with their bombs on board, the rest were required to bomb through the clouds, which was not the most desirable effort considering that our troops were not too far away from where the bombs were dropping. Ground troops reported that the B-17s' bombs dropped harmlessly two or three miles ahead of them.

3,467 heavy bombers, 1,645 medium bombers and 5, 409 fighters flew on D-Day. No enemy fighters scored on them but the German flak batteries shot down 113 aircraft.

The day after "D-day", I wrote to my aunt Babe:

"Well the big day has come and gone, and where do you think I was? On pass I was, and enjoying myself, too. To my great surprise, the British took the news very calmly and no celebration was visible anywhere. I'm afraid my plans have been changed by the big event, and now I don't know when I'll finish my tour. In other words, missions unlimited until further notice. It doesn't seem so bad when I think of all the help we can be to the boys on the ground by flying to the limit of endurance. They need all of us now and I'd hate to be the one to let them down. I'm very well, so don't worry."

CHAPTER 7:

MY PROMOTION TO LEAD NAVIGATOR - DUE TO A CLERICAL ERROR

On June 14th I wrote:

"Your letters, having been bunched together, aren't lasting as long or coming as often. I guess it's the postal service to blame, so we might as well forget about it."

"We fly formation, as you probably already know, but you don't know the task of the navigator who isn't in the lead ship. The lead navigator does the navigation for the whole wing and the other navigators keep track of where they are rather than where they are going. You can see then that his main duty is to keep track in case they lose the formation. I have been doing this for twenty-three missions and then, on the twenty-fourth they told me to lead the Wing - about 36 planes and 360 men. Well, I started to worry right then and didn't stop until we landed again."

"Everything went well until we got to the target and found it clouded over, so we went around to a point from which to start our 'through-the-clouds' bombing run. We dropped our bombs and, when we started to turn off the target, we found ourselves sandwiched in between two groups and couldn't turn. My job was also to avoid any Flak, so I started to sweat blood. The weather was getting worse, so we had to let down to keep in formation and we ended up at 9,000 feet - B-26 altitude - cold turkey for anti-aircraft. Well, we made it without a shot fired by Jerry and preceded home."

"When I got back to our base - we were leading a Wing from another field - they told me that it was a mistake that I was sent to do the job. Ever since then they have had me doing 'deputy lead' - sort of a sub. Who knows, I might even get a promotion."

"That's all for today. I hope you enjoyed my little adventure. I didn't until I was back on the ground."

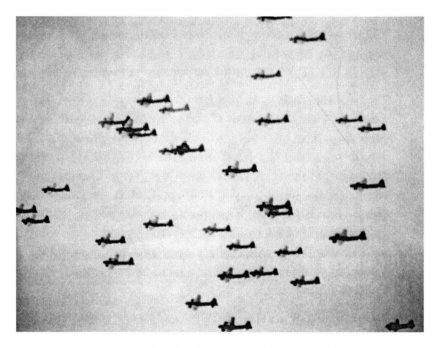

Figure 26. B-17 Combat Formation in attack mode.

My recollection of this mission is still very strong. We, the Jolls' crew, flew to another base on orders - which turned out to be nearby "Bassingbourne"- and boarded the lead plane with the base commander, a full Colonel, riding the right copilot's seat. Lew Jolls was flying the plane. We also had the newest, top secret, through-the-clouds "Gee-H" bombing equipment on board along with a Gee H operator/navigator who rode in the nose compartment with me and the bombardier. We were the Wing leader for the day. There was no room to spare in the nose with three men in that small space.

At first, I said nothing. I was waiting for the other navigator to tell me what I was supposed to do that day. He introduced himself as the Gee-H operator and that was it. It didn't occur to me to ask about my assignment and in the next few minutes we were airborne.

I had never led a mission before as navigator and was completely untrained as such (actually there was a two-week course conducted away from the base which leader trainees went through to qualify for the job.) There were things you had to know about maneuvering a large group of planes in formation which I had no idea of. Until we got on course for the target, the pilot was in charge of assembly, or at least I thought he was. We circled; it seemed endlessly, as the 36 B-17's joined the formation one by one. The sky was clear at altitude. No one told me that I was supposed to be in on the job of watching departure time and a full three minutes got away making us late departing the English coast. When we arrived there, two other groups were also there. They were on time, we weren't. The Colonel said nothing but the pilot began a weaving course in order to slow us down so we might be able to drop back behind the other two groups. It hadn't yet occurred to me that my ignorance might have put us in danger of a disaster.

We were heading for the invasion front to bomb close behind the enemy lines - a Luftwaffe airfield was the target. As I wrote in the letter, we approached the target for a visual bomb run, but just as we were about to reach the "IP" or initial point, we found clouds blocked the bombardier's view of the target. The wing commander ordered us to go to the alternate IP for Gee H bombing. I gave the direction to start a slow turn to the left and sat back and watched as the Gee H operator took over. In minutes we were at the new IP and we changed course again heading toward the target in a southwest direction. The Gee H operator flew the plane from the navigator's desk and dropped the bombs, all with his special equipment and then we were ready to turn due west and head for the ocean.

Again, we encountered other groups of B-17's, probably because of the course change and the resulting loss of time, and we had to drop down to a lower altitude to stay clear of them. Our heading was 270 degrees until we approached another turning point to head back north to England.

I was in charge again and the pilot was following my directions, completely. The Gee H guy was taking a nap or something. We were supposed to make a 90 degree turn according to the routing on my map to be on course for England. But, applying my own intuition and ingenuity, I informed the pilot of a new course to cut the corner. It may have appeared as a change designed to make up for the lost time - but, actually, it was just my fecklessness. It never occurred to me that this might be risky or dangerous, but nothing happened and nobody said anything about it. It's reasonable to guess that at least one of the following navigators in our formation was paying attention and in doing so must have wondered about the change in course.

After completing our turn to due north, it was a straight shot to the base. We landed and our crew re-boarded our own plane and headed for home.

When we got back to our base, I was summoned into Headquarters. I didn't know what to expect, maybe to be chewed out for something I did or didn't do. The mission wasn't perfect but it was a success and there were no losses. The officer in charge told me that what I had done was a mistake to be the leader because I hadn't been through lead-navigator's school. But, he said, since I did the job, they were going to promote me out of the Jolls crew to fly "deputy leader." (Take that, Colonel Preston, in response to your disdain for kid navigators!)

Well, I was popping my buttons. But they omitted to tell me that being deputy lead meant flying alongside the leader and the lead ship was always the prime target for the anti-aircraft gunners. Good duck hunters aim at the lead bird in the flock. If they miss, there's a possibility they might hit the next nearest bird. My chances of getting shot down had just doubled and it would be twice as likely we'd be hit. I had worked myself up from being a live duck with problems in the back of the flock to a dead one up front.

Unbeknownst to me, the Group had already lost three deputy leaders but never a lead ship. Maybe that's why nobody warned me about what I was getting into. My new crew was led by 1st Lt. Steve King. His regular navigator, Jack Sinise (uncle to be of movie and television star Gary Sinise - "Forest Gump" and "CSI New York" and many other popular shows), had been bumped up to Squadron Leader, Steve was informed he was getting a new ace navigator. At least that's what he told me. Not in my mind, I wasn't. But maybe I really was.

Figure 27. The King Crew: L.R. Czarnecki, Rutishauser, Hagen, Lt. Henry, Miller, Lt. Sinise*, Ray Weehler, Lt. King, Lt. Olson* (*Not flying on the last mission; replaced by author and M. Miller, respectively.)

King was a comer with the Group and had already volunteered for a second tour on the colonel's promise of a captaincy and a real chance to move up to the leadership level. I had more missions but it was easy to follow a fine airplane commander like Steve. We already knew each other and it was a comfortable change for both of us to make.

Unbelievable as it may seem, the Jolls crew was left to fly without a navigator for its last five missions. Lew told me years later that without me aboard he was so stressed that on his return to the States he spent a few weeks in the hospital in Miami Beach, Florida being treated for combat fatigue. He said that he had complete confidence flying with me but none without me. It was my number one compliment of the war.

As for me being deputy leader, you don't buck odds like that. On June 18th, my second mission with the King crew to Hamburg - which happened to be my 28th (I only needed that mission and two more to go home.) we were bombing the vital synthetic oil refineries. It was Sunday at around 10:00 a.m. The enemy's strategic fuel supplies were vulnerable and we were going to try to make things even worse for them. The sun was shining brightly but disaster loomed.

CHAPTER 8:

DESCENT INTO THE
MAELSTROM

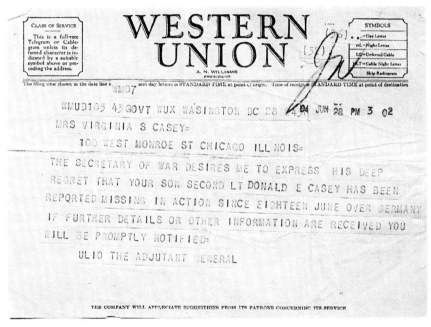

Figure 28. Fateful Telegram to Author's Parents to notify them their son is Missing in Action as of June 18, 1944 over Hamburg, Germany.

It was Sunday and mission number 28 for me, but the feeling of tension was the same if not more so. We went through our routine of briefing, collecting our maps and readying ourselves for another worrisome sortie over Germany, Hamburg to be exact. We were flying as deputy leader. 1st Lt. Steve King was the airplane commander, my old copilot Milton Miller, and Charlie Henry, bombardier also were on board. The enlisted men were all King's crew. They put us in a shiny new B-17 and ours was a really important ship in the formation. If the leader became disabled, we were in charge. I had the very latest navigation equipment aboard and we were looking good. Yet, there was that nagging feeling as I was nearing the end of my tour. I had been extremely lucky, but I was taking no unnecessary chances. The empty feeling in the pit of my stomach was larger than ever. I had received communion from Father Sullivan that morning and I was as ready as I could be. And I knew my stuff. That was not what worried me. What was on my mind was just how many times can you fly through to the target before your luck runs out? Max Hastings in his book "Bomber Command" wrote of the Russian roulette of flying through a flak barrage. I made up my own version of this which was that flying in combat with any feeling of confidence because of prior successes was like playing Russian roulette and thinking you were getting good at it because the gun didn't go off.

This was an over-water mission until we made a landfall to the Hamburg area. Our target was the docks and oil installations there along the shipping channels. This kind of target was Germany's Achilles heel above all. Apparently even the high command hadn't been able to agree for a long time on the importance of oil to the enemy's war machine.

We began the bomb run and it was the longest I had ever been on, an incredible thirteen minutes. The Flak was heavy at 25,000 feet, but nothing unusual. What we didn't know was that the Flak gunners had our altitude exactly. We must have looked like a flock of geese heading south. As hunters learn to do, the German gunners aimed at the lead ship. They missed and hit us instead.

Figure 29. 88 mm Flieger Abwher Kannonen (Flak) manned by experts in rapid fire mode.

It was the first time I had ever heard a Flak shell burst - yes, from the hail of falling shell fragments bouncing off the hull, but never the explosion itself. There were two very loud sounds, one right after the other. "Wham, Wham." Aircraft commander Steve King announced over the intercom' that we were hit and were on fire and that we should "bail out." The aircraft had been struck twice in the right wing, about where the gasoline tanks were located. There were no conditions or reservations about that order.

Figure 30. Pilot Steve King's drawing in Prison Camp of the burning ship's death throes.

A moment later, just a couple of feet away in the catwalk between the nose compartment and the flight deck, I saw copilot Milt Miller pull the release handle which opened up the nose hatch and fall out head first.

It did not take long to figure out that we were doomed. I have no memory of our dropping our bombs notwithstanding the report that we did. I had worn my parachute beginning with takeoff and I had the flak vest on over it as we approached the target. I was ready to jump as soon as I removed the vest and oxygen mask, disconnected my throat microphone and headset. I positioned myself on my knees over the open nose hatch, and, after pausing momentarily, Facing the open hatch, I began debating with myself about what I was about to do. I had to go now or pass out soon from anoxia. The thought went through my mind as it must for everyone whoever received the bail out order over enemy territory, "This airplane is the only way you have of returning to home base alive. Now you're going to leave it without any chance of returning, parachuting into a place we just bombed. This is crazy!"

I overlooked two important things. First, I left my street shoes by my navigator's desk. I had taken them off in order to slip on the heated slippers which I wore inside my flying boots; and second, I left my brief case with some maps and splashier frequencies in their plastic cases. Neither were on my mind at all. I had received the order to jump and I was about to carry it out.

Gritting my teeth and doing the unthinkable, I bowed my head and tumbled out of the hatch, head first. I was on my own now. All was silence. There was no feeling of falling at all because there were no reference points against which to compare. I lay on my back looking up at the sky. It was an absolutely clear and sunny day. I was all right so far, as they say, but what lay below, I wondered and worried, a lot. It was a feeling of sheer terror.

We had been told not to open our parachutes at high altitude, but to wait as long as possible. On the wall back at the base there was a poster which said: "DELAY OPENING YOUR CHUTE." There were two good reasons for this advice: first, without oxygen at bombing altitude, one would be in danger of passing out; but second, German soldiers and civilians were watching from the ground below and an open parachute is visible for miles. Why give them any lead time in tracking you down?

Not knowing the tricks of skydiving (a term which had not yet been invented or thought of at that time) I did not know how to right myself into position so that I could watch the earth coming up to meet me at about a 120 mph, "terminal velocity." I waited and waited, and waited some more.

As I fell, I noticed what appeared to be silver flecks like confetti in the sky above. I thought it might be the remains of my airplane but I am sure now that this was only "Chaff" which was tinfoil dropped by other planes to block or jam the enemy's ground radar.

I kept on falling for what seemed an interminable length of time. I had to crane my neck to see over my left shoulder and look down. Our parachute training had been only verbal instructions. We never practiced jumping in any way, but I remembered being told to wait to pull the ring until things appeared to be moving on the ground. I didn't have a good perspective but it just seemed like a hell of a long time had already gone by. My father used to joke about parachute training. He would say "How do you practice something you have to do right the first time?" This was a funny saying but still an oversimplification because the paratroopers in fact did practice jumping off 12 foot platforms built for that purpose in learning how to roll into a somersault on landing to protect against leg and ankle fractures which might otherwise occur.

Finally, I lost my nerve and yanked on the ring. Suddenly, and with a jerk, I became upright and hung there in my parachute harness. At the same time, one of my fleece lined boots fell off leaving me shoeless on one foot. Now reality at last sank in. I prayed to the Blessed Mother to save me, from what I did not know. I said to myself in these exact words, "Kid, what have you gotten yourself into now?" In no time at all I was on the ground, standing up with my chute falling down around me. I was in a grove of trees but had missed them completely. I looked around and found myself in what appeared to be suburban surroundings. Across the street was a low-rise military hospital in which there were young men wearing bandages and missing limbs hanging out of the windows watching me.

CHAPTER 9:

UNCLE EMMETT M. CASEY JOINED IN DEATH 26 YEARS LATER?

My father still had wrenching memories of his beloved older brother Emmett who was killed in action in France in World War I on August 8, 1918. Now he was faced with a new and possibly tragic situation. After the first War, on each anniversary of his brother's death, dad had to fight off the depressing recollection of August 1918. He was 19 then, two years younger than Emmett, and was a 2d Lieutenant, and a combat observer/ photographer in the U.S. Air Service also in France. He flew over the battle lines to take pictures for the Intelligence Service. He was making a special trip to see Emmett at his encampment. When dad arrived at the place, his heart was broken on hearing the news of his brother's death in action only two days previously. All dad recovered of his personal effects was his bloodstained soldier's handbook and a diary in which Emmett had written briefly. Dad never got over that experience and now there was this terrible news of the loss of his second son who bore the same name.

Figure 31. Author's Father Lt. J. Douglas Casey in World War I uniform in 1918.

Figure 32. Emmett M. Casey, Killed in Action in France August 8, 1918.

Emmett was the apple of his father's eye and my dad's idol, best friend and protector in school. It couldn't be true that he was gone forever. Emmett volunteered as a combat engineer when war was declared by America and our nation began raising its Army to save the French and British from certain defeat by Germany. He didn't have to go and fight but it was his nature to be in the thick of things.

He wrote to his father the day before his death:

"You asked me to send you some souvenirs. There are all kinds of them around here, German guns, helmets, gas masks, and all sorts of stuff, but you cannot send anything. I am collecting a bunch of buttons and badges. I have them from nearly every army in the war. The fellows use the helmets for wash basins. I sure have met some fine fellows over here and some of them have been in the war since it began."

To his mother a few days before his death, Emmett had written, "Everything is going along fine so far and I am still in good health. Don't worry about me for I think we will be together again soon."

Emmett was in the 108th Combat Engineers. As reported by his friend, Corporal John Corrigan, they were notified to be ready to move into action as part of a new drive in their sector. It was to be the largest one of the war in that region. Wrote Corrigan:

"We went over the top at 4:30 a.m. Thursday, August 8th (1918). About five minutes after our barrage started a call came for volunteers to work ahead to keep in touch with the infantry. Emmett was one of eight to volunteer. We filled in one of our trenches and then we moved up to what was left of the Huns' front line. We were caught in his counter barrage which he used to keep back any reserves we might bring up."

"We dropped flat for a few minutes and Emmett and the others of his party went into a shell hole, because it seemed impossible to carry on any work. He was hit while were waiting. He was only about eight yards from me when he spoke of being hit and started to walk back. Two of our boys helped him and he never showed any

signs of fear, but stood it like a man. He passed away in the dressing station behind the lines while the doctors were working over him. I don't think he suffered much pain for he did not speak of it. He was game all the time and made the sacrifice. We pushed the Hun back in one week almost as far as he gained in four years."

"Emmett did not have an enemy in the company, but was liked by everybody and the boys certainly felt very sad over the loss of their friend. He lived a good life and was brave to the last."

Figure 33. Death Certificate of author's uncle Emmett Casey signed by Gen. John J. (Black Jack) Pershing 1918.

It is sad now to think that had they had blood plasma as we had in WWII, his life might have been saved.

CHAPTER 10:

LETTERS OF SYMPATHY TO THE BEREAVED

The folks received many letters from friends, one of whom was Colonel J. Henry Pool from Air Force Headquarters in Washington, DC dated July 6, 1944. Dad took advantage of his acquaintance with the Colonel and had written to him on July 3rd asking for whatever information he could get on my fate.

The Colonel wrote:

> **"I was terribly sorry to hear that young Don had gone down over Germany. I immediately called the Adjutant General's Office to see if they had any advance information, but all they had was what they had forwarded to Mrs. Casey. I find from the A.G.** (Adjutant General) **that reports from prisoners of war are sometime three or four months in arriving in our hands. A friend of mine went down three months ago and just last week we learned that he was a prisoner of war and everyone had been almost sure that he had passed on. Tell Mrs. Casey to keep her chin up."**

Dad's best friend in the service was Colonel Gus Minton at Headquarters of the AAF Training Command in Fort Worth. Colonel Minton wrote to Dad on July 10th that he had asked the Commanding Officers of the Redistribution Centers at both Atlantic City and Miami Beach to interrogate any returnees assigned to my squadron or group that might have any information as to what had happened to me. He also asked A-2 (Intelligence) in Washington to see if they had any information.

John Clarke, one of dad's colleagues in the investment banking business in Chicago and a close friend of the family wrote a letter to me dated July 20, 1944 and sent it to my folks:

> **"Dear Donny: I heard the other day you were missing over Germany and that's tough, kid, but I know you weren't destined to do other than come back and add to the joy of living in a postwar world. So I know, somewhere in Germany, or even in neutral country, you will be found safe and sound. When and as your Dad gets your address, I am asking him to send you this rosary, blessed for you by the Pope, and also this St. Christopher medal blessed by the pope for your next crate!"**

Another good friend of Dad's was Clifford Roberts, famous in later years as the tournament chairman and major domo of the Masters Golf Tournament at Augusta, Georgia. He wrote to say that he had heard about the bad news.

> **"For the past week, I have been trying to think up a good message to send you, but I am still unable to express myself as nothing seems adequate. I know how proud you are of the particular boy. There is one thing about it, however, and that is that he may have inherited some of the good luck you have had all these years, and you may get further word that he is still alive."**

Finally, on July 14th, another telegram came from General Ulio stating that a report had been received through the International Red Cross that I was a prisoner of war in Germany and that an explanatory letter would soon follow.

Mother received a touching letter from Mrs. Thurston Richardson in Houston. She had last seen me at Ellington Field as an aviation cadet and wrote as follows:

> **"I can only tell you what the news about Donny did to me when I received it the other day. I was alone and found myself crying and talking to myself, and I kept seeing his sweet innocent face as he sat on our davenport just a few months ago. If you never realized it before, I**

want you to know and believe me when I say that of all the children of all my old friends, Don has always been one who somehow or other tugged at my heartstrings. For that reason - and for your sake, too, I shall be hoping as hard as you are that he will turn up as a prisoner of war."

"I know that all of the parents of sons in this war have steeled themselves for such news, but I am sure it still does not make it any easier to hear. I shall be thinking of you - and hoping - and even praying for you both and your son."

At least I knew where I was but mother and dad had no idea what to think. "Missing in Action over Germany" did not sound good at all. It was another fourteen days before they got the somewhat better news from the Red Cross. Dad wired the news to Mother in Three Lakes, Wisconsin: "Received Wire from Adjutant General through Red Cross Don German Prisoner Letter of Information following From Provost Marshall General."

The local newspaper featured my picture in the "Service Men's News" column telling of how I was now a POW of the German government after being reported missing in action on June 18, 1944.

"Nineteen year-old Lieutenant Casey was a deputy lead navigator and led the formations on their missions, and is a veteran of many missions, having received the Distinguished Flying Cross and Air Medal with Oak Leaf Clusters."

Not long after the news of my erstwhile demise two army officers appeared at my Mother's front door and delivered to her my DFC and Air medal with my name engraved on the back.

The Chicago Sun newspaper listed my name on October 11th along with 46 other unfortunate - or fortunate depending on your point of view - who were "Chicagoans Prisoners."

CHAPTER 11:

HIDING MY PARACHUTE IN PLAIN SIGHT

The first thing we were told to do once on the ground was to hide your parachute before preparing to escape. I began to look around for a place to hide both my chute and my bright yellow life preserver. I had an excited audience across the street watching my every move. The air raid was still going on and I could hear bombs exploding in the distance. Within two or three minutes, a car pulled up about 25 yards away and two armed soldiers got out and came toward me with their pistols drawn. I was crouched under a bush now, but not at all well hidden.

Seeing no purpose in pretending they couldn't see me, I stood up and out from my supposed hiding place with my hands up as I faced their automatic pistols which were aimed right at me. They wasted no time collaring me with my life preserver on backwards and gathering up my chute and stuffing it into my arms while simultaneously nudging me with their weapons to walk ahead of them.

We walked a short distance to a small underground air raid shelter. The place was full of people who would gladly have torn me limb from limb but for my captors who had become my protectors. I was wearing my dark green heated flying suit, my aviator's helmet and carrying the white bundle of parachute, it was obvious what I was one of the "terror fliegers" (terror fliers) the Nazis wrote about daily in their newspapers and propaganda materials.

Soon the raid was over. My guards marched me out of the air raid shelter with a flourish of disdain. The huddled people said nothing and did nothing. I learned later that Hitler had announced to his people - over the strong objections of his own military leaders - that they should feel free to take revenge on any downed fliers they found, even to the point of execution, if desired, and that the soldiers were not to interfere or try to stop them. Fortunately, I was in the hands of two men who disagreed with that order. Whether they knew it or not, retribution awaited murderers of helpless prisoners if Germany surrendered.)

They took me to their car and I got into the back seat. We made our way slowly through the city which was in shambles from prior raids. In August, 1943, the British and Americans had firebombed the city, relentlessly killing some 75,000 civilians in the space of a few days and nights. I don't recall our superiors telling us anything of this or of Hitler's exhortation to the civilians to feel free to destroy us on ground, if not in the air. One thing we did know not to do was to carry a sidearm, such as a forty-five automatic which we all were given as standard equipment. We were told it was not mandatory to carry any side arms because it might give the Germans the justification to kill us on the spot. There were already enough reasons for the Germans to shoot fallen enemy aviators but an armed man could be killed on the ready pretext of self-defense.

CHAPTER 12:

"FUEHLSBUETTEL" - A FRIGHTENINGLY FAMILIAR NAME

Finally, the car pulled up to a fenced-in compound. The arch over the gate bore the name "Fuehlsbuettel." I knew that name. In fact I was quite familiar with it and it did nothing to give me any comfort at that time. In High School I had read a book entitled, "Out of the Night" by Jan Valtin. It was a true horror story told by the author who was a German communist labor organizer arrested by the Nazis and taken to a prison right there in Hamburg with that very same name. While there, according to the author, he was tortured and beaten along with many other political prisoners. The cruelty of the Gestapo was unrelenting according to Mr. Valtin, an assumed name. I did not know what to expect inside the walls, but my recollections of the book were not what I needed at the time.

Where were the other men in my crew? Steve King told me later that he and the bombardier, Charlie Henry, stayed with the ship after it was hit to determine whether the crew in the rear had heard the command to bail out. Charlie crawled back from his position past the open escape hatch up into the cockpit. When he got to the flight deck to ask Steve if he could be of any help in controlling the now flaming bomber, Steve ordered him to bail out immediately. He did so and was taken prisoner and wound up in the same place as I did.

The plane careened on as Lt. King prepared to jump. He put it on autopilot and worked his way back toward the empty bomb bay with the doors still open. He looked back toward the waist section and saw our radio man, Charles Rutishauser, clutching the sides of the rear door apparently unable to decide what to do. Steve said he shouted and gestured for him to jump and just then the ship exploded. Rutishauser may or may not have been wounded by the flak bursts but he died in the explosion. Steve and the ball-turret gunner, James Hagen, were blown clear and survived.

CHAPTER 13:

ONLY ONE OF OUR PLANES IS MISSING

The official report pursuant to "Field Order 397" of the 379th Bomb Group for Mission #145 to Hamburg on June 18, 1944 was as follows:

> **"CREW OBSERVATIONS AND UNUSUAL TACTICS (AERIAL BOMBS, ROCKETS, ETC.). Time: 09:48 1/2, Place: Target, Height: 24,000;**
>
> **A/C (aircraft) #628 of our group hit by flak. No. 3 engine and portion of wing on fire --- plane under control losing altitude.**
>
> **Of the 20 planes dispatched from our Group that day with 1 A/C P-628, 526th Bomb Squadron, lost. Bombs on target, 342; size 250; type G.P. (General Purpose) Casualties: -0- killed, wounded: 4, missing: 9, rescued: -0-. Battle damage: minor - 14, major -4. No (enemy planes) destroyed, probable or damaged. Leaflets 10 (parcels) of type 203."**

In a narrative report of the same date, Captain John J. O'Connell, Group S-2 Intelligence Officer wrote:

> ***1. The 379th Bomb Group furnished the lead and low groups in the 41'st 'B' CB on the mission to attack Hamburg. Ten units of G-44 leaflets and ten units of ZG-3 leaflets were dropped over Hamburg.**
>
> ***2. Due to 8/10's undercast, bombing was done on PFF equipment. However, there were some holes in the clouds and our first photos show our bombs away in the port**

area. Accordingly, it is felt that good results were obtained and that the bombs fell well within the port area.

   *3. No enemy fighters were seen by this group. No claims.

   *4. AA fire at Hamburg was described as being moderate to intense, black and accurate. No other flak was reported.

   *5. Weather over the target area ranged from 8 to 10/10's undercast and required that bombing be done on PFF equipment. Weather over England on the route out was 10/10's, but broke to 3/10's on the route back.

   *6. A smoke screen was reported at Hamburg. Several large vessels, about 15 in number, were seen in the bay at 5355N - 0655E. At Neumunster, 17 planes were seen parked close together on the ground.

   *7. Our A/C 628 was hit by flak over Hamburg at 0949 hours and its number 3 engine and a portion of its right wing were seen to be on fire. After dropping its bombs, our plane was seen to go down under control. No chutes were reported. Friendly escort was very good."

The Group's lead bombardier reported that we were on the bomb run for 13 minutes and that the results were unobserved because of the cloud cover. "Our heading was 200 degrees and bombs were away at 9:28 1/2. The 'Gee' (British radar set) went out of range at 8:51 at 0630 E. The group departed the enemy coast at 1008 and entered the English coast at 1138 1/2 over Cromer at 8,000 feet. The Group landed at 1230."

No doubt the reporting officer was taking pride in the fact that *only* one ship was lost that day. A tolerable percentage at that time but not if your plane was the one that did not come back. For us it was 100%.

The Group had taken off at 5:40 a.m. and formed over

Molesworth at 0635. "We departed the English coast at 0709 over Louth. Our fighters rendezvoused with us at 8:10. We crossed the enemy coast at Amrum Island at 0916 at 23,500 feet."

The Battle Casualty Report showed our aircraft No. 42-102628 and our crew as "missing." Later, the true results were written in by hand. Copilot Milton Miller, Radio Operator Charles Rutishauser, Tail Gunner Eugene Miller and Waist Gunner Zygfryd Czarnecki were listed as "KIA" (killed in action). The rest of us were missing or P/W (prisoner of war). We five survivors, Pilot Steve King, Bombardier Charlie Henry, Engineer Ray Weehler, Ball Turret Gunner James Hagen and myself as Navigator had somehow come through "the eye of the needle."

CHAPTER 14:

NEWS OF OUR DEMISE
ANNOUNCED AT THE AIRBASE

Back at the base, Jack Sinise, my good friend and a fellow navigator whose place I took on the fated mission, was in our barracks killing time, waiting for our planes to return from the mission. When we met after the war, I asked him what was going on that day after the planes landed without us. He said that people rushed in with the news. He said that he had to be "philosophical" about it and that he went on with his work.

Perhaps I expected more than that from him, but why should I? After all, that was how we kept going previously - just brush off the other fellow's bad luck and resume thinking that it would never happen to you. Had it been the other way around, would I have acted any differently? I like to think that it was harder than he made out to ignore the loss of friends who were that close - a good reasons not to get too close to any one in combat.

Jack told me that he never forgot my sense of humor and how I put on a show for them in which I acted out what it would be like to be shot down and captured by the Germans. He remembered me saying that when they put my nether parts in a vice, I would immediately tell them everything I knew. My audience laughed long and hard. Now the laugh was on me and it wasn't at all funny. As this book is written, Jack is still around and somewhat of a celebrity for being the blood-uncle of movie and TV star Gary Sinise. ["Forest Gump" and CSI New York" to name just a few roles he has played.] When Jack and I get together as we still do occasionally, I remind him of his debt to me for taking his place that June day in 1944.

My new pilot, Steve King, had a world of guts, to be sure.

Shortly before this last mission, he had volunteered to fly a second tour when C.O. Col. Preston promised him 30 days leave in the States and an immediate promotion to Captain. Steve apparently had decided as a young man that a military career was what he wanted. He was thinking that if he could finish two combat tours, he would be promoted again to Major and receive a bundle of decorations in the process, all of which would stand him in good stead later on. He did not know the meaning of the words "give up" in any way and he willingly put his neck on the line to prove it. The colonel had sensed this and marked Steve for higher levels of command. Had I known this at the time, being deputy leader would have meant that much more to me.

As Steve tells it, when the plane blew up, he was knocked out briefly and regained consciousness in mid-air in a free fall. He immediately pulled the ripcord on his parachute, just in time to save his life. He landed south of the city in a rural area and managed to escape detection for the next 10 hours. He hid himself until night fall and began the rather hopeless task of trying to escape from deep into Germany. He stole food where he could find it and managed to remain on the loose for a brief but frightening period of time.

Finally, he was caught by some farmers who, following the Fuhrer's exhortation, put a rope about Steve's neck and were ready to string him up. Before they could accomplish this brutality, soldiers came on the scene and saved him. Steve said that the soldiers were quite rough on the civilians in the process and made no bones about showing their total disapproval.

Steve was taken away and soon rejoined our flight engineer and top turret gunner, Sergeant Ray Weehler who had also been captured. Weehler, too, was an Errol Flynn (the movie actor) type when it came to danger. Steve tells the story of how Ray had shot down five German fighters while on his crew and how, as aircraft commander, he reprimanded the sergeant severely one day for waiting until the Jerry plane was dangerously close before opening fire from his two gun top turret. Steve asked Weehler what he was waiting for and Ray responded that he was letting the enemy pilot get closer so that he could get a sure kill. Steve angrily replied that he didn't want that to happen again and that instead of holding his fire, Weehler should be shooting at the attackers even out of range of the guns to warn them off.

Later on a train that night to an interrogation center, they found themselves unguarded and broke a window and jumped out. The train stopped and the soldiers quickly recaptured them and re-boarded.

The Germans told Steve that copilot Milton Miller had been shot to death in his parachute from the ground. One can only speculate that Miller had panicked and pulled his ripcord too soon. It was a fatal mistake and made himself clearly visible, inviting the very thing that happened. Steve, Charlie Henry, Weehler, myself and gunner Jim Hagen survived. The other four died. 8th Air Force statistics showed about a 60% survival rate for shootdowns.

CHAPTER 15:

A CAPTURED OFFICER AND "TERROR FLIEGER" OR A BOY SCOUT?

Adolph Hitler and his chief propagandist Dr. Goebbels came up with the tags for us enemy airmen: "TERROR FLIEG-ERS" and "LUFTGANGSTERS." My captors took me inside the Fuehlsbuettel compound and began asking questions. Four or five others joined them, possibly expecting to see and hear something unusual. What it was I did not know, but quite apparently, they were impressed by my youthful appearance. Perhaps I gave them renewed hope that America was at last running out of front line troops, scraping the bottom of the barrel and sending over the boy scouts.

I was a fuzzy-cheeked kid of nineteen who had not even begun to shave yet. Not an impressive sight, to be sure. (Their of-ficers had life and death power over them so how could the Ameri-can Army give that kind of authority to a mere boy?) One of the Germans spoke a little English and began to ask me in halting fash-ion: "How old is you? When is you born?" I shook my head and held up my hands as if to say that I did not understand what he was saying. Again, I remembered the orders to give them "name, rank and serial number," but nothing else. This I did faithfully.

Finally, they gave up the interrogation and put me in a cell by myself. After what seemed quite a long time, but still that day, I was given a little bread to eat. There was a cot to lie on which I did and slept through the night. My only communication with the guard was his signal that I could relieve myself. This was not a ma-jor problem because I was still too scared. I felt like crying, but it didn't come and soon I was asleep. For lack of any idea what was coming next, I didn't even have a nightmare about my sad plight. Tension ebbed and exhaustion took over.

The next night, I was taken away under guard and put on a passenger train. I was closely watched at all times by an armed soldier who carried a bulging brief case which contained enough food for the two of us. I had no idea where or in which direction we were going.

At daylight we were in another city which I learned was Frankfurt on Main. From the railroad station, my guard and I boarded a trolley car and rode some distance through the city. The trip had been uneventful, so far.

CHAPTER 16:

IN SOLITARY CONFINEMENT

We got off the trolley and I was marched to a foreboding building where I was turned over to a new array of captors and put into a small, closet-like cell with a small high window, a cot, a mattress and a soiled pillow covered with ticking. I supposed I was being softened up for the real interrogation. They fed me with a modest amount of soup and bread and water as I sweated out their next move. I was very lonely and not at all comfortable with my circumstances. I prayed a lot and hoped for the best.

Solitary Confinement is a well known punishment and has been popular for centuries. There is scientific evidence that human beings deprived of contact with other humans long enough will inevitably break down, mentally and cease to function. The Germans knew this very well and used it whenever appropriate. The first day in my new cell was a test of wills. Since I knew nothing about our war strategies and merely flew bombing missions per orders from my superiors, there was very little to gain from my confinement. Not knowing what they were going to do to me, if anything, was worrisome and not at all pleasant but otherwise seemed to have no effect on me of which I was aware.

The morning of the 3rd day, the door to my cell was opened and the guard motioned me down the hall to a small office in which sat a smartly dressed German officer. He spoke flawless American English. To my great surprise there on his desk was my brief case from the airplane. I knew it was mine for sure because I had painted my name and number on the outside myself. There was no mistaking it. Now he knew everything I knew, and more.

He offered me a cigarette and asked me where I was from. I blurted out: "Chicago." "Oh," he said, "I was at the World's Fair of 1933 in Chicago." I also told him my father's office address. He hinted that I should tell him what Group I was in, but he already knew very well which one it was. Not that it was all that important. I was just a young punk second lieutenant, and I looked it. German Intelligence was not interested in interviewing kids like me. They saved their best efforts for Majors and Colonels who had knowledge of more important things like strategies. Before too long, he signaled my guard saying in English: "Take this officer to ...," then lapsing into German so the guard could understand, "Zimmer Sieben" (room seven), my cell.

After three days of waiting for the other shoe to drop (I only had one boot left), I was assembled with some other prisoners and marched off to what we came to know as "Dulag Luft" - meaning a temporary camp for air force prisoners - for transshipment to the more permanent "Stalags," a shortened version of "Stammlager" or permanent camp. I limped along with a flying boot on one foot and the electric slipper on the other. Fortunately it was not too far a distance, because my slipper was soon in tatters leaving me with one mostly bare foot.

CHAPTER 17:

BY TRAIN TO STALAG LUFT III, THE "GREAT ESCAPE" POW CAMP

It was still June and the weather was clement. They had taken the electric lining out of my flying suit without which it hung on me in baggy fashion. At Dulag Luft, we boarded a passenger train heading east for Poland and Stalag Luft III, the already in-famous - later to become known as the "Great Escape" camp. No one knew it by that name yet. I remember one of our guys trying to speak English with the guard who replied in German using the word "Lager." The airman mistook the word to mean a type of beer. The guard, a middle-aged man, shook his head affirmatively that there would be "lager." He meant camp. I grasped what he was saying, even if my new buddy did not, but I had no idea what was waiting for us.

Figure 34. Map of locations of Prison Camps for American POW's in Germany.

Figure 35. German photo of the author with his cellmates taken at Stalag Luft III in Poland in July 1944, Back Row to Front: Lee Hamaker, Bill Shapiro, Jim Ferguson, (unidentified), (unidentified), Jim Crouch, Freed Warren; Second row (seated): Phil Corkin, Don Casey, Morrie Bauer, John (Bud) Elliott, Joe Varhol; Front row: Valleau Wilkie and Sonny Fisher.

Figure 36. The stump-ridden confines of Stalag Luft III, Sagan, Poland.

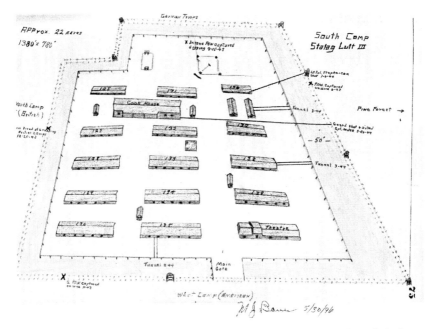

Figure 37. Fellow Kriegie and cellmate the late Morrie Bauer's drawing of the layout of our South Camp at Stalag Luft III. Barracks 135 - low center - was our "Block."

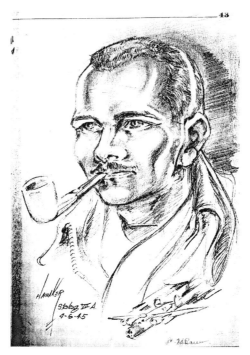

Figure 38. Portrait of the late Morrie Bauer drawn by fellow cell-mate Lee Hamaker, deceased.

About a day and night later, we were there. We were put off the train and marched through the gates of "South Camp." (The other compounds were the North, the Center, West and the East camps). My first impression was of northern Wisconsin where I used to go with my parents for summer vacations. The weather was pleasant and the camp was surrounded by fir trees. We were "fresh fish" to the inmates. They also referred to us as a "purge," as if the Germans were cleaning up the bomber crews we sent over, or purging the unfit from the fit, the unlucky from the lucky. We were "Kriegies" now and forever. This was an American/British word made up from the longer German word, "Kriegsgefangener" or war prisoner. Translated back into English, "kriegie" would be "warry," a nonsense term to them, but not to us.

Figure 39. Prison personnel card with photo of vanquished author.

I was interviewed by two American senior officers and assigned to a cell block or barracks right near the main gate and, within the block, to a room with eleven other men, all victims as I was. They turned out to be a great bunch of guys. They were very solicitous at first, but once you told your "there I was" story about being shot down, you merged into the flow of things and never spoke about it again. Everybody there had lived through his own personal tragedy in being shot down, so it was no big deal.

Actually, to me, things seemed reasonably tolerable. After all, I was only two years away from the Jesuit boarding school where 400 boys were restricted to the campus and our custodians watched us every minute, just like here. The important difference lay in the fact that the German guards carried guns at the ready. Make the wrong move, and they shot you dead. At boarding school the punishment had been only an extra hour of study hall or confinement to the campus. Otherwise, our "campus" held a bunch of very aggressive and bright young men who had volunteered to fly and now were imprisoned for an indefinite period of time. If our side won, we could go home. If their side prevailed, we were their prisoners for as long as they needed us. In fact, Oberfeldwebel (Master sergeant) Glemnitz regularly chided us by saying that after the war we would remain and help rebuild Germany. We couldn't accept that but one never knew for sure.

Figure 40. Oberfeldwebel (Master Sergreant) Herman Glemnitz in charge of our compound, so highly regarded by the prisoners that we invited him after the war to come to America and attend our POW Reunion.

Eventually I was told about a German guard shooting and killing U.S. Corporal Myles when he stuck his head out of the Cook House in our compound during an air raid in spite of strict directions to remain indoors until further orders. When our Senior American Officer, Col. Goodrich, complained to the prison commandant about it, that officer replied with a question: "When you give an order to your men, sir, do you not you expect it to be carried out?" The Germans had ordered every prisoner to stay in his assigned place indoors until the air raid was over or suffer the consequences.

Another camp shooting involved a guard's random bullet fired into one of the barracks and wounding Lt. Col. Stevenson as he sat in his room. That time, no excuse was offered for a clear mistake. Stevenson was partially crippled as a result but maintained his spirits.

There was sufficient food in June 1944 so that no one was starving. The Red Cross saw to that, delivering an eleven-pound package of food to each prisoner, once a week. In the box was a package or two of cigarettes, a pound of powdered milk or "Klim" (milk spelled backwards), cans of Spam, corned beef, liver pate', salmon, cheese, margarine, crackers, jam, prunes or raisins, sugar, crackers and one good old, heavy solid chocolate "D" bar, some powdered coffee and a few other things like soap and tooth powder. The food was wholesome, tasted reasonably good, and it was keeping us alive. Sure, the allies had landed and had been in France for about three weeks already, but our captors gave no sign that they thought it was all over. To the contrary, the saying they used on us was, "For you, the War is over." Which it was, unless we were somehow to escape or be repatriated. After the Great Escape murders of 50 men, escape attempts were no longer obligatory, just optional and approved by the camp's Escape Committee. Sagan was about 80 miles southeast of Berlin, not a particularly opportune jumping off point from which to expect to make it back home.

The camp was run from the inside as a standard military regime. A second lieutenant was low man on the totem pole. We had plenty of captains, majors and lieutenant colonels. Our colonel was a ramrod type by the name of Goodrich, but a solid citizen, well respected and in no way a jerk to his men. We lieutenants were kept in the dark as to discussions between our seniors of field rank, Major and above. Behind the scenes, there were many decisions being made daily by the Senior Officers without any notice to peasants like me.

Figure 41. Unidentified prisoners around room cookstove at Stalag Luft III, 1944.

Weekly Ration ½ parcels Sept 8 **91**

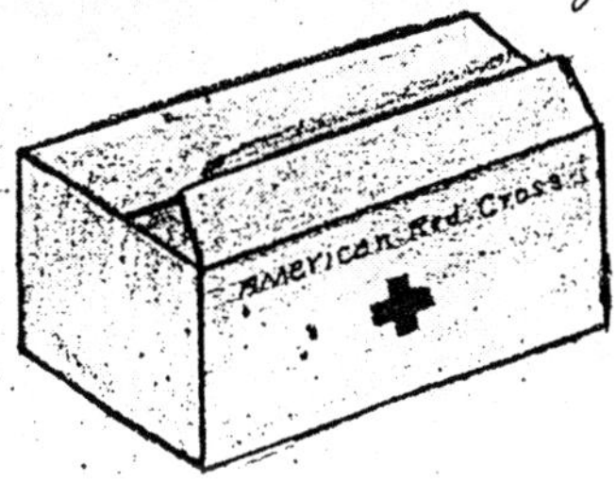

Evaporated Milk (Klim, Milko, or Nestles)	1 - 14½oz Can
Hard Tack	1 - 8oz pk
Cheese	1 - 8oz pk
Liver Paste	1 - 6oz can
Corned Beef or "C" Ration	1 - 12oz Can
Spam	1 - 12oz Can
Raisins or Prunes	1 - 15oz Box
Sugar Cubes	8 ozs.
Orange Beverage Powder or Jam	12 oz.
Nescafe Coffee	1 - 8oz Can
Chocolate "D" Ration	4 oz.
Margarine	1 - 1lb can
Sardines or Salmon	1 - 8oz Can
Soap	2 - 2oz cakes
Cigarettes	5 packs

Reich Issue

Bread	1 Loaf per week
Potatoes	350 grams
Beet Sugar	¼ lb per week
Meat	¼ lb. every other week
Margarine	6 oz per week

Figure 42. List of contents of Red Cross Parcels at Stalag Luft III, 1944.

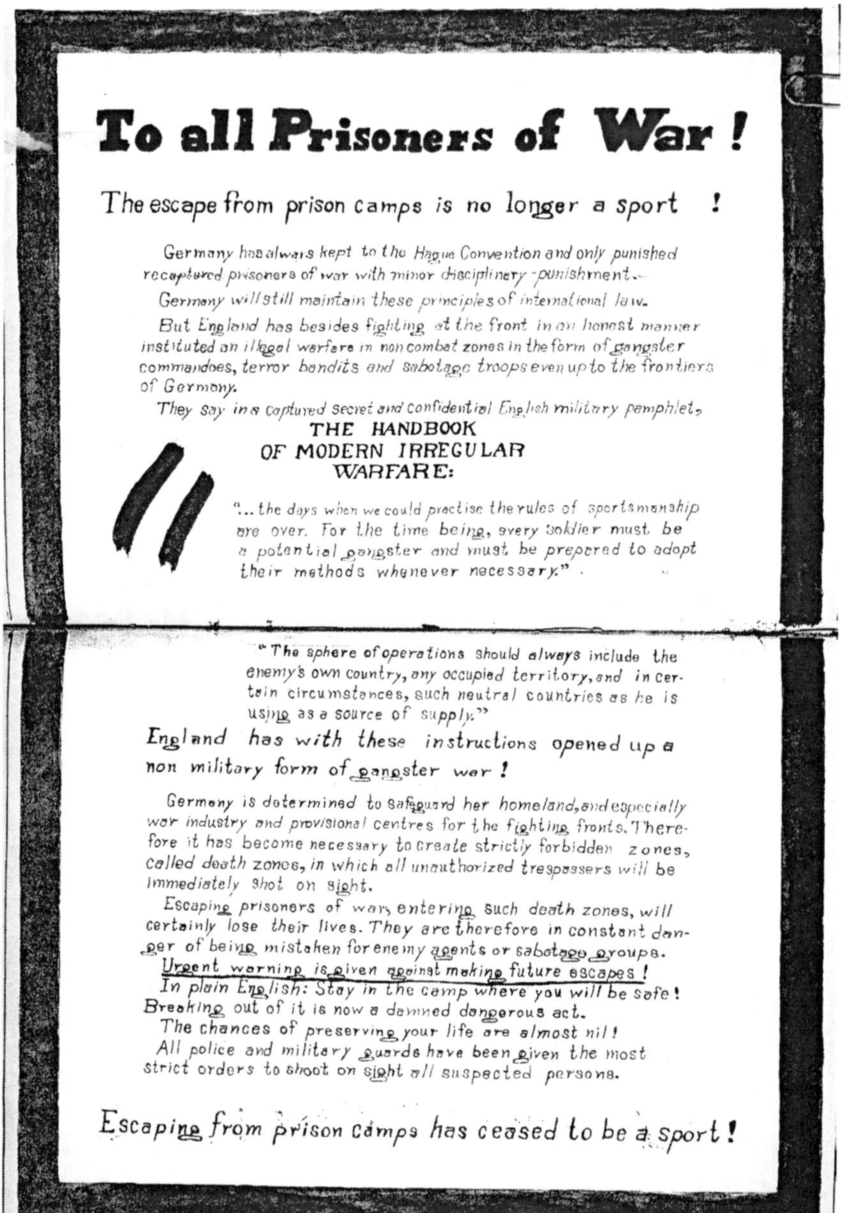

To all Prisoners of War !

The escape from prison camps is no longer a sport   !

Germany has always kept to the Hague Convention and only punished recaptured prisoners of war with minor disciplinary punishment.

Germany will still maintain these principles of international law.

But England has besides fighting at the front in an honest manner instituted an illegal warfare in non combat zones in the form of gangster commandoes, terror bandits and sabotage troops even up to the frontiers of Germany.

They say in a captured secret and confidential English military pamphlet,

THE HANDBOOK
OF MODERN IRREGULAR
WARFARE:

"... the days when we could practise the rules of sportsmanship are over. For the time being, every soldier must be a potential gangster and must be prepared to adopt their methods whenever necessary." .

" The sphere of operations should always include the enemy's own country, any occupied territory, and in certain circumstances, such neutral countries as he is using as a source of supply."

England has with these instructions opened up a non military form of gangster war !

Germany is determined to safeguard her homeland, and especially war industry and provisional centres for the fighting fronts. Therefore it has become necessary to create strictly forbidden zones, called death zones, in which all unauthorized trespassers will be immediately shot on sight.

Escaping prisoners of war, entering such death zones, will certainly lose their lives. They are therefore in constant danger of being mistaken for enemy agents or sabotage groups.

Urgent warning is given against making future escapes !
In plain English: Stay in the camp where you will be safe!
Breaking out of it is now a damned dangerous act.
The chances of preserving your life are almost nil !
All police and military guards have been given the most strict orders to shoot on sight all suspected persons.

Escaping from prison camps has ceased to be a sport !

Figure 43. German Bulletin to Prisoners of War at Stalag Luft III following the murders of 50 British officers in the "Great Escape."

CHAPTER 18:

THE REAL PRISON VERSUS THE MOVIE

For readers who have seen the movie: "The Great Escape" starring Richard Attenborough, Steve McQueen and James Garner, the set was remarkably like the original place. After that, the script made serious departures from the facts. The opening scenes of new prisoners arriving and immediately being caught up in an escape attempt was complete fiction. First, there were no fir trees or loose branches around because the place had been hewn out of a forest leaving only stumps which dotted the landscape. Second, there were no Americans in the British Compound (North Camp) because they were all moved to other compounds days before the actual escape took place in March 1944.

Figure 44. StalagLuft III Commandant, Col. Von Lindeiner, disgraced for presiding
over the camp at the time of the "Great Escape."

McQueen's character in the show closely resembled that of Major Jerry Sage who tried to escape so many times he got the name of "Cooler King" because of all the time he spent in solitary confinement as punishment for trying and failing to escape. Sage was an extraordinary man who worked for the Office of Strategic Services (OSS) later to become what is now known as the CIA. During his time at Luft III, he was referred to as "Silent Death" because he could kill a man with his bare hands. The intrepid Major finally did escape without using a motorcycle but from another POW camp at Schubin, Poland to the East of Sagan. He made his way through the East Front battle lines at night, linked up with the Russian forces there.and was repatriated. On his return to active duty, he volunteered his services to help in the liberation of Moosburg (Stalag VII-A) but his offer was declined.

What I liked about the casting of the movie was that British actor Donald Pleasance, who played the prisoner who became blind, had actually been in the camp during the war. What did not impress was the depiction of the German camp commandant in so many scenes which made it appear that his presence among the prisoners was an everyday thing, His headquarters were completely secure from the prison Compounds. Nor did I ever see or hear of German cars being driven in and out at any time I was there.

My room was number 5 in block 135. There were 12 of us there later to be increased to 14. Prisoners in similar rooms customarily formed a combine to spread the burden of cooking and serving our own food, we carried our own water from the Cook House to the room and did our own dishes in hot water from our stove.

Inside, there were four triple decked bunks and one double decker placed up against the inside walls in our room. The new guys got the top bunks, as one would expect because the lower beds were taken. The Germans gave each of us a burlap mattress stuffed with straw and excelsior. The paliasses (mattresses) fluffed up quite well until you laid on them a while. Then they would pack down into a large bag of very uncomfortable lumps. Every so often - like a bowel movement, you could easily tell when to do it - we would take them outside to break up the clumps and re-pack them. The mattresses were held in place over wooden slats which in the Great Escape were removed and used to shore up the tunnels.

The slats were very hard. More experienced Kriegies made their own mattress supports out of strips of the large Klim cans opened at the side, flattened out and grommeted together in lengths. With six or eight strips fastened crosswise to the sides of the bunk and stretched across where the slats had been, the play in the wooden the sides of the bed provided flexibility and therefore more comfort. If you knew how to do this, you didn't need any of the wooden slats. I never did learn how, so I suffered with my lumpy mattress on the bed boards.

Each day, a Luftwaffe contingent consisting of about eight enlisted men and the "Hauptmann" or captain, would go through a drill in front of our block. The corporal or sergeant would line the men up as in "dress right dress" and tell them to move up or back in order to present a straight line for inspection. "Komme Hier, Komme Hier", he would say to them as though it was an important moment before they were to greet and salute the officer in charge of the "Abteilung" or detail. Hauptmann Gallathowicz was his name, a burley fellow in his forties with one shiny gold front tooth, neatly dressed in his medium blue Luftwaffe uniform with a highly polished orangish-tan leather belt and a small pistol on his left flank. He would receive the troop leader's salute and address them briefly. One of the more prominent soldiers of the group was Unteroffizier (corporal) Hohendahl who spoke English with a British accent, only occasionally tinged with German. He was a small man, but quite arrogant for his size and rank. We might have been officers, but we were in his charge all the same.

Every morning and every evening, we assembled on our exercise/parade ground for roll call where we stood in place in company sized groups of four ranks each totaling approximately

100. I can still see in my mind's eye the Hauptman accompanied by the Feldwebel or sergeant, walking up and down counting us carefully. At the end of a line he would announce smartly, "Ocht (8) und neuntsig (90)"

Eating was the main occupation of every day. Within the room, we pooled our food and divided it as evenly as possible. Even when we were being fairly well fed, we counted the crumbs, almost. At breakfast time, the usual fare was a piece of German "schwartzbrot" or pumpernickle type black bread sliced very thin spread with jam and washed down with tea or powdered coffee. We cut cards to see who had first choice of the arrayed slices of bread. The men would take turns choosing their portions as they crouched down at the table's edge to get an eye-level perspective of the thickness of the appetizing spread. It is important to understand that this bread was a major staple of our diet. It was an acquired taste - the bread was sour tasting at best - but it was solid and nourishing. One of the essential ingredients was "wood flour" estimated to have been between 10% and 15%. Don't try to buy it at the super market because it is sawdust.

Each loaf of schwartzbrot was about the size of an unwrapped Pepperidge Farm loaf but weighed a healthy 3-4 pounds or so and was stamped with a date of baking. The date often predated our consumption by several years, as incredible as it might seem, the oldest one I saw being 10. Inevitably there would appear a little mold which could be cut off - very carefully, almost surgically, to save as much as possible. The Germans had been preparing for war for a long time and Hitler had seen to it that there would always be a supply of this bread and provided for its storage so that it was preserved, even unwrapped, indefinitely. The German soldiers usually carried a chunk of it in their knapsacks. They knew what they were doing, because one could literally live on the stuff.

Mid-morning we had tea and a biscuit. Lunch usually included some prison-issue soup with which we would eat a little more black bread with perhaps pate' spread on it. Dinner was the main meal consisting of canned meat, occasionally some German vegetables, potatoes or sauerkraut, and perhaps more bread if available. Never having eaten sauerkraut before, it took me a little while to learn how tasty it could be when one was hungry. But for the Red Cross food, our prison fare consisted of schwartzbrot, soup, potatoes, vegetables and sauerkraut along with hot water for coffee, plus a very occasional - once a month if lucky - serving of fresh horse meat which made tasty burgers.

The day was concluded with the closing of all shutters; and finally, just before lights-out, or "licht aus," we ate a sweet snack of some kind, usually a Kriegie pie or cake. The favorite dessert was condensed milk pie in a cookie/cracker crust which became known more popularly in Kriegie vernacular as "condaggers pie". Adding lemon abstract to the condensed milk caused it to set up like whipped cream, even without refrigeration of which there was none in the summer time. Cakes were made by rolling out into flour the small grains of millet which the Germans gave us, adding sugar and the salt and baking soda, the ingredients of Pycopay tooth powder, to make them rise. Each process was watched carefully by everybody in the room. Doing so helped build one's anticipation while at the same time making sure that no one got more than his share - or less.

One of our senior officers in another compound, Col. Delmar Spivey, wrote:

"We strive to set up a model community designed to keep our bodies, minds and souls healthy and alert, awaiting the day we can return to our homes within our own land. We have our moments of loneliness and hunger for the companionship of home and the home folks. The rest of the time is spent studying, and reading, working, hoping and praying. We shall hold firm to our faith in all of you and are ever assured of your love and consideration."

Almost all of us prisoners were in excellent health, even the so called "early birds," men who had been shot down and captured as early as 1942 and 1943. These men had an aura about them that inspired the rest of us, particularly the recently "purged" like myself. Each man had passed through "the eye of the needle" to get there. It was a true statement. When your aircraft was mortally wounded, it could do so many bad things to you if you stayed with it long enough. You could be trapped easily, upside down or pinned against the fuselage immobilized by the force of gravity, for example. The plane could burn or explode. In every instance it was a split-second experience where you either do or you don't survive. Nevertheless, recent captives like myself were looked down upon because we had not suffered enough, yet. No credit was given for having just come from fighting the war to free them.

My cell mates were great people. Bill Shapiro (he pronounced it Shapyro and claimed he was a Catholic), from Far Rockaway, New York. Bill was a tall man and had suffered severe wounds to the head, left eye, left knee and heel in the fall of his plane. And his Achilles tendon had been severed on one ankle. He was taken to a German military hospital and when the surgeon came in to see him, the two were alone in the room. Suddenly realizing that he still had his 45 automatic, but with no intention whatsoever of using it, Bill pulled out the gun. The Doctor immediately threw up his hands, probably frightened out of his wits. Bill told us he then turned the gun around and handed it butt-end first to the doctor who took it gladly.

By the time he got to Stalag Luft III, Shapiro was recovered, except that he now had a permanent drop-foot, which made it difficult for him to walk. He kept up his spirits, though, and tried to participate in whatever way he could in the sporting activities in camp of which there were several. We even had a couple of golf clubs and Kriegie-made, pretend golf balls but I could not even think of the game at that time. I told Bill that when we got back to the states I was coming to see him to buy one of his used cars. His reply was in the negative because, he said, "Our motto on the lot is that you can really screw your friends because they trust you."

Our minds were occupied, even if we were caged up. There were books, card games, chess and music. There were two accordions in the South Camp and I latched onto one of them. The good one, though, was kept by Lee Forsblad who had played it professionally in civilian life. He was so good, it seemed hopeless to think that I could ever play anything well on the thing, even when I had a beautiful Italian Dalape' hand made accordion at home which my father had bought for me when I was only thirteen years old.

Forsblad, it turned out, didn't even like the accordion, although he was a master of the instrument. He was a music scholar as well, and out of dissatisfaction and/or boredom, he took up and taught himself to play the saxophone. There was almost a full orchestra in the camp with trumpets, saxes, clarinets and drums, all furnished by the YMCA. Those guys were professionals and first class musicians some of whom played with the big name bands in the United States. They cheered us up many times with their musical shows. Forsblad was so talented that he was able to write out the music of all the popular songs at the time including separate pages for each instrument in the band. Ultimately, all of this had to be left behind, except for Lee's accordion which somehow managed to follow along when we finally had to move out. I will never forget one dreary winter night at Stalag VII-A when Lee played his accordion for us for the last time. He played the Hungarian Rhapsody so beautifully it brought tears to my eyes. The last time I saw Lee in May, 1995 at our 50th POW reunion in Cincinnati, Ohio, he asked me how my own Dalape' accordion was. I guess I made some sort of impression on him after all. Lee has passed on now but after the war he became a PHD in music and taught at the University of California. He also became known for his talent as a composer.

At Stalag Luft III, I played my accordion almost every

day. In order not to disturb anybody while practicing, I would go into the block's laundry room - which was literally that, a place where you did wash or washed yourself. There was an indoor urinal but no toilets. Outside there was a large 20 hole outhouse - called an "Abort" in German - not too far away. Nobody could leave the block after lights out.

I would sit in the washroom playing scales and various tunes by ear. For some reason, no one ever actually asked me to play a tune for them, except Lee Forsblad. Knowing that I was at least trying to play and had no music of any kind, when he would come into the washroom he would suggest scales and asked me to work up a tune, which I did. It was the Russian song entitled: "Dark Eyes." He had perfect pitch and could name the notes I was playing with his back turned. I was obviously a hacker and he couldn't take me very seriously. At least I had a very good memory for popular music and could work out some semblance of any song I could sing.

I happened to overhear a chap one day - I don't remember who - say: "If you want to see someone who is over the wall and out of here, take a look at Casey with the accordion." It was true. I could escape any time I wanted to and disappear into my instrument, now and then grimacing as I strained for the notes I tried to play. As soon as I stopped playing, I was back behind the wire again. My own music always did that for me and was a great source of comfort on many occasions in later life when things were going badly.

One of the Kriegie actors who made it in the big time after the war was Chicago personality, the late Ray Rayner who produced and starred in daily kids TV five days a week. Ray called his pet duck "Chelveston" which was also the name of his air base in England. He did two years behind the wire but never talked about it in public. At our South Camp reunions he was just one of the guys. Another of the camp's best actors, Bud Gaston, played a small role in the movie "Stalag Seventeen" starring William

Holden.

Figure 45. **Author with Ray Rayner at POW reunion, 1985.**

A regular form of recreation was walking the circuit around the inner perimeter of the compound. The soil was sandy and comfortable to walk in. The only thing you knew for sure not to do at any time was to step over the little warning fence bordering the walk path which was only about a 20 inches high. There was a guard tower every 30-40 yards or so with a rifleman at the ready. These people weren't fooling for a minute.

As a relatively latecomer I took for granted that there were things available such as furniture and even a theater capable of seating about 400. These things were constructed entirely by the Kriegies before I arrived and made out of whatever passed through the camp. For instance, the Canadian Red Cross parcels came to us in large wooden boxes about 3 feet square with plywood sides. These boxes, when taken apart into six pieces, furnished the wood for chairs and even the theater seats.

The powdered milk "Klim" cans were about 4 inches high.

There were many uses for the leftover tins to make things like shredders, cracker grinders. Klim cans without tops and bottoms could be made into a very workable stove (also called a "Kriegie burner") These stoves could burn slivers of wood and paper scraps to produce enough heat by the Venturi process to boil water and cook. Almost anything the mind could think of (other than an airplane) could be built with the raw materials we had on hand.

Escape was on everyone's mind, of course. The so-called Great Escape from Stalag Luft III had taken place the previous March and resulted in 50 British officers being executed for the attempt. Thereafter, our superior officers ordered that there would be no escape attempts without prior approval. The only escapes I heard about happened during our evacuation westward the following winter.

In the Great Escape, Three RAF officers had gotten completely away. Two were Europeans with a fine command of the German language and knowledge of how to move in civilian society unnoticed. I met one of them years later at a POW reunion. His name was Bram (Bob) Vanderstok and a real hero if there ever was one. He wrote an outstanding book about his war adventures called "War Pilot of Orange" in which he related how he had escaped German captivity twice, once as a Dutch air force prisoner in 1940 and again as an RAF type in the "Great Escape." In 1944, he tunneled out dressed as a Dutch worker with enough German currency to buy railroad tickets back to France. Once there, he made contact with the French underground who guided him to the Spanish border and freedom.

Figure 46. Author with Dr. Vanderstok at POW reunion., one of the three men to escape in the Great Escape.

Once Vanderstok got back to his air base, he was soon flying again but not beyond the British Channel. His new assignment was warding off Nazi V-1 flying-2000 pound bombs. One of the more dangerous tactics the RAF used was to fly close to the projectile, put a wing under the V-1's wing and tip it over.

The conclusion we American Prisoners reached was that there was hardly any point even trying to escape from deep in Germany unless you were a European or had extraordinary talent and pluck and could speak the language well enough to use public transportation. There was no way a POW could ever get away on foot from behind the wire.

I kept myself as busy as possible. We played a lot of bridge in the room and I became quite good at it. Chess was something else. The way we played, it was a good thing there was no time clock running. What the hell, time was all we had. No one complained if the other guy took five or ten minutes to decide on his next move. We weren't going anywhere, so what was the hurry? I read the thickest and heaviest books I could find, all fiction. I made myself stick with them until I was finished. In the process I surprised myself by really enjoying every book.

Some of our guys were former teachers and even taught courses there. I decided to take some more Algebra because I failed the course in first year college. I found a teacher among our Kriegie population who helped me understand it a lot better.

Other Kriegies taught foreign languages. For some reason none of them was German which I would have liked to have learned. As it was, I heard bits and pieces of that language every day enough to be able to say some of the commonplace phrases like: "Haben sie Essen?" Do have anything to eat?" There were others I still remember such as "Hande Hoch" (hands up), and "raus" for move out, "Brot" (bread,) "kartoffeln" (potatoes), how to count up to a hundred, and so forth.

There were special uses for obscure languages such as Gaelic. Padre Murdo MacDonald was a British Army chaplain who, on his capture, actually refused an offer from the Germans to be repatriated so he could stay with the prisoners. He was fluent in Gaelic and became a messenger helping to pass important information that way from one compound to another. The German Guards could not translate it at all. In his book "The Man From Harris" the Padre tells an amazing story about his work among the POW's. He did God's work with us and kept our spirits alive with his sermons.

One of my closest friends in our room was James M "Fergie" Ferguson from Vardaman, Mississippi. He was an "early bird" who had been shot down over St. Nazaire in January 1943 on his fifth mission while bombing the German Submarine pens there. He was then taken to a POW camp at Schubin, Poland, East of Sagan. (The early bird POW's would tell us newcomers that if we thought things were bad at Sagan, we should have seen "Schubin.")

Figure 47. Jim Ferguson and the author in 1955 at Prisoner of War Reunion

Fergie and I and a few others from Room #5 stuck to-gether throughout our captivity, even after we marched out of Sagan that coming winter. After the war, we got back together in the States a few times at reunions and once when I visited him and his wife, Doris, in Mississippi with my first wife and our four young boys. They loved him, too. Poor Fergie died in an accident in a grain elevator when he was in his fifties. He was smothered to death when he fell into a silo full of grain. He was a natural born philosopher and always had an encouraging word for everyone.

Joe Varhol was from Minneapolis, Minnesota. He looked

and was of Slavic origin and could speak some Russian and German. He was a little guy who might remind you of the movie actor Charles Bronson who appeared in the movie, "The Great Escape." Joe was shot down on his seventh mission in February 1943 over St. Nazaire, France and suffered a severe wound from a 30 caliber machine gun bullet through his right arm. His ulnar nerve was destroyed and the skin covering his inside elbow joint looked paper thin. He was loose for 24 hours and had walked some fifteen miles before being captured by the French police. Then he spent almost a month in a German hospital or "Lazarette."

Varhol and John B. (Bud) Elliot from Grand Rapids, Michigan seceded from the room's combine and cooked their own meals, largely fried food. Bud, then age twenty-six, was shot down on his second mission in January, 1943 over St. Nazaire, France and swam ashore. He wound up in Schubin, Poland at "Oflag" (officers camp) 21 B.

The rest of us coped pretty well with a variety of meals, whether boiled, baked, mashed or fried. Our favorite delicacy was fresh red meat which we got about once every four to six weeks. It was horse meat, but there were no leftovers. (Years later, while in a Chicago shoeshine parlor, an older gentleman accosted me as I sat getting my cordovan leather shoes shined. "Don't you know," he said, "that they had to kill a horse to get those shoes?" My unhesitating comeback with true conviction, which no doubt took him aback, was: "Sir, I love horses. I have eaten horses to stay alive." He huffed off without another word.) Another sort of animal food we had, which I wouldn't turn down, even today, was "Blutwurst" or blood sausage. It was clumps of animal blood with gristle and God knows what else. If we couldn't slice it, we spread it on our bread.

We could listen to the German radio playing at the central cook house whenever we wanted to. Personally, it did my heart good to hear them talking frantically when our bombers were over their territory as they were regularly. The announcer would say, very officiously, "Achtung, Achtung, Schnelle Kampflugzeuge uber die Westen," translated as: "Attention, Attention, fast battle planes were over the West." Another regular broadcast I heard but seldom understood completely was the German High Command announcements which began with another "Achtung," and then the announcer would say: "Der Oberkommando Die Wermacht, Gibt Bekant" (the High Command of the Armed Forces Announces - or at least that's what I think it meant.)

There was a secret radio in the camp. Very few were allowed to see it or know its location. Prior to use, it was assembled from several hiding places, played and then taken apart again and re-hidden. Almost every day we would have a secret briefing on the real news from the Allied forces radio. One of the regulars would come in the room and tell us what was going on according to the BBC radio news. We had reason to believe we were winning the war and we knew it would be over some day, but when? When? The radio was built by prisoners with material stolen or "scrounged" from the enemy.

CHAPTER 19:

HITLER'S NEAR ASSASSINATION IS DISAPPOINTING NEWS

July 20, 1944 was an exciting day. We got word that there had been an assassination attempt on Hitler but no details. Little did we know how close the conspirators came to succeeding. (Would it have made a difference if they had? I think it surely would have.) The next morning, the German guard detail of six or seven men entered the gate near our block and lined up for inspection by the Hauptmann. Things had changed overnight. This morning, after the dress-right lining up process had been completed, the Hauptmann sang out to his troops in a clear voice: "Heil Kamerad," to which the men replied in unison: "Heil Hauptmann." This was the Nazi reminder to the men that Hitler was still in charge and that they had better not forget it, or else. In a few days the German papers proudly related the story of the heroism of Major Remer in Berlin who refused to believe that the Fuhrer was dead or that the leadership had passed to a new regime. He insisted on talking to Hitler personally by telephone refusing to accept new orders from the conspirators. On talking to the Fuhrer over the telephone, he ordered his troops to seize the usurpers and take them prisoner, which they did immediately. The disappointment in camp was noticeable but soon faded into resignation that the war would continue indefinitely.

Summertime was fairly pleasant. I got a tan and was out of doors as much as possible. We walked the circuit for exercise. There was ample sports equipment available for basketball, baseball and football but it was not something I was interested in at the time.

There was at least some "busy work" to do, such as laundry. Someone made up wash buckets out of cans and for agitation of the suds put an open Klim can on a stick to push down into the wash and move the soapy water through the clothes. There were clothes lines to dry things on, too. If you wanted a hair cut, there were guys who would take care of it for you. I just had my hair cut as short as possible so I wouldn't have to bother with it. Taking care of one's bedding was also important. Sleeping gave one time to get away from the boredom of captivity. Talking about favorite meals was enjoyable. Sex was only a distant memory and thus not an important topic of discussion.

One of my cell mates was Lee Hamaker, a professional artist. He drew a sketch of me carrying a steaming pot of food to the table and entitled it: "The Bride's First Stew." I still have the drawing and know it is of me, for sure. Lee captured me in my butchered-tailored shorts with the pockets hanging out below the cuffs. It was my first effort at re-styling clothes. The shorts seemed too long so I took a scissors and cut the cuffs parallel to the belt line making them very short but leaving only a half-inch of crotch.

CHAPTER 20:

FALL WEATHER A HARBINGER OF A TERRIBLE WINTER

As the days ran on into early fall, we experienced a 50% cut in food rations and a rising concern for proper clothes to wear with the change of seasons.

For Thanksgiving 1944 I was in charge of stooging the meals for the week. I'm proud to say that I cooked dinner for fourteen, the whole room, all out of cans. There was Spam, mashed potatoes, German bread, Kohlrabi, and, for dessert, a very rich condensed milk pie with a crumbled cracker crust. It was a real feast enjoyed by all.

Speaking of Kohlrabi, we had some of the worst looking stuff I ever saw. (To be honest, I never had seen it before Sagan.) We cooked it boiled, fried, baked, every way imaginable. It was picked too late and was full of unchewable fibers. Sauerkraut also became a delicacy for me. I couldn't stand the smell of it at home, but this was different.

In order not to give the impression that Stalag Luft III was the main prison camp of the war, it should be understood that there were at least six such airmen's camps, along with countless others for ground soldier POW's. The Stalags were scattered all over Germany. For some reason, the Stalag Lufts were in what came to be known later as East Germany and Poland. There were also "Oflags" or offizier lagers; and there were "lazarets" or hospital camps for sick or injured prisoners. If a prisoner was sufficiently disabled because of his wounds, "repatriation" could be arranged, eventually. Even the Germans recognized the humanity of such an act, and besides, the subject prisoner obviously posed no further threat to them.

There were thousands and thousands of prisoners of war all over Germany: Americans, Russians, British, French, Polish, Dutch and Belgians. Whenever they needed, the Germans put the enlisted prisoners ranked corporal or private to work doing manual labor. Officers and noncommissioned officers (sergeants and above) were not required to work. There were sergeants in Stalag Luft III as aides assisting the senior officers in anything they were requested to do. If we didn't get together with them it was because we didn't usually do much outside our own cells or combines in terms of socializing.

At Sagan, rules for a civilized society were formulated. It was perfectly all right to visit with a friend in another Block or even in another room of one's own Block. But, roommates kept to themselves, only occasionally visiting in other rooms. You felt that you could always go in another room and talk to anyone you liked, but you did not hang around for any length of time. As an example, my pilot, Steve King, was in another Block and we rarely saw each other or talked. Steve seemed to be having a particularly hard time getting over his experience in being shot down. I believe he felt he had lost his chance for promotion and a promising career in the service - which he was told he would have had by completing a second combat tour.

People I remember best were in South Camp were the men in my room and in my Block. I have named some of the room-mates. Here were some of the others: Leonard (Lee) Hamaker from Santa Ana, California, age twenty-four and a pilot of a B-17 shot down near Paris in late December 1942 on his fourth mission. Lee was a football player in college in California and looked every bit the athlete. I would liken him to a blond Burt Reynolds. He was an artist for Disney Studios in Hollywood before the war and cartoon-ist in residence in room 5 and was a friendly easy-going guy to boot.

Then there were later comers like Morrie Bauer from, Portland, Oregon, age twenty-three. Bauer, a B-17 pilot on his fourth mission, bailed out near Berlin three days after I was shot down. Perhaps because of his German name, he said he was roughed up quite a bit by his captors.

Valleau (Val) Wilke, a B-17 pilot, age twenty, from Morris Town, New Jersey was shot down in January 1944 near Osnabruck, Germany. He made it all the way to Antwerp, Belgium where he was identified by an informer and captured by the Gestapo in early June after five months on the loose. Incredible! With him throughout this experience was one of our other roommates, Freed Warren, from Memphis, Tennessee. Freed was reddish-blond haired but, upon opening his mouth, was immediately revealed to be 100% "red-neck."

Freed told the most interesting story about having to learn how to ride a bicycle while on the run - which he had never done as a kid. He found himself practicing on a bike in a Dutch farmer's barn for weeks. They lived with the farmer in very close quarters in the farm house, but they were fed and warm that winter. The Dutch farm families, he said, were not as clean as their propaganda made them out, such as scrubbing the streets in Amsterdam, and largely lived unbathed in rural areas.

Another long-term kriegie in our room I almost forgot about was the genial Clarence (Sonny) Fisher from San Antonio, Texas. Sonny was a B-17 pilot and was shot down by flak on April 5, 1943 over Antwerp, Belgium. He was 24 years old at the time, a quiet fellow but excellent company in such a crowded place.

Later on came Leonard "Pops" Poskitt, from Palisades Park, New Jersey. He was an ancient, 27 years of age. Pops' story was one of the saddest. He had been flying out of Italy where they had to do 35 missions and was shot down in August 1944 near Budapest, Hungary on either his last or next to last mission, one he didn't have to go on that day. Hell, he was 7 years older than I was, practically old enough to be my father. He was a mechanic in civilian life, married but with no children. A peach of a guy who never let his bad luck get him down.

A story "Pops" told was about his wife and his sister-in-law at their home in New Jersey. His wife and her sister conspired one day to have the sister-in-law make a pass at him so that he became aroused. The wife was in the kitchen, and, at the point when Pops was feeling the effects, the sister-in-law jumped off his lap and went into the kitchen with the wife. They then called to Pops to come and join them, knowing full well he couldn't stand up without embarrassing himself. When he didn't come immediately, the two women came where he was and howled with laughter. Well, it was very funny at the time.

Each Kriegie had a story to tell about being shot down (some excellent ones are compiled in a 1992 book entitled, fittingly, "Through the Eye of the Needle".) Being that we all had suffered some hardship or frightening experience to get where we were, the view among Kriegies of what we called "There I Was" stories was necessarily jaundiced. The old saw about "I thought I had it bad when I had no shoes, and then I met a man who had no feet" applied here in spades. For every horror story, there was always was a worse one around. For this reason, we did not spend a lot of time crying in our tea about where we were and how we got there. Each one of us had been through it. We cried together but separately. There were always some distractions, the main one being the ever-present question: "when do we eat?"

I began writing letters home again within a few days after being taken prisoner. My mother faithfully saved each one. On June 23, 1944 I wrote (printed) a small post card to my Mother. In the upper left hand corner of the card was the word "Kriegsgefangenlager" (War prisoner camp).

"This is not a permanent address so don't write! I'm OK and unwounded so don't worry. Letters will be few but they'll come! I hope I haven't ruined Jim's vacation

and you haven't worried too much. Give my love to all and be patient as I shall have to be. The end of it is near and I'll be with you then. Watch your health! I miss and love you all."

On June 29th I wrote again:

"Dear Mother," The Red Cross will give you the dope on packages. Send concentrated stuff and, mind; these old boys can really cook. Use your imagination. I'm not too lonesome yet but I may need your encouragement. I love you all and I'm hoping for the best."

By July 14th, I was able to write a letter to Mother and Dad on a one piece folding letter and envelope combined:

"It's beginning to look as though your packages and letters will never reach here because they take from three to five months. This letter has probably taken that long. Yes, I'm really holding high hopes now and I don't think I'm going to be disappointed. Do you?"

"I'm in a room with 11 other men and we take turns cooking out of red cross parcels which we get one per man per week (later one half a parcel per man and still later, none at all.) We have German bread, butter (from the Canadian red cross) or margarine and often jam and tea for breakfast. Lunch is bread, toasted, with sardines, a cheese or liver paste and coffee. Dinner is the big meal and we have corned beef, or spam or salmon, potatoes, tea or coffee, and always a pie, raisin, apricot or lemon, or prunes. The Germans give us bread, barley and margarine and occasionally fresh vegetables. Hot barley meal or pea soup is issued for lunch about four days per week. Of course, there are exceptions in the routine. Our quarters are comfortable and I'm not losing any weight."

Mother clipped out a contemporaneous news article by Beulah Schacht which she saved for me.

> **"Ever make a chocolate cake using ground biscuits for flour, powdered milk, oleomargarine, chocolate bars and tooth powder? Just leave it to the American prisoners of war in Germany to make an attempt at concocting some of the delicacies that remind them of home."**

> **"The German government did not obligingly give the Yankees these ingredients, but they did offer them one bowl of turnip or cabbage soup, three or four boiled potatoes and three slices of black bread per day - everyday. All else came in the Red Cross prisoner of war packages which reach American prisoners in Europe weekly and those in the Orient whenever Japan permits. That is all except the tooth powder. After using the German tooth powder a few times, they found it was composed mostly of baking soda and made a moderately successful leavening agent."**

> **"The boys spend hours each day working out menus that will supplement the too-meager German rations and add zest to the simple but nutritious foods in the Red Cross packages."**

Apparently the folks ordered and paid for cigarettes which I never received. The American Tobacco Company sent a card confirming that the Provost Marshal General had returned the package so he enclosed a check to cover the cost of the cigarettes.

Headquarters Army Service Forces put out a letter to families with "Mailing instructions - Germany." The letter directed that in regard to mail:

> **"There is now available, at all U.S. Post Offices where required, airmail letter sheets for use in corresponding**

with American prisoners of war. Experience has shown that use of such a form greatly reduces the time required for the delivery of a letter to prisoners of war in German custody. There are several reasons why this letter sheet, *WD, PMG Form No. 111, facilitates delivery of mail: (1) letters written on this form, with a six-cent air mail stamp attached, are, after censorship, flown to Lisbon, Portugal. From that point they are forwarded by German plane to a central point for German censorship and thence dispatched to the various camps in Germany: (2) the use of this form greatly facilitates censorship both in the U.S. and in enemy territory by providing a standard size unsealed letter. Advice received through Swiss intermediary channels states mail addressed to American prisoners of war held in certain prison camps under German control will not be delivered to the addressee if it bears endorsements or slogans intended to promote the war effort."

The letter went on to quote a senior American Officer POW who wrote explaining that the unsealed letter form received prompt handling by the Germans, while sealed letters were left unopened, unread and undelivered. There was no limit on the number of letters - probably because they weren't going to be delivered anyway.

The Red Cross published a monthly "Prisoners of War Bulletin" which my parents were able to obtain. In the April 1944 edition, two months prior to my capture, news from several of the German camps was published. A separate report dealt with service pay and credits for POW's and related that prisoners would be entitled to receive their same pay and credit for service equivalent to active duty. The publisher quoted from the Geneva Prisoners of War Convention regarding the obligation of the "Detaining Power" to pay the same pay to their captives the same pay each month as officers of corresponding rank in the armies of that Power, on the condition that this it did not have to exceed the pay to which they

were entitled in their previous service. Our government also continued to pay to servicemen's dependents the same allotment the
men had provided for prior to capture and maintained in force the
life insurance.

Not that my mother needed it, but I had made provision for
a monthly allotment to her of $100. She continued to receive this
sum each month and wisely used it to purchase War Bonds for me.

The Bulletin also printed letters from American POW's,
one of which was from my camp at Stalag Luft III dated October
18, 1943. It was delivered in America on January 15, 1944 which
demonstrates the length of time that it took to get messages back
and forth. The unnamed writer spoke of having been relocated to a
new American compound after being moved from the British compound where the Americans could now concentrate on real football
and baseball instead of beating the English at rugby and soccer.
The biggest job was to keep busy, which he was able to do by
studying two foreign languages and reading and taking part in athletics. "So the time goes fairly fast," he wrote, "and that great day
everyone is looking forward to is not too far away, I hope." This
was the theme of every Kriegie's hope for liberation. Thank God
we had some reason to hope, or it would have been a pretty desperate lot. Americans just weren't used to a defeatist attitude and we
weren't about to start here in Germany, as bleak as things came to
appear in the coming months.

Amazing. In the next Red Cross Bulletin dated May 1944
there appeared a cartoon by my roommate, Leonard E., "Lee," Hamaker, illustrating the setups of the bunks in our room. The issue
included a report from the camp as follows:

> **"The strength of Stalag Luft III is continually increas-
> ing, the latest report available giving the number of
> American officer-airmen there at over 2,000. The South
> Compound which is all-American and has men from
> practically every state was only opened last September.
> Within two weeks the men there had begun to build a**

new theater and to prepare a playing field by digging up tree stumps and roots. They were permitted to use the fire service reservoir as a swimming pool." (The number of us prisoners matched the number in each compound but not the entire Stalag which was 10,000.)

The camp grounds were like a stump forest. The Germans had simply marked out the boundaries and cut down every fir tree in the area. The fallen trees were removed leaving only the roots and the bases. We prisoners took to pulling up the stumps for fire wood and it was great busy work. Clearing the land and our recreation areas also gave us an opportunity to plant some of our own vegetables to eat. The Germans provide a stump puller which was a crude lever consisting of a length of tree trunk approximately 6-7 inches in diameter on a bi-pod base with a hook on the end. One or two men would dig out the soil around the base, chop through the roots and set the hook. Two more on the other end put their weight into leveraging the stumps clear.

In the Army back home there were what were called: "Officer Candidate Schools" which turned qualified soldiers into lieutenants in 90 days. They were called "90 Day Wonders." My innate sense of humor caused me to create in my warped state of mind the need for a "Stump Pullers OCS." One of the shorter guys in our compound, "Shorty Kahl", was in fact nicknamed "the Stump Jumper," probably because at his height he could not easily step over them like the rest of us.

Every once in a while, a German fighter plane would fly over the camp. At a low altitude, the sound was quite loud. The motor noise was not muffled in any way in order not to detract from the aircraft's power and speed. Then one summer day, a strange looking aircraft came over at incredible speed. It looked to us just like the twin-engine American A-20 light attack bomber, except that it was going too fast. We were unable to articulate that it was a "jet" because that term was still unknown to us. So it was dubbed the "blow-job" because of the whooshing sound of the air through the pipes or engines. It was the new German jet Messer-schmitt 262 which flew at about 450 to 500 mph and for a short time was the terror of the skies as far as our air forces were concerned.

Had Hitler allowed these jets to be built earlier and in sufficient quantity, the air war could very well have been won by the Germans because it was simply unstoppable with the equipment we had. This was the kind of decision that was left to the Fuhrer and it proved too much for one man to handle. Undoubtedly, it was this propensity of the Germans to let the leader do all the thinking and to follow him to the death rather than disobey a superior's orders that led to their downfall in the end. That inclination was enhanced by the Gestapo and Hitler's private army, the "SS", who did their worst to keep the people in thrall out fear of punishment or death.

The Red Cross Bulletin went on to advise families of POW's to send parcels containing useful things such as name tags that might be stitched into a prisoner's clothing. Other suggestions were "peanuts; seasonings (except pepper), hard candy, tea, dehydrated or dried fruits, toilet expendables like toothpaste, soap, razor blades, and a cribbage board. If any prisoner receives unneeded supplies, he can always arrange trades with fellow prisoners." The paper warned that "transportation disruptions, or other accidents of war, retard deliveries to the camps" and that it might take months to reach the addressee. Still another Bulletin warned that if two packages arrived for the same prisoner in one month, one would be held until the following month. And a two-pound package and a three-pound package could not be sent in the same month as the rule was strictly "one package a month" up to a maximum of five pounds.

One package my Mother sent which I never received contained a sweater, gloves and scarf and suit of winter underwear, plus two pairs of socks and six handkerchiefs along with some food and several different candies.

Books were also reported to be popular with the prisoners. I certainly agreed with this and read as many books as I could get my hands on, the longer and more turgid the better so as to challenge myself to finish them. The "Modern Library" set was quite readily available to us and I set about reading the classics which I usually found slow going at first and then very diverting and comforting once I really got into the story. The Red Cross discouraged sending current or topical books because they would most likely contain forbidden references to the war. "The prisoner of war," it went on, "lives in monotonous and drab surroundings, but through books he can escape into another world."

In a "Question and Answer" part of the April 1944 Bulletin, in answer to a question about whether officer prisoners of war held in Germany were put to work, the editor wrote: "No, officers do not have to work; but privates, providing their health is good, may be put to work in factories, mines, sawmills, breweries, cold storage plants, glassworks, railroad yards, etc., or on roads, farms or in the forests." Such prisoners were supposedly given better food than that provided in the POW camps. This was the reason our Air Force made all enlisted crew members sergeants in order to exempt them from such duties.

Another letter from a Stalag Luft III Kriegie spoke of receiving phonograph records (of acetate because that's all there were at the time) and that they had arrived unbroken and were being played carefully by the men. Apparently the big bands were featured because the writer mentioned how everybody seemed to like Benny Goodman's band.

One prisoner wrote a letter at Christmas time of 1943:

"Tonight my thoughts drift home and to my loved ones. Christmas Eve here at Luft III will be ideal tonight because we have the opportunity to celebrate midnight Mass and to receive the Sacraments. My heart flies back to you all."

Christmas was a very difficult time for all of us as I was

to experience for myself in 1944. Imagine how prisoners felt on Christmas in 1943, when things looked far less favorable for the Allies. Feelings of desperation were even more prevalent back then.

In the June 1944, edition of the Red Cross Bulletin there appeared a picture from Stalag Luft III which must have been heart-warming for the folks at home. The men were apparently warmly dressed and engaged in reading or playing chess or checkers. A closer look revealed tables and chairs, maps on the wall and one of the ceramic jugs in which we transported our hot water from the cook house. Speaking of water jugs, in addition to the ceramic ones, we had others made of metal on which were labeled with the warning: "Kein Trinkwasser" (don't drink water) because of possible metal contamination. We all laughed about this warning as if we were ever going to worry about endangering our health. We used the "Kein" to heat water for dishwashing and tea at night when there was no hot water available at the cook house.

Another article the folks saved was a"Repatriate's Report" by a Kriegie named Lt. Louis Means of Whittier, California who was returned to America in January 1944 after a long hospitalization and who had resided at our camp for one month. He painted a pretty nice picture for the folks at home who no doubt pored over every word for a glimmer of hope. The lieutenant spoke well of the supplies of regular GI clothing which were available including shoes, underwear, shirts, pants, overcoats, gloves, etc. The Germans also issued each man two blankets. "Hot showers are allowed at least once a week," he said but this became rarer as time went on. In the summer of 1944, I don't remember any hot showers, but we could do with the cold showers as long as it was reasonably warm out.

Exercise became a real focus as well. Walking was the main activity around the inner perimeter of the compound which was about 15 yards inside the barbed wire fence. There was a low wire which marked the outer limit of the circuit track beyond which one did not go for fear of being shot. The intermittent guard towers were manned constantly and the guards kept close eye on us at all times. One of the "roomies" would say, "Anyone for a turn on the circuit?" We usually walked together with someone just to chat about things on our mind.

Another important exercise was "flapping" our gums in the room, which went on day and night. The guys liked to talk about food - far more than sex, for sure. There was one hard and fast rule about talk that prevailed at all times. That rule was that there should be no "flat" statements about anything. A "flat statement" in the extreme would be like pronouncing that the world is round. Now, everybody there knew that already so no one ever brought that up for discussion. However, if one were to say that blonde women have better breastworks than dark-haired girls, or perhaps that Massachusetts was the 33rd largest state in the U.S., an argument would immediately ensue, and I mean a bitter one. It was almost as though the audience was just waiting to pounce on the speaker's pronouncement that could not be supported with substantial evidence.

One example I can recall was made by cell-mate Jim Crouch. He told us a long story about one of his buddies who was constantly disassembling his 50 caliber machine gun and reassembling it, even in the dark, so that he could do it with his eyes closed on a moment's notice and at lightning speed. "Why," Jim said flatly, "I remember one mission when this guy's machine gun wasn't firing fast enough to suit him and he completely stripped down the gun and fixed it right then and there and was back firing it before you'd know it." It was my turn to jump him for this and so I said, "Jim, that was completely unnecessary to tear down the gun just for that because all one had to do was to stick a screw driver in the butt end of the gun and turn the 'oil-buffer setting' a little to the left and the gun would automatically fire faster." Everyone who knew about the 50 caliber machine gun knew I was right and Jim was mad as hell at me - for a short while, at least.

Figure 48. M/M Jim Crouch and author at 1985 POW reunion.

Crouch had the hands of a sculptor. When he was on cooking duty, watching him prepare each dish was like watching an artist at work. First of all, they were scrupulously clean so that there was never a concern for contamination of the precious food. And, he enjoyed what he was doing.

I never heard Jim Crouch talk about his last flight, but his experience was truly inspiring compared to many others. Jim was a member of the fated 306th Bomb Group, and was shot down over Antwerp on April 5, 1943. According to Jim's story, told in 1992 in a book of Luft III "there I was" stories, his Group was under the same kind of head-on attack by German FW-190's that I had been in May 1944. His plane was hit by flak setting an engine on fire and leaving the left landing gear hanging by one small strut. Jim himself was hit by a piece of a 20mm shell and after ordering his crew to bail out; he jumped himself and opened his chute too soon. His wounded airplane was circling out of control and falling at about the same rate as he was. The dying craft came within 150 feet of hitting him in his parachute.

Jim was bleeding. Once on the ground, he attempted to find a doctor while, at the same time, trying to hide in a nearby farmhouse. Soon a German soldier took him into custody having been tipped by a Belgian collaborator who pointed Jim out to him. In the hospital under treatment, he was nevertheless singled out to be turned over to the Belgian civilians who were ready to hang anyone, particularly an officer, who had been allied with the bomber which accidentally bombed and killed some civilians a few days before. Jim had the presence of mind to warn the German official that if he did so, he would certainly receive equivalent retribution if America won the war for turning a wounded American officer over to a mob.

Jim attempted to escape again while en route to interrogation in spite of his wounds. The Germans didn't even draw their guns, Jim said, knowing full well that he was incapable of getting away from them in his condition. His tale was finally told in the outstanding compilation of Kriegie stories in the book "Through the Eye of the Needle."

Friendly needling easily turned into argument, which, if it got too heated, sometimes someone had to say something to quiet things down. Flip Corkin was one of the newcomers to the room that summer and he had a particularly thin skin for criticism. For some reason it's in my nature to be the peacemaker. I much prefer that people get along rather than pick at one another. Finally, one day when Corkin had been needled into a frazzle, he stormed out of the room saying he was going out on the circuit. I followed along and we talked for quite a while until he calmed down and returned to the room. People who know me long enough may have noticed that tendency to help reconcile differences among others. Maybe that's why post-war I came to enjoy the practice of law as much as I do.

My letter to the folks dated July 29, 1944 was retyped and distributed to all of the family, including my father's business partners. I told them:

> **"I'm still alive and kicking and hoping. My only worry is winter for lack of warm clothing. I have an overcoat, sweater, and light jacket, 2 wool shirts and long underwear and 2 pair of wool socks and 2 blankets. I hope I don't have to use them."** (Contemporaneous Red Cross Bulletins received by the folks at home quoted POW's' letters saying, 'don't send any more clothing, just food.')

> **"Hot showers have just been installed, so you can see it has been pretty cold bathing till now. It's pretty hard to find something to say without any answers from you as you know. On the whole, the camp is comfortable and pretty well stocked with things to do. But there is still plenty of time to think which one can't help some of the time. We get German Communiqué's over the camp radio and spend a lot of time talking about the war. It's also a favorite pastime to argue to great lengths over anything just to be arguing. We combine our food parcels - 12 roommates - and 2 men do the cooking with a change every week. I'm glad these boys have the experience and can cook as they can. Needless to say, we eat well for POW's. Give my love to all and take care of yourselves. Don't worry too much because I'll do the same."**

In a letter dated the following day, July 30th, I wrote:

> **"Still healthy and getting tanned when the sun is out. There is not much news in a prisoner of war camp, so don't expect any. I am getting back to my accordion playing here under professional instruction. We have church service twice a week and I am praying hard for**

the day. Hope your are helping out on that.”

I was serious about my lack of clothing. In the summer-time, I had a pair of cotton twill, knee-length shorts and a tee shirt of sorts and got along just as I would have had we been up at the north woods of Wisconsin at the same time. In my compulsive haste, as usual, I had taken the scissors to my shorts in order to shorten them for greater exposure to the sun. What I did not take care to do was to pay attention to reasonable tailoring concepts for shorts. As a result, I just sawed them off straight across leaving virtually no crotch. Having no underwear, I just hung out of my shorts, but so what. Who cared and who looked?

My high school alumni magazine dated July 1944 asked for prayers in my behalf:

> **“Lt. Donald E. Casey, ‘42, holder of the Distinguished Flying Cross, the Air Medal with five Oak Leaf Clusters, reported ‘missing in action’ over Germany on June 18th. Lt. Casey was navigator of the Flying Fortress, ‘Hells Bells’, is now known to be a prisoner of war in Germany.”**

The bombardier from my original crew, Jack Ellenberger, wrote to my folks on his return to the States in September of 1944:

> **“Dear Mrs. Casey. Received your letter and was glad to hear about Don. I knew he would make it OK, but your letter made it the real thing. I wouldn’t worry about him, he can get along swell.”**

> **“To answer your letters or questions, my writing and thinking clash at times, Don and Lt. Miller were flying together on the same plane that day. Lt. Miller was our original co-pilot. Sgt. Taylor was retained as an instructor and the rest of us came on back.”**

"I don't remember when he went down, but the raid was Hamburg Germany that day, really a rough target. To get promotions you had to fly on a lead crew. Don flew with them (King's crew) for his 1st Lieutenancy. I flew the same position the next day for mine."

"All I know is they were hit with flak and went down with Lt. King saying someone had been wounded and that was the last we heard from them. But that was the best news I'll hear for a long time. I'm going to write the rest of the crew and let them know Don is OK. I know they will like to know."

"That's about all I can say, but I will write to Don. And if I can ever help, please let me know. Sending Don's things home was the least I could do as we were great friends. I have a few snapshots of Don we took overseas. I will have some more prints made and send them. Sincerely, Lt. Ellenberger."

About the same time, the folks began hearing from the families of my other crew members. The parents of our waist gunner, Ziggy Czarnecki, wrote asking my folks to ask me if I had any news of their boy. They still had not heard.

The much sadder letter was received from copilot Milton Miller's folks. They had not yet heard of Milt's death and were still clinging to a faint hope that he might have survived in spite of the Red Cross report that he had been killed on June 18th.

There was another Miller on our crew, Staff Sergeant Eugene. Another letter to Milton Miller's parents a copy of which was also sent to my folks from Eugene's parents recited additional facts obtained from the War Department. "The Group reached the target at Hamburg at 9:50 a.m. and upon leaving the target, an anti-aircraft shell hit the wing of the bomber and when last seen they were losing altitude but were under control as they

dropped into the clouds. The next report indicated that Lt. Steven King, Lt. Donald Casey, T/Sgt. Ray Wheeler, S/Sgt. James H. Hagen and S/Sgt. Czarnecki were taken prisoners by the German Government. At the same time, it was reported that T/Sgt. Charles E. Rutishauser and our son (Eugene Miller) **were killed in action on the date originally reported as missing. The information from you** (the parents of Milton Miller) **that Milton was killed makes the third crew member so reported."**

On September 30, 1944, Milton Miller's father wrote to dad that his family was thankful that I had **"escaped the fate which has been the lot of many other boys, including our son. We also want to express our thanks to you and Mrs. Casey for the kindness you bestowed upon our son when he was a visitor at your home for several days with your son, Donald. Milton spoke very highly of Donald."** (On a short leave from Dyersburg, Tennessee, I had taken the officers of my crew, including Milton, to Chicago to show them around. We visited the Chicago Athletic Association which impressed them no end as we enjoyed the cuisine and the liquor package offering available to members.)

> **"I wonder if it would be possible for you, in any correspondence which you have with Donald to ask him if he could tell you whether or not the entire crew was able to bail out. I ask this because we, of course, still cling to a thread of hope because we have not received Milton's dog tag."**

Steve King's parents also wrote to dad about the same time from Akron, Ohio. They had received the good news about Steve's survival and that he was also at Stalag Luft III. Steve had written to them advising about how lucky he was to have made it. They, too, had been informed about the three known fatalities - there was eventually a fourth.

Still another letter was received in October from the parents of Sgt. Rutishauser.

> **"We were advised that our son, Charles was missing, and later advised that he was killed June 18th. Needless to say that this was very hard to take. We hoped that some of the crew members were safe so some day we may learn just what happened to their plane. We have had letters from Mr. Martin Miller whose son was also killed. Also received a letter from pilot King's mother. Her son is also prisoner."**

> **"We do hope that the war in Europe will soon be to an end so that the prisoners can be released. We will appreciate any further information if you receive any."**

These sad letters must have been a chilling reminder to mother and dad of how close it was to being the end of me, too. Rutishauser and Eugene Miller were the gunners Steve King reported were still on board when the plane blew up. Eugene survived but Rutishauser did not. Steve said he tried to signal them to jump, but they could not bring themselves to accept the end of the mission in time to save their lives.

Charlie Henry's wife wrote to the folks, as well. She had received a card from him saying that he was safe and well. "I met Steve King when the crew was in Tennessee and he was the pilot. I met a few of the fellows in the crew and they were all a bunch of swell kids and Charlie told me time and again that Steve was a very good pilot, so I guess their going down was out of the pilot's hands."

Still another letter the folks received from Sgt. Hagen's mother told of her receiving news that he had survived and was at Stalag Luft IV. "I am sorry that not all of the crew were able land safely. My heart goes out to the parents of all the boys. I know how they feel, as the suspense and anxiety of those days were terrible. I hope and pray that our boys will return home safely."

My closest pal in grammar school, Tom McCracken of River Forest, Illinois wrote to the folks in August that he too had heard about my being safe in Germany. Tom went on to say:

> **"Don was one of the few fellows I've seen who wanted to go over and fight as soon as possible. I see he was awarded the DFC and Air Medal. It's to him and guys like him that those honors should go. His attitude wasn't to make the best of bad deal, but to do the best he could at a tough job - which was what he wanted. He's not leading the life of Reilly, but you don't have to worry about a guy who got his commission at 18 and is a real hero at 19."**

Jack Ellenberger wrote again to the folks:

> **"Don and I flew together as navigator and bombardier on the same crew for 26 missions. We met about two years ago and were on the crew together up to his last mission. He flew with a lead crew so he could get a promotion that day. And we had a new navigator that day. I don't have the report on Don, but one thing I know is he's OK. He used to sit on the escape hatch when the flak started. All he had to do was pull the handle and he was clear. His ship was hit by flak and went down under control. Two chutes were seen to have come from the nose. One must have been Don. I'm really sorry about Don but I am confident he is all right over there. We all liked him for he was one swell guy. Do let me know if you hear anything about him."**

The mother of Milton Miller wrote again to the folks on

September 28th.

> **"We received word by telegram on September 16th saying Germany had reported through the International Red Cross that our son had been killed on June 18th and no further details given at all. We are simply crushed at this news as we had been so hopeful all along. I'm writing to ask if you will let us know as soon as possible what news you have received of your son. We still cling to the hope that there might have been a false report sent in by the Germans as so many have received word like ours, which later was proved to be false."**

I never learned whether the Miller's parents got the whole story as Steve King had heard it from his German captors that Milton had been murdered in his parachute by gunfire from the ground as he came down. It could have happened to any one of us.

Also collected by my folks was a copy of the "Gefangenen Gazette" about the American POW's in Germany. On a lighter note, the Gazette quoted the following letter received by a Kriegie from his wife in the States: "Darling, I'm having a baby but it's not yours. He is an airman too and he's very nice about it. He promises to send you cigarettes while you're there." This was known as a "Dear John" letter which heartened the recipient no end, to be sure. After all, how long is a girl expected to wait alone and lonely at home? How does she know if her "Johnnie" will ever make it back, anyway? This Gazette included several Kriegie drawings which did quite well at portraying the living conditions inside the wire and the walking circuit with the wooden barrier over which one did not step for fear of being shot.

Some of the German guards had a sense of humor, but not all of them. Oberfeldwebel Glemnitz was a stern but practical man who found amusement at the goings on of the Americans. The boys called him "Popeye," perhaps because of his muscles. Popeye one day came out with the crack "This camp will be the garden spot of Germany," speaking of the gardening attempts of some of the Kriegies.

Mother tried writing to me in November but her letter was returned undelivered.

I again wrote to the folks under date of October 18, 1944 as follows:

> **"Dear Folks, Have received 14 of your letters since October 13 and I'm glad to hear that you're receiving mine. I stopped writing back in Aug. for obvious reasons and I still hope to beat this one home."**

> **"Selling the house is not pleasant, but if it's worthwhile, I guess I'm agreeable. The apartment idea sounds good, especially if you like it. It's going to seem strange living in the City, though."**

> **"I hope you're right about Dick changing schools but I think Campion would have been better, all four years of it. Helen and Jim are wasting too much time waiting until June 1st. What makes any one think he'll be available and why?"**

> **"Education facilities here are not what the bulletins make them out to be, but I am taking algebra. Also, brushing up on literature - books. The accordion is coming along but I wish that I had a real teacher. Why don't you start John on the piano? But make it stick for once out of four tries. Who knows, we might get something. Love, with supreme patience."**

To a girl friend, I wrote also on October 18th:

> **"The weather here is tending more toward winter every day. I hope it doesn't last too long and that I get the clothing my folks**

sent. I sure miss all of you and home, but that's war."

Mother wrote to me on October 20th but the letter was re-turned.

> "**Lew Jolls** (my original pilot) **was in to see me and was so glad to hear about you. I took him to dinner. He was on his way to Las Vegas where Dad used to go. I told him if there was anything special he wanted, to let us know. Dad may be able to help him.**"

> "**I got a big kick out of your imitations Lt. Jolls told me about. Wonder if you're still doing them. Bet not.**"

> "**Am still watching for a picture of you in the Red Cross Bulletin. I enjoy them so much. I couldn't find one single thing to put in your box to make you think of X'mas. I'm so sorry. We are all well and hope you are, too. Hope you will like the books I sent. Just found I could send them. Expect them every month. Love and Kisses, Mother**"

The books mother referred to were never received, but the package she was referring to was, and it included a fine pair of fleece-lined house slippers. They turned out to be a Godsend for me, although I never wore them on the floor at any time. Only on the march to come while resting and in bed at night.

On October 23rd, Mother wrote:

> "**How's my pet today? Hope you are well and getting along all right. Just wonder if you received the boxes I sent. Do hope they are things you needed and wanted. It is hard to know at this end just what you need most. We all pray for you - John burns five candles every Sunday.**"

The letter came back undelivered.

Mother kept on writing and told about the new apartment she also related how well Johnny was adapting to the city life and was taking tap dancing and swimming lessons. She acknowledged without explanation that Mrs. Miller, Milt's mother, was writing to her for solace but that there was little she could do. None of this was received.

Dad also tried to write with the same lack of success. He tried to tell me about the nice fall weather and that he was not playing golf for a change because of his business entanglements. He always tried to cheer me up.

Another letter of mine got through dated October 31'st. I reported to the folks that one of the new Kriegies was from my Group and told me what happened to my clothes back at the base when we didn't return. It made me very angry because it had simply never entered my mind at any time when any of our crews went missing. I was incredulous.

> **"I gather that they** (my clothes) **have been distributed among the 8th AAF so I don't have to worry. Tell Ellenberger and ask him to do something about it."**

> **"It's turning winter here so I'm sweating out those clothes. Please send food in portions for 12: muffin mix, baking soda, coffee, spaghetti, sugar and saccharine. Also bridge cards, Books - Ken Roberts Arundel, Shakespeare, no mysteries. I hope I won't need these, but what can I lose? I'm playing the accordion daily and you'll be glad you didn't send mine when I show you what I've done - or have you sold it? I can also cook, wash and sew due to necessity. What a wife I'll make someone. Keep writing and praying."**

On my twentieth birthday, November 6, 1944, I wrote to the folks:

> "Here I am in a POW camp and twenty years old. It's criminal. I'm having a big party: corned beef, potatoes, raisin pie, coffee and all the water one can drink. What a 'bash'."

> "I'm taking college algebra and trig' and progressing. There are no study rooms available so it's rather hard to concentrate. I'm trying, nevertheless, to glean enough knowledge to enable to pass a test in these subjects at college. I think I'll try Purdue again, but I would like to discuss it with you first."

> "Your letters are coming in very well. The latest one is Sept. 20. No parcels have appeared as yet. I'm still optimistic but am beginning to change my views slowly. I'm praying and I know you are, so we'll have to wait and see. Give my love to all the folks."

On November 18th, another letter I wrote to the folks told how I had still not received their parcels.

> "The weather is rapidly becoming suitable for those clothes. I hope I'm lucky for a change. It is all right for one outside the family to write occasionally, so please tell the rest. It is best for you to do most of the writing, but others can do no harm by a few letters. After the clothing parcel, send only food except for a few pairs of socks (all I had was 2 pair and they began to wear out fast)."

> "Ready-mix baking dough, eggs, beans, coffee and chocolate and sugar are needed most. I have ample vitamin pills, so you can cut down on them. Soap, tooth powder and (tooth) brushes and sundries are not on a

very high priority."

"Johnny sounds like a full time job for mother. I hope you give him a try at music. I know I wish I had worked a lot harder when I had the chance. I'm working on an accordion here, but I'm not progressing as I could with a teacher." Give my love to all and don't worry."

Mother wrote again about my Brother Dick's struggle with school and told about my grandparents coming to visit the apartment. Grandpa Casey, she reported, had an automobile accident and was somewhat shaken up but all right.

Dad wrote on November 20th that they were still reading my letter dated July 14th and that mother had read and reread it about 40 times. He said that Dick's most successful course was French "which he needs like another set of teeth. The only good French would ever do him is in talking to waiters, and there's certainly no money in that."

CHAPTER 21:

MOTHER RECEIVES MY DFC AND AIR MEDAL

Mother received two letters from the Army. One was a form letter from the Prisoner of War Division dated November 22, 1944 stating that my POW number was 6100 and that this number should be used in addressing future correspondence to me. The other was dated November 23rd from Brigadier General Dunlop at the War Department about my medals:

> "Dear Mrs. Casey: I have the honor to inform you that, by direction of the President, the Distinguished Flying Cross, the Air Medal and three Oak-leaf clusters, representing three additional awards of the Air Medal, have been awarded to your son, Second Lieutenant Donald E. Casey, Air Corps. The Citations are as follows:

> ### DISTINGUISHED FLYING CROSS

> For extraordinary achievement while serving as Navigator of   a B-17 airplane on a number of combat bombardment missions over *** and *** occupied countries.

> ### AIR MEDAL AND THREE
> ### OAK LEAF CLUSTERS

> For exceptionally meritorious achievement, while participating in five separate bomber combat missions and in sustained bomber combat operations over enemy occupied Continental Europe. The courage, coolness and skill displayed by this officer upon these occasions reflect great credit upon himself and the Armed Forces

of the United States.

Since these awards cannot be presented to your son at this time, the decorations will be presented to you. The Distinguished Flying Cross, the Air Medal and the Oak Leaf Clusters will be forwarded to the Commanding General, Sixth Service Command, Chicago, Illinois, who will select an officer to make the presentation. The officer selected will communicate with you concerning your wishes in the matter."

And so they did. One wonders why the symbol "***"

was used to keep secret where I had been and where I now was,

in Germany. In the Air Medal citation there is a clear reference to

"Continental Europe."

No one ever explained how I won the DFC. However, it is

fair to guess that having completed 27 1/2 combat missions and

needing only 30 to qualify for this award, some weight also was

given to the fact that I did fly once as "lead navigator" (the equiva-

lent of two missions) and flew twice more as "deputy leader"

which together might have been accounted for what was needed.

There were approximately 75,000 DFC's awarded during

the war, which seems like a large number, but not compared to 16

million in the service, most of whom never had the flying duty nec-

essary in order to earn this medal. Also to be considered was that there were multiple winners and that it was occasionally awarded for strictly aviation achievement not involving combat. However, it was the highest award given by the Army, Navy and Marine Corps- as distinguished from the higher-ranking Silver Star, Distinguished Service Cross and Congressional Medal of Honor which were awarded throughout all branches.

> **"Some people say the award was 'automatic' and in WWII. If you flew a number of missions you received the Air Medal, and then for so many more you receive the DFC. Well, if you consider flying over an area where flak is as thick as steel snow flakes and enemy fighter planes are filling your path with lead and cannon fire, then you can consider a mission an automatic checkpoint on your eligibility list to be awarded the Distinguished Flying Cross. All who received the DFC received it for acts of heroism while participating in aerial flight."** DFC Society newsletter #3-6/95.

My mother clipped out a contemporaneous news article naming me as the recipient of these awards which were presented to her by Captain Lawrence Gennardo of the 6th Service Command in Chicago. I know she was very proud of them because she bought a glass display case for them which she hung on the wall in her apartment. She also had the small white and gold flag in the window with the 2 blue stars for her sons in service which was commonly displayed on the home front. Just so it wasn't a gold star, which meant a deceased service person.

Another undelivered letter from Mother dated November 19th mentioned receiving my first letter dated July 14th and how thrilled she was to get it. She said that I sounded cheerful, which made her very happy, and got the impression that I was getting enough to eat.

On November 30th I wrote another letter:

> **"Dear mother and dad. The weather is becoming extremely cold and your parcel is yet to arrive. I hope it's soon for I need those clothes. Please send some pictures when you write using the regular stationery you use at home. I saw my second American movie last week and it was quite a treat. The sound wasn't very good, but I hope we get more like it."**

> **"I'm still working at Algebra and occupying most of my time reading. That's about all I do besides sleeping and eating, so there's not much to write about. I haven't had a letter for a couple of weeks, but my mail situation is comparatively good. I'm learning bridge by a Culbertson book and play whenever I can get up a game. It's a great game and it's pretty important, as you know, so I'm not wasting my time learning all about it."**

> **"Keep in good health and it won't be too long? Give my love to all."**

The November 1944 Red Cross Bulletin reported somewhat ominously that at our camp, the water was cut off intermittently and that the place was becoming "overcrowded" with 5500 POW's by the end of August, an increase of 1,000 for the month. It was about this time that our room contingent increased from 12 to 14 men.

The Bulletin reported that morale was high among our POW's.

> **"After the first weeks of despair and shock on finding oneself a prisoner of war, the average American, under**

the splendid leadership of American captive officers and enlisted men who serve as camp spokesmen, begins to dig in and to take part in the activities of the camp. He finds that Red Cross parcels of food, comforts and clothing are on hand. The men are not idle. They mark time with a purpose; each day is filled with activity designed to help the time pass pleasantly and profitably. There are scheduled classes under capable teachers. Well-organized sports programs exist. Constantly growing libraries minister to their reading needs. Fresh vegetables grown during the summer augmented the food provided by the Germans and the Red Cross. Many camps have their newspapers; all large camps have their orchestras and theaters. Most camps have religious services. No camp is a country club, but the American prisoners are determined to keep up their spirits."

One of the chaplains was quoted as saying:

"Not for an instant have we forgotten that our duty to our God and our country still binds us. Though captive and restrained, we are still active and free. Poor and needy, we are rich as Americans in Jesus Christ."

"Morale depends a lot on the number of years of internment, said the Red Cross. Among some of the prisoners who have been interned for over four years, there is a tendency to lose interest in life. In all camps, however, there are those who do their utmost to encourage the prisoner to study, play, enjoy music and look to the future. All look forward with the greatest eagerness to returning home."

My room #5 was one of nine (not counting the senior officer's quarters and the washroom) in "block" (barrack) number

135 which was located right near the outer gate and across from the Kriegie Theater. The word "washroom" should not be misconstrued. There were no toilets in the building because there was an outside "abort" or toilet building nearby. But we did have cold running water, electric lights and showers.

The room was fair-sized, about 15 feet by 18 feet. Against the walls were four three tiered bunks made of plain, unfinished pine. There were four windows on one side which were covered at night by shutters to conceal the lights. In the center of the room was a table for ten with benches. In the corner by the door to the room was a stove for cooking. There were no ladders for the beds and one had to climb up using the bed frame. As a newcomer, I had a top bunk, naturally. There was just enough space between the bunks and the table to negotiate one's way around the room. In other words, we were on top of one another at all times. But we made do, and, as I previously mentioned, the main activity was eating, anyway.

Figure 49. German tunnel hunters we called "Ferrets." Man at right was called "Blue Boy" by the prisoners. The German guards were called "Goons" ala the "Popeye" cartoons back home.

Compare this with how the American flyers interned in Sweden were treated. The Red Cross reported that they were doing "splendidly," which is not too hard to imagine "The men live in small hotels in some of the most beautiful spots in Sweden. They were permitted to roam the countryside within a large restricted area. They met the civilian population and had facilities for study and play (probably mostly boozing and womanizing). Sometimes these were not taken advantage of because of the wonderful weather this summer (of 1944) which was not conducive to study and serious activity. All these young men are restless because they are out of the war and in comparative safety." (Comparative safety, my foot. What about Cirrhosis of the liver and sexual exhaustion?)

The next letter the folks received from me was dated December 8th.

"One of the fellows that came in with me here received his first parcel, but mine has not shown. It's not too cold here yet, but it's going to be soon. Stephen King is here with me and Charlie Henry is in another compound. Wheeler and Hagen are at another camp."

"King told me about your invitation to his mother and I'm quite pleased about it. Christmas is rapidly approaching and wouldn't it be my luck to cook that week. Two of us take on all the work duties every five weeks and it's quite a task, for --- (the number was censored) **hungry mouths are your responsibility to feed. We get six Red Cross parcels per week and potatoes and usually fresh vegetables. I miss you all and I wish I could be with you, but I'm still hoping. Don't worry about me and don't let me spoil your fun. Keep sending food parcels and occasional clothing. Love, Don."**

A further letter from me was dated December 23, 1944:

"Those socks you sent were a godsend, especially since my present issue had just about worn through. I had picked up darning and was practically darning new socks around the few fragments of the pair I had. A new Red Cross (clothing) **issue is due any day, so I will be just about set."**

"The camp entertainment staff is putting on a couple of shows and an American movie is rumored to appear soon. At least I won't have much time to sit around

and moon about home. The cold weather has really set in now and I'm thinking of moving to Florida when I get home. As the English say, I have 'had' this frigid climate. After morning roll call, I spend my time in the room as near the stove as I can get doing mostly reading and card playing. What we're looking forward to the most is an early spring, and I hope I'm not disappointed. Love, Don."

Mother wrote to me on Christmas Eve.

"If you could only be here, our Christmas would be a happy one. Our tree has been up one week. It is a large one with all the ornaments and tinsel. We haven't a fire place, so the four stockings - yours with John's silver cross on it - are hanging on the Capehart radio. Brightly wrapped gifts are under the tree - a suit for Johnny, sweaters for the girls, dresses for Aunt Babe, (dad's sister) Alice and Gram'. A jacket for Gramp (her father), my presents for Dad, Dick's wrist watch, yes, another one."

"We were so thrilled to receive your Christmas greetings. There were greetings from all over the world, and at the end of the radio program they said 'The boys from Stalag Luft III send their best wishes for a merry Christmas to their next of kin, friends and relatives." It gave me 'duck bumps'. Jack Benny repeated it on his program."

"Well, darling, I hope you are able to keep well and warm. We all send our love." The letter came back unopened.

Mother wrote to me again on Christmas day in a letter that sadly was returned. She said that she had gone to Aunt Babe's for dinner and how they missed not having me there.

"You were the center of the conversation," she said.

"Many people called to tell me of the Christmas message sent from your camp, in case I didn't hear it. I sent another box off to you - hope they are getting through to you. Had a sad letter from Ziggy Czarnecki's mother. He died the 19th of June. All this time she thought he was getting along fine. You are always in our hearts and our minds. Just hope you are well. All our love and kisses, Mother."

Brother Dick tells the story that over Christmas dinner, Dad, who still kept in touch with his old Army buddies, Col.'s Minton and O'Toole announced that the U.S. was working on a secret weapon which would end the war by Christmas time, 1945. Dad really did not know what the weapon was but he could guess that it was something awesome. No one then could even imagine an Atomic Bomb of the type which was used on Japan the following August.

The December Red Cross Bulletin included another cartoon drawing by my roommate Lee Hamaker depicting Santa with an ax and live turkey. An on-looking Kriegie was sticking his head through the barbed-wire, hopefully. The report from Stalag Luft III was as follows:

"Gen. Arthur W. Vanaman, a recent arrival at Luft III, is now senior officer for all three American compounds. His quarters are in the Center compound, but he is permitted to visit the South and West compounds.

The story going around our compound about General Vanaman was that he had gone on a mission as an observer and bailed out in his parachute thinking the airplane was going down. After he jumped, the pilot was able to fly back to base after all. He was the only American General captured in Europe and was a particularly important prisoner because of his knowledge of some of the still secret strategies of the Allied battle plans. For a while, there was real concern back in England as to what might be done to him. I saw him once in our compound briefly but heard later that he was taken to Berlin where he received special treatment because of his rank.

A report received of a visit to the camp by a representative of 'War Prisoner's Aid' of the YMCA spoke of the

> **"Wonderful spirit of discipline and exceptional order. All activities are animated by 100 per cent participation; cleanliness is exemplary; and good comradeship among the officers extraordinary."**

> **"Religious interest among the prisoners was reported to be 'remarkably strong', with about 20 per cent of the men attending services which were held in the theater in each compound." A picture of some of the men in various dress was included. Some of the guys even had ties on.**

Mother received a letter from Mrs. Czarnecki at Christmas time to let her know that they had been advised on November 4th that their son had died June 19, 1944 from gun shot wounds in the lungs and a fractured neck received in action on June 18th. (Those gun shot wounds had to have been inflicted on the ground, by the German civilians, more than likely.)

> **"To think** (she wrote) **we had been waiting, hoping and praying for approximately four months that he was living and all this time he has been dead. The news was very shocking to us and we know we'll never get over our son's death, but we're still having hopes that this report has been a mistake and that he'll return to us."**

> **"It just doesn't sound true to think he died a day after his bomber was shot down and it took them so many months to let us know. We will never give up hope."**

> **"Are you hearing from your son? Does he ever mention any of his crew members? If there's any news at all you can get from him regarding our Zig', we would appre-**

ciate it very much. Please write. Sincerely Mrs. Stella Czarnecki"

I had written about Steve King and Charlie Henry, but I knew nothing of the fate of our other crew members. Steve King told me about seeing two of our gunners in the waist area (Hagen and Rutishauser) when he was blown clear of the plane. My survival had been strictly a matter of chance, I now believe. It could just as easily have been my fate, too. Were those German civilians justified in shooting our fliers that way? I doubt that they considered the possibility of retaliation against their own soldiers and aviators who would inevitably be captured. Hitler's approval of such brutality was ruthless and unconscionable. I can't speak about the RAF's bombing but I know that our targets always had a good military purpose to them.

A letter I wrote dated December 21, 1944 announcing the arrival of the parcel my mother had sent.

> **"I wish to commend your judgment in everything** (socks, scarf, sweaters, etc.). **It was just short of terrific and I can hardly wait until the next one arrives."**

> **"I'm no longer dreaming of a white Christmas, but maybe we'll have a happy new year. The Red Cross Christmas parcels have arrived with turkey and several other precious articles, so at last our stomachs can have a little yuletide joy."**

> **"I have ordered a Patek Philippe watch from Switzerland and had the bill forwarded to you. Our retainers allow no gold watches, so I'm getting a stainless steel case which I am told can be replaced with gold for about eighty dollars. The watch itself costs around $100 and I'm sure it will be well worth it. Give my love to all the folks and keep praying. You're doing a fine job, just keep it up. Love, Don."**

Ordering a watch that way was only a shot in the dark. Ap-

parently some of the guys had been successful at it. If something
turned up, so much the better. It was worth a try, I figured, but the
watch never arrived.

Mother wrote January 3, 1945 from Sebring, Florida where
they were visiting with my brother Jim who was stationed there.
Apparently Jim was not going overseas. He was very unhappy
about it.

Fortunately, I now had a wool hat and overcoat, a wool
shirt, sweater and trousers. My shoes were simple high top boots,
the source of which I did not know, but they weren't American issue. When I had come down in June, I had no shoes on. For several
days I limped along with a felt slipper on one foot and a fleece-
lined flying boot on the other. When they finally gave me some
shoes, I was not paying attention to the fact that I was still growing, including my feet. The shoes were comfortable and fit up to a
point. Eventually, however, I experienced what Chinese girls did
when they had their feet bound. It became an unseen form of tor-
ture for me as I continued to grow.

The November 4th issue of our camp newspaper "THE
CIRCUIT" celebrated an anniversary of sorts. W.J. "Kriegie" Hall,
our oldest Kriegie, was starting his fourth year as a POW having
been captive since July 2, 1941, three years before my capture. The
paper named four other 1941 captives. So no one thought they had
it so bad in comparison with those fellows.

That November, there was a rumor that the Germans were
about to confiscate any excess food. There was nothing else to do
but to consume the extra supplies as quickly as possible before
any confiscation could be carried out. People made milk cakes out
of two 1lb cans of Klim, something we never would have done
under normal circumstances. We were already on half parcels and
had been since September, but we were still able to save food for
emergencies. Then, it was announced that parcels would be doled
out daily which didn't evince confidence in our captors good-faith
adherence to the Geneva Convention.

Christmas Eve was as memorable as it was depressing. The Battle of the Bulge was important news at the time, but it was very discouraging news. The German radio was claiming victory over the Allies. Had they succeeded in pushing through to the sea, our hopes of an early recovery would have been dashed indefinitely if not permanently. The show people among us put on a special faux radio broadcast from home. On stage was a set made up like someone's living room with an easy chair facing the radio. A Kriegie sat in the chair as though dreaming of home. There was a Christmas tree there too, decorated with ornaments and pretend gift packages all around. On the wall above the living room was an outline of America on which were drawn radio waves rippling out over America. It was almost more than we homesick ones could bear. The weather was very cold and there was snow on the ground. Still, there was caroling and music to cheer us up, if possible.

Colonel Goodrich announced that things would get worse before they get better. We knew that the Russians were moving west inexorably. We dreamed of their coming to free us, but it never happened.

We knew pretty well by the January, 1945 that something was about to happen. Either we would be overrun by the Russians or the Germans would have to evacuate us to prevent that from happening. There had to be a point of no return after which evacuation would become impossible and rumors were rampant that the hour was coming soon. We began making preparations anyway, storing food and preparing our clothing for a trek, if it were to come. There were many different ways of doing this. I came up with my own invention which was to take my blue denim shirt, cut off the sleeves and sew up the shirt tales to make pouches, front and back, for what I would need to carry with me.

It was January 27, 1945, another very cold day. The Russian Army was a mere thirty kilometers away, a spearhead of tanks having just reached the river at Steinau. Many of us were at the theater that night for a presentation of the stage show "You Can't

Take It With You." The show was in progress when suddenly, Col. Goodrich stepped onto the stage and announced that we were to return to our rooms and to be ready to march out of camp within the next 30 minutes. It took a little longer than that, but we hustled back to the block and packed up everything we could carry and got ready to move. We ate a last meal with hot coffee and tea. I took some of the precious margarine and spread it over my shoes for protection against the snow.

Everything I owned and all I would have to eat for an in-definite period of time was now on my back, either being worn or in my pack. I had an overcoat and scarf and gloves. On my head was a balaclava type wool hat. Mother's last gift of the "house slippers" was in the pouch. My blankets were rolled into a horseshoe and tied at the bottom so as to fit over my head and shoulder. My makeshift pack was heavy with all I thought I would be able to carry and I knew that in time it would be cutting into my shoulders. The pack was a good idea, all right, but I forgot to pad the shoulder straps. We had some German bread, some dried fruit, powdered milk, but we were leaving behind a lot of good food that was just too heavy to carry very far.

Roommate Morrie Bauer tells the story that our artist-in-residence, Lee Hamaker, came to him at that time and handed him his sketch book, saying: "This is going to be too heavy for me to carry, do you want it?" Morrie accepted the gift and carried the book in his pack. At one point, he considered discarding it in order to lighten the load and ultimately carried it all the way home at war's end. The sketch of me as the harried "stooge" was saved in the process to be included in this book.

The bride's first stew

Figure 50. Sketch by Cell-Room artist Lee Hamaker of author stooging. Note butchered tailoring on author's shorts. "Bride" equates to "Rookie."

Then we were outside by the gate in company-size formations ready to march. The temperature was definitely below zero.
One report it was minus fifteen degrees. In fact, that winter was
the coldest in 25 years. No matter what we had in the way of clothing, it was surely not enough for such conditions. After waiting for
a time standing around in the snow, the gate was opened and we
headed out under heavy guard, including guard dogs. It was about
11:00 p.m. It was exhilarating in a way to be out from behind the
barbed wire, but I wondered what was coming next.

Along the way, more bread was issued to lighten the loads
of the wagons which accompanied us. We ate it as fast as we could
and kept moving. All night we marched. I can remember one rest
stop on the road that we made. There was no protection from the
wind out there in the open, and there was real danger of frost bite.
Nevertheless, I laid down flat on my back on the packed snow on
the road to get a bit more rest than I thought I could standing up.
I remember my buddies yelling at me to get up. It warmed my
heart to hear them calling me to stand up. It was nice to know they
were worried about me, but I knew I was all right and that there
was no numbness, yet to worry about. When the order was given, I
got back on my feet and moved along with the rest. No order was
given by our superior officers not to try to escape but it was not
recommended.

En route, many Kriegies began lightening their loads by
dumping things like log books and personal articles they had
wanted to keep but which became too heavy to carry. The way was
littered with these treasured works which had taken many hours
to create while in camp. I never kept a diary so all I carried was
food which I consumed as we went along and a change of stockings. Many men suffered numbness in their feet and legs. A lot of
fellows experienced frost-bite the effects of which were going to
plague them for the rest of their lives.

As it became daylight, I could see that we were in open
farm country. There was nothing in view but an occasional house

or barn. By noon we had gone about 20 kilometers. A farmer came out with some hot water and we filled our cups and drank it either with coffee or just plain. Word came that we were going to stop soon so we could lie down and rest.

Figure 51. Winter 1945 march from Stalag Luft III Westward to evade surging Russian Army. Temperatures were 15 and more degrees below zero and the snow was deep and blowing. Courtesy of R. W. Kimball's book "Clipped Wings."

When we finally did come to a halt, our guards put us in

some barns where we could lie down at long last. Once inside, I rolled myself up in my blankets in the straw, but not before taking off my shoes and socks. I put on my other pair of socks and Mother's gift fleece-lined house slippers and my feet were warm and dry again. I tucked the damp stockings in my arm pits to dry. My shoes were also under the blankets with me, to keep them from freezing. Sleep came easily. I was exhausted by that time.

By dark, we were on the way again, and it was snowing hard. I didn't see it myself, but I learned later that some of the men had dropped out along the way and simply couldn't keep up. Those that couldn't go on were put in wagons until they were able to resume walking.

The next day, we passed little children at play in the snow. They chattered in German as though what was going on was an everyday event; but somehow, it seemed strange that they didn't sound like our own American kids. We paused for a few minutes nearby and, to my embarrassment; I had to relieve myself out there in the open. There were no facilities, and even if there were, there were too many of us. No one seemed to notice. After another 18 kilometers or so we stopped at about dark and moved into available barns and chicken houses for the night. It was a place called Graustein.

Reverend Murdo McDonald (Padre Mac) wrote about the "death march." It wasn't apparent at the time to me or among my group on the march, but there may have been some fatalities along the way.

> **"On the second night out, Lieut. Jenkins, an All-American football player, decided to die. I heard the summons passed along the straggling line. 'Padre Mac, you're wanted'. Retracing my footsteps, I found Jenkins lying on his back in the snow. He insisted on giving me what remained of his scanty rations. I stayed with him till he died, closed his eyes and ran to catch up with the main column some three miles away. The summons came again and again."** (A fellow-Kriegie,

Charlie Mueller of Center Camp and of Chicago, told how he totally passed out on the road that night and was carried to a nearby farmhouse and given a chance to rest and recuperate. After a few hours, Charlie said, they put him on a wagon and carried him until he caught up with us again.)

Our guards were middle-aged men. I saw one of them pull out of his pack a small chunk of the black bread and cut himself a slice with his pocket knife during another rest stop. He was as miserable as we were, but he and his cohorts kept on moving along with us. To fail or refuse to do so would have meant death for them, too. They were doing worse than we prisoners were because they had to carry their rifles. One exhausted soldier allowed a prisoner to carry his gun for a while because he could not keep up.

That single act epitomized the spirit of the marchers and our individual captors in those terrible conditions. The Geneva Convention prohibited this sort of abuse of prisoners of war but, in and of itself, the ones primarily to blame like Hitler and Goering paid the ultimate price with their lives rather than face the humiliation of trial and hanging which was due them. The Gallows were too good for both them and their regime.

After a few more hours in the blowing and drifting snow we made a much needed stop for a little while in a Church to rest. About 1:00 a.m., our procession came to a town called Muskau. We stood in the cold a while longer until word came to move inside a factory building nearby. It was warm and there appeared to be room for us. It was a pottery factory. At last we could take our outer clothes off and our shoes. We made ourselves comfortable on the concrete floor. After eating some bread from our packs, we slept the sleep of the nearly dead.

There was hot water there, enough for bathing, shaving or doing laundry for those who cared to. It couldn't last, I told myself. How soon is it going to be before we have to move out again? Some very good news came from the Colonel. We would be allowed to stay through the next night. No explanation was given, but who cared as long as we could be warm a little longer. We learned later that our senior officers had insisted that we be allowed to remain for another day for fear for our lives.

The second morning, we were "Raused" out and ready to march on. Before doing so, we stood in a courtyard and the Germans passed out boiling hot porridge, made of barley. It was our first food from them since leaving Camp. We had our cups at the ready and wolfed it down as fast as we could.

We resumed our march on a small side road wide enough for our mass of men or perhaps two wagons. Passing through villages, we saw German refugees fleeing the Russian onslaught, too. It was pitiful to see women and children pulling a wagon - perhaps the horse had been eaten - with an elderly man riding along with all of their belongings. Occasionally, an automobile would pass us to the West. There was no gasoline available and the cars were powered by coal gas or methane. One I saw burned wood for fuel.

A Chicago newspaper article told of the movement of prisoners of war that winter. The writer quoted a dialog between Hitler and Goering about it. Hitler wanted the prisoners moved back into central Germany. "They've got to be taken away, even if they have to march afoot in the mud. We will give the job to the Volkssturm. Anyone who tries to get away will be shot. It must be done with available means," said Hitler. Goering's response was that there were 10,000 men at Stalag Luft III.

Hitler opined that it would take 20 transport trains for 10,000 men, but less if transported according to Russian ideas. Goering chimed in saying, "Pull off their pants and boots so they cannot run away in the snow." Little did we know that we were being discussed with such low regard at such high levels.

Then we were off again, but this time it was a shorter walk, only 9 miles to the railroad tracks on which stood a long train of unheated box cars, "forty and eights" (40 men or 8 horses) of the same size and description as used in World War I. We were officers and therefore entitled to special accommodations, no doubt. Actually, I knew otherwise. The cars would have to accommodate 50 or more of us. Some cars reeked of animal waste freshly shoveled out.

Figure 52. 40 men or 8 horses unheated freight cars —We rode 50 per car taking turns sitting down for lack of space.

My car was at least clean, after a fashion, and dry. They packed us in and the doors were closed and locked. There was not enough room for everyone to lie or sit down all at once, so we took turns standing up. Our close proximity to one another generated some warmth, but not all that much. The bitter cold kept us shivering in the limited space we had. The train lurched on, westward. We could only guess where we were headed. It was not until the next day that we stopped and the doors were unlocked. The guards let us out to relieve ourselves. I remember one of our German-speaking fellows shouting out the question: "Wie Heist Diese Stadt?" (spelled phonetically), meaning what is this city? I wasn't sure I heard the answer from our guards.

The next afternoon the train stopped at dusk. The place was said to be Regensburg. Just after nightfall, the air raid sirens sounded. The guards checked to see that our doors were securely locked and then hurried off to air raid shelters. We had no idea whether our box cars were marked or whether our train was the target. It was possible that the bombers - which soon would be overhead - did not know we were inside. We waited in silence, huddled together. Could it be that our own planes' bombs were going to smash the train and us into the ground? We heard explosions at some distance but could not guess what the target was.

The all clear sounded not too long after that and the train moved out again. Further along the way, we were allowed another relief stop and received some rations from the Germans. Then our train continued on to our destination, Moosburg, near Munich. Not being ready yet to deal with the mass of humanity on board, the Germans left us locked up in our coops for still another night.

The next morning we detrained. What we could see was nothing pleasant. Tents were to be our home for several days more at least. It was February, and sleeping out doors was no picnic for the animals, let alone human beings. After a few more days, we were taken indoors and given a hot shower and then billeted in the barracks buildings there. The place was cold, dirty and wretched. Seeing each other stripped to the skin in the one hot shower they allowed us confirmed the effects of the march and the lack of proper nourishment over just a few weeks time.

Figure 53. The Hell-Hole of Stalag VII-A at Mossburg, Germany where the prison population reached over 110,000 by April 1945.

The barracks were furnished with 12 man, 3 decker bunk beds built as one unit occupying a 6X12 foot floor space. Imagine four triple decked bunks, two bunks wide and two bunks long joined together in a square and you have the picture. We drew lots for beds and I lost out and wound up sleeping on the floor for the first month. The wooden floors were very hard. Also, what we didn't know was that under the floor boards were ferocious fleas by the hundreds of thousands which came out at night and feasted on our unsuspecting bodies. This is how typhus epidemics started, the disease being transmitted by infected fleas.

Stalag VIIA was like starting over again compared to Stalag Luft III. All of the laboriously constructed tinware that had been left behind had to be remade so that we could have cooking pans and stoves. There were no books, no musical instruments, or athletic equipment, except what the guys had been able to carry on their backs. In short, nothing to do and nothing to do it with.

Figure 54. Abominable "Abort" (Outhouse) at Stalag VII-A.

Now survival became our first and only concern. We weren't getting any healthier and the food was miserable. We had our limited ration of German bread, but beside that there was an awful dehydrated soup. The vegetables, if that's what they were, were disgusting looking, rancid and practically inedible. Not completely. Somebody named it "green death." We found a way to get something into our stomachs, no matter what. Often I would find in my bowl what looked like the leaf off a tree and I never tried to eat any of that. Now we were starving in fact because the Red Cross parcels were so scarce as to be of no real help. The flow of them from Switzerland stopped completely and the parcels from Sweden had no way of reaching us now that the East and West front lines of the war began retreating inward. Any attempt to move food our way was being obstructed by the German population which was also starving. The fact that we had company in our suffering did not change the impact of our dire straits.

My routine each morning was to disrobe completely and pick through my clothes to remove the fleas. They would hide in the seams of our clothing. When you found one, it would jump away if you were not quick enough to catch it. To kill one, I found I had to seize it between my forefinger and thumb nail and press down until I was able to break through the hard shell. Blood would spurt out in doing so. My blood. It was a useless effort because there were so many more waiting to hatch again at night and coming out from under the floor. Needless to say everybody was covered with welts from the bites of these creatures. But at least I could feel that I had cleaned myself for the day.

At night, I would put on my overcoat, take off my shoes and put on my fleece-lined slippers and roll up in my blanket and go to sleep. By morning, I would be stiff and sore and scratching again. But now, I noticed something else about myself. When I put my shoes on and attempted to walk a few steps, my feet hurt much like I was stepping on hot coals. The soles were as sore as they could be and I was developing large calluses and corns. It simply didn't occur to me that my growing feet had finally begun to experience the torturous binding effects of shoes that were too small and getting smaller by the day. The bones were being compressed into each other, but continuing to grow. After a few minutes, the pain would subside and I would be able to stand and move about again.

A major chore of the day was cooking. From what tins we could find or "scrounge-up," we prisoners created stoves, or "heatless smokers," made up of three or four tin cans stacked one on top of the other, in which we could burn small splinters of wood about the size of three wooden matches bundled together and scraps of paper which mysteriously, when ignited, created a gas which burned quite hot and could warm up food. (Somebody opined that the result was the "Venturi" phenomenon.) It could take as long as an hour to cook one dish. The Blower or bellows device, if you knew how to make one, was much more effective in generating heat, but it also consumed more fuel. The Germans seemed not to notice when some of the men, in desperation, found a way to get under the barracks and tear out much needed wood fragments for cooking.

Our 14 man Stalag Luft III Room 5 combine was scattered from the time we marched away never to be together again. Fergie, Morrie Bauer and I and two or three others stuck together and continued to share food and cooking duty. It was better that way and you had some one at least to commiserate with over it. We got along, somehow. It was a sight to see the small corner cook room where everyone gathered to heat their food. The smoke from all the make-shift cookers would send you out every few minutes choking and teary-eyed for a breath of fresh air.

What was most depressing about Moosburg was the filth and mess of the place. At Sagan, we were able to keep our rooms, ourselves and the environs fairly clean and picked-up. Here there were no brooms and no way to straighten anything up. Add to that the discontinuation of Red Cross parcels by the end of February. From then on we were on Prison rations only, pitiful as they were.

The Red Cross Bulletin for February, 1945 reported that the routing of parcels for prisoners through Switzerland had been cut off and that the only source now was from Sweden - which made it virtually impossible for them to reach us in Bavaria. There was even mention of the possibility of the war continuing through 1945 and how relief goods would be moved through Sweden to the prisoners. I know now that had the war continued another three or four months beyond its eventual end, very many of us would have died. We were sick now and getting sicker and we were slowly but surely starving to death on the little food we were receiving. We were surviving on hope. And the news about the war was sounding better each day. Rumors started circulating that we might be moved south into the mountains to a Nazi "Redoubt" where we could be ransomed off or even executed. This kind of talk was not at all helpful to our morale.

"Suffering produces endurance, and endurance produces character, and character produces hope, and hope does not disappoint us, because God's love has been poured into our hearts through the Holy Spirit that has been given to us." (Romans 5:3-5)

We prisoners were hoping against hope.

Another letter from Dad dated January 6th, which never reached me, talked of receiving my letter of October 18, 1944 and that the previous one was dated July 30th. The long delay was worrying them considerably. They both were writing almost every day in hope that one or more might get through to me. They worried also that they were not sending the right things and detected from my letters that I needed clothing more than food. Mother must have thought about me having just as bad winter as they were at home in Chicago and not knowing what our living conditions were.

My brother Jim was engaged to marry his fiancée', Helen Jackson of the neighboring suburb of Oak Park, Illinois. Brother Dick was beginning to wonder if I would be home by the time Jim and Helen were due to get married in the summer of 1945 and even talked about how he might have to be Jim's best man.

The folks were still debating about returning to our family home in River Forest, a close-in western suburb of Chicago. Since dad had been released from active duty the previous spring, they had been trying but could not regain possession from renters because of rent control. Mother wasn't well enough to take care of the house, he said, and dad was afraid she would be too lonesome there as compared to their new apartment in the city. Mother stayed in Florida and was near my brother Jim's air station in Delray where he was still in training. She wrote that it was bitterly cold in Chicago making her glad she was down where it was warm. They had no idea when they wrote these letters what was going on with me in Germany. She mentioned that she was feeling guilty knowing that it would be cold where I was, also.

My letter of January 23, 1945 arrived at home.

"Dear Mother and Dad. Your latest letters are November 30 and December 4, and along with them arrived my birthday letter. Jim must really be "working the rackets to be doing what he's doing, but more power to him." That new high school of Dick's (Lawrenceville Prep' in New Jersey) **really sounds like a country club and I imagine he's playing around. I think he was better off at Campion High. He might not have met Lord Fauntleroy and he might not have been as well prepared for college, but he would get something just as important and even more and that is his religion."**

"I didn't realize it myself while I was there but I know it now and I am grateful. As a prison philosopher once said: 'We live only in the past and the future. The present is but a vague transition period.' We live only for the day of freedom. The spirit is high at this moment and we're laughing and hoping and praying. Love, Don."

Somehow a brief post card I wrote from Moosburg dated March 12th got through.

"My health is good and I'm praying that my high hopes will not be in vain. I miss you all but it won't be too long. Take care of yourselves and try not to worry. Give my love to all. I'm with you always in spirit until that great day. Love, Don"

CHAPTER 22:

LIBERATION AND VICTORY IN THE SPRING OF 1945

By the end of March 1945, our German guards themselves seemed to want to get the war over. An American news article dated March 31st reported their soldiers were signaling from the ground trying to surrender to our airplanes. Our air force so dominated the skies over Germany by then that nothing could move in daylight in the air or on the ground that wouldn't be shot up or dive-bombed. How could the Germans fight a war under such circumstances? They couldn't. Contemporaneous wisdom blames Hitler and the Nazis for letting the war go on as long as it did. Germany was still turning out fighter planes right up to the end without pilots or gasoline to fly them.

One sunny afternoon in late March, we were sitting out in the prison yard when the American bombers came over. We could see them clearly as they flew toward Munich, hundreds of them. We could not see the bombs falling, but we heard them, even from a distance of 30 miles or so. It was like rolling thunder as the bombs landed in the same grouping as the planes from which they had been dropped. Imagine 36 bombers, each carrying two tons of high explosives, flying in close formation and dropping simultaneously. It was the 8th Air Force's method of bombing that wiped out everything in its path.

Figure 55. Kriegies at Moosburg cooking outside with Kriegie stove and blower device made out of empty cans 1945.

Dear Jack Ellenberger, my friend and original bombardier, wrote again to the folks in an undated letter. He was trying to explain what had happened to my clothes. Even my leather flying jacket with "Hells Belle" on the back, which he had painted for me, was being traced to no avail.

Figure 56. Ellenberger's Flight Jacket showing missions flown with the Jolls' crew. Taken at crew's reunion in 1995.

Figure 57. Post War 1995 in San Diego, California, L-R, Steve King, Jack Ellenberger, Lew Jolls and Author.

Figure 58. Drawing by Lt. Ellenberger of B-17 crewman in fleece lined flying gear. Once we started flying for the 379ᵗʰ Bomb Group, electrically heated suits were made available which provided excellent protection against the 50 degree temperatures experienced at 25,000 feet in the air – as long as the electricity was available. A loss of power could mean serious frost-bite injuries for the crew.

"There's an old tradition in the 8th Air Force. I don't know where it started, but the fellows spread out the clothes (of the presumed dead) **among the group. I think it is the outgrowth of the shortage they had. I tried to keep all of his things together. I sure hope Patton frees every one of the boys. I'd sure like to hear from Don and see him again and I know that's what you want very much."**

"Most of the boys who flew with us are back here in the States or missing. I sure hated to hear about Ziggy (Czarnecki). When they went down and I saw a chute, I just knew it was Don because he used to sit right over the escape hatch on the bomb run (not true at all, but reasonably close). **When this is all over, Jolls and I and Don will have to have a meeting to talk about all the wild missions."**

"I can just see Don sewing and cooking. We used to kid him about making beds and being a poor cook, as we cooked a lot of things over our charcoal stove in the hut. We once had a chicken one of the boys found wandering around outside the door. We built a spit out of a coat hanger and tried to cook it. Don wanted it stuffed so we crammed about a loaf of bread into it. The outcome was burned bread and raw chicken. He claimed that was the way to stuff a chicken."

"I pray Don will be home soon. I guess all the fellows who got through give thanks. On every mission, just before the bomb run, we all said a prayer and I can say if it didn't help, it made you feel a lot better. If you find out anything about Don, please let me know as I'm sweating him out and I'll see about his clothes."

In the brief three months I spent at Kimbolton flying with the 379th Bomb Group, I never once had occasion to touch, let alone scavenge, the personal effects of one single person. We had losses of aircrews but none in our barracks. Such a cruel act generally brought anguish to the lost fliers' families at home. It was wrong, inexcusable and ghoulish. There were worse things going on than that. According to my friend 379th BG lead bombardier, Chuck Olson, there was an officer he knew who, preyed on new air crews by borrowing money from them secured only by a well-kept promise to repay by the next payday. If the lender survived, the exact sum due was promptly repaid as promised. If not, the proceeds stayed in the borrower's pocket by default. This same man, according to Olson, would retrieve abandoned bicycles of missing crews and sell them for cash.

Many years later I asked Jack Ellenberger how he felt that day in June 1944 when I did not return from my last mission. Jack earnestly replied that he was "devastated." This was in contrast to my friend Jack Sinise's response but Ellenberger and I had flown 26 missions together through thick and thin and we had bonded through that experience as even brothers can't do. He and I always sat at our posts in the nose of the ship where we were sure to be killed if the pilot lost control in those most dangerous moments of flying and never gave it a thought.

By April 1, 1945, living conditions for us prisoners were worsening by the day. We were trying just to stay alive. Our secret radio brought news from outside that the American forces advancing from the West and the Russians from the East were getting close to making contact with each other.

A Chicago Tribune article written about that time from Germany with the U.S. 1st Army Advance Headquarters reported that between 600 and 1,000 allied war prisoners, most of them Americans, were liberated at Duderstadt, seven miles east of Goettingen. "Early reports indicated that most of the men are suffering severely from malnutrition and that the Americans had been given extremely harsh treatment." Said a Scottish prisoner interviewed by the embedded press. "When I saw the Americans coming to free us, I could hardly speak,"

Another news article the folks saved for me dated April 12, 1945 related how there were numerous deaths among the prisoners from freezing and sickness and of guards' cruelty during forced marches from Eastern European camps as the Germans fled before the Red Army. This had to have been discouraging news for them.

CHAPTER 23:

LIBERATION DAY
APRIL 29, 1945

The Fourteenth Armored Division of General Patton's Third Army was closing in on Moosburg and by April 28th. German troops, including a division of SS Panzer Grenadier troops and an infantry division, were gradually falling back to the east. Before dawn a German military car bearing a white flag made contact with our forces and requested a truce which included a pause in the fighting. The enemy wanted time to withdraw from positions around our camp and asked for a cease fire long enough for the Germans to retreat in order. This offer was rejected for fear that prisoner hostages might be taken along for the sake of leverage in further negotiations.

The Division commander ordered the attack to continue and seize the one open bridge across the river preventing its destruction by the Germans. The defending SS troops were only lightly armed and had no defense against our tank forces but were still able to destroy the bridge. The remaining German forces surrendered and the firing ceased.

Inside the camp, that morning we had heard cannon fire in the West. Then we heard the guns firing at close range. I for one could only think at that point of how to stay alive a little longer and not die just at the moment of our liberation. I positioned myself inside the tiny cook room of our barrack where there was at least some masonry half way up the wall, behind which to crouch.

The battle had lasted almost 3 hours. At one point during the struggle I had to answer the call of nature because of my dysentery and found myself running across the prison yard to the "abort" to relieve myself. There was plenty of excitement to get the bowels moving, anyway. I made it over and back on the dead run and back into the cook room. All the while, there were guys cooking in the room which was filled with smoke from their tin-can stoves like nothing was happening outside.

On my mind was Eric Maria Remarque's WWI story: "All Quiet on the Western Front" and the last scene in the movie in which the actor, Lew Ayres, playing a German soldier, reaches out of his trench to catch a butterfly and is shot dead by a French sniper. I was desperate over the same thing happening to me so close to liberation.

We didn't know about the "SS" troops in the area who were completely and ruthlessly devoted to Adolf Hitler. My guess is that we were being guarded to preserve The Fuhrer's last opportunity to ransom us for a better settlement with the Allied forces than "unconditional surrender." A few prisoners were wounded but none fatally.

The American tanks rolled right through the barbed wire fences into the camp. We were free at last. The leaders of our rescue forces made it clear, however, that it would be best for us to stay where we were and wait for transportation out. That was easy for me because I was still in a daze and lacking any spunk or inclination to do otherwise.

A Chicago newspaper headline dated April 30th reported that Patton's 3rd Army had liberated 110,000 Allied prisoners from the German prison camp (our prison) at Moosburg, north of Munich. "In the greatest single mass liberation of the war, Gen. George S. Patton's troops overran the camp and freed the cheering Allied captives. Among them were at least 10,000 American prisoners." I was one of those 10,000.

CHAPTER 24:

PATTON VISITS MOOSBURG

Figure 59. General George in all his glory on May 2, 1945 at Moosburg Prison Camp.

Three days later on May 2, 1945. General George S. Patton, "Old Blood and Guts" himself, came into our camp to review us. He was standing up in his jeep bearing his three-star General's flag in all his glory with his ivory-handled pistols, one on each hip. (Some people referred to the handles as being of made of pearl. Patton consistently rebuked that misconception by saying that pearl-handled pistols were something found only in French whorehouses.) He dismounted and walked toward us. We were standing at attention in a semi-military formation on two sides of the area.

He walked down the middle, looked over our gaunt and ragged assembly and in a loud voice said: "Have you enough to eat?" Our appearance answered the question. Actually it wasn't so much a question of having enough food but whether we could even swallow regular food, our stomachs had shrunk so.

We cheered. But Patton scowled which I mistook as an expression of disdain. I thought perhaps it was his practiced General's face. It prompted me to guess that he might be thinking: "You men must have screwed up somewhere or you wouldn't be here." If so, he was right. We had zigged when we should have zagged and there we were in our parachutes. My suspicion was that he never had given much thought to what an airman could do to avoid capture while falling from thousands of feet in the air and hundreds of miles deep in enemy territory, by himself and out of uniform.

We air crew prisoners held in camps all over Germany represented what was left of the Air Force's casualties counted in calculating the 60% average survival rate for downed air crews in Europe. The unfortunate non-survivors killed-in-action were not to my knowledge counted according to the way they died. I can't recall ever seeing the number of downed-fliers murdered by German civilians. Those who paid with their lives were the real heroes.

We were the lucky ones who hadn't fallen victim to the angry mobs and to their thirst for revenge on us "Terror Fliegers" and "Luftgangsters" (terror fliers and air gangsters). The German civilians in Hamburg the previous June had murdered three of my crew and their Flak got one more. My pilot, Steve King, and our flight engineer, Ray Weehler, narrowly escaped being executed. How many more were similarly mistreated during the war?

I forgave Patton in a hurry. It was an historic moment to see him up that close and hear him speak to us. Many years later, I read his diary about that day. He called us "A fine bunch of men." Quite an understatement in my estimation. We were the luckiest people I ever knew and proud we were, too, of what we had been through and lived to tell about it. It was reported that the General's scowl was an expression of his anger over how we had been mistreated. Maybe so, but I preferred my version. He could have smiled or laughed or shaken hands with us.

It was reported that one of the prisoners asked the General how soon we could leave the place. He is said to have asked, "Do you have wire cutters?" In other words, what's holding you back? This was not the point at all. Our new orders were to stay put so that we could be evacuated in an orderly fashion and accounted for. Some of the fittest guys "liberated" automobiles and headed for Paris where there was civilized life again. Army discipline was no longer observed, especially for liberated POW's who were wandering around France. There was, I was told later, both money and clothing available so they blended right in and were not even noticed except perhaps for their lean visages.

As for myself, I was still in shock even after we were freed. It just couldn't be over that quickly and simply, even though there were those moments of panic about possibly being killed by the last bullet of the war. I and most of the others followed orders to hold our places and stick around because they were coming to get us. We were pleased with our new circumstances but still very lethargic. Of course we were also very anxious to go home.

CHAPTER 25:

WHILE WE WAITED TO BE EVACUATED FROM MOOSBURG

That time is just a blur. I do remember that on May 8, 1945, Victory in Europe (VE) Day, the day the war in Europe officially ended, one of the guard towers was set on fire as part of the celebration. We were still there in the camp, though, and feeling and acting like we were still prisoners. We continued sleeping in our flea-ridden barracks. The Army brought in K-Rations but I passed on most of that. It didn't fill the bill just then. More tolerable food would come later after we got to France.

A buddy and I decided to walk out of the prison camp one day and explore the environs. I picked up an abandoned German soldier's forage cap, a belt buckle stamped with the words, "Gott Mit Uns" (God is with us) and a "soldat's" epaulet. The surviving enemy soldiers stripped off their military clothes and insignia in order to hide among the civilians to avoid capture. It took a while but they were rounded up and fenced in with other German prisoners of war. There were hundreds of thousands of them and photographs showed looks on their faces of utter defeat and despair. Adolph Hitler's 1,000 year Reich had ended in less than six years.

We hitched a ride in an Army truck which took us to a nearby field kitchen where they were cooking for our combat troops. We must have looked, acted and smelled like the worst looking bums you ever saw. We were dirty, ragged and starved in appearance. The mess sergeant offered us their food but our shrunken stomachs really couldn't handle it. It was too heavy and rich and we realized instinctively that we shouldn't gorge ourselves, even if we could have gotten it down.

On the way back to camp, the two of us rode in the back

of another troop carrier. On the floor lying loose and rolling around under our feet were German hand grenades - "potato mashers" they called them resembling a can of peas on a 12-inch wooden handle. The driver told us not to worry about them. He said the GI's used them for fishing - they pulled the pin and threw the grenades into the river or stream. When they exploded, up came the stunned fish which they just picked out of the water.

The next day, some of the former inmates who had gone out foraging for souvenirs brought back wine and liquor. I tried some brandy, but it didn't seem to do anything for me. They carried in barracks bags full of so many items; they couldn't possibly take them home to the States. I accepted the invitation to help myself and chose an officer's dagger - a short form of dress sword German officers wore on parade. Also, I helped myself to a full-sized dress sword in its scabbard. There were plenty of "Ost (East) Front" rabbit fur hats available so I got one of those, too. It's still in my possession in a Plexiglas box on the shelf and in brand new condition as it was when I got it. My friend Fergie Ferguson cut off a piece of the prison barbed wire for himself and for me to take home.

It was several days after May 8th when the army trucks pulled up at the camp and we boarded with everything we could carry. From there we were driven to Landshut airport a few miles to the North. It was noon when we arrived. There were wrecked German planes everywhere, but a runway had been cleared for our C-47 (DC-3) transport planes to land. We were wearing our Class-A rags and they lined us up for delousing with DDT to kill the fleas we still carried.

Figure 60. Transport from Moosburg to Landshut Air Field for evacuation.

Figure 61. At Landshut Air Field ready to board C-47 Transports for Le Havre, France.

Figure 62. C-47's lined up and waiting for POW's to board for last flight to Le Havre, France, May 1945.

When the transport planes landed, we cheered enthusiastically. It took awhile to organize our boarding. And then it was like a miracle was happening. I was airborne again for the first time since June 18, 1944. I could hardly believe we were out of the clutches of the Germans at long last and headed for France. After a few minutes into the flight it was as though I was back navigating again. I went up to the pilot's compartment and talked briefly with the crew. We were free and among the living again for the first time in almost 11 months.

CHAPTER 26:

CAMP LUCKY STRIKE, LE HAVRE, FRANCE

I would guess (I had no watch) that we were in the air less than two hours and then we landed on a temporary air strip at Le Havre, France. It was a new facility called "Camp Lucky Strike," the name of the cigarette, and we felt very lucky. Other similar camps were called Chesterfield and Camel after other popular tobacco brands. We were now designated officially as "RAMPS" - Recovered Allied Military Personnel.

Figure 63. "RAMPS" wait in line for food at Camp Lucky Strike, Le Havre, France.

We had a chance to bathe in hot water at long last and get into some clean clothes. I threw away every bit of clothing I had except my green Barathea flight jacket (sans the electric lining which, when plugged in, kept me warm at high altitudes in temperatures of 40 and 50 degrees below zero), a pair of over-darned, thread-bare stockings and my mother's gift of the fleece-lined house-slippers which I slept in but never wore on the floor. Everything else was rags. We were outfitted with olive drab (OD) slacks and "Eisenhower" jackets that were the standard blouse cut off at the waist, British style. They gave us new wool shirts, underwear and socks, and overseas caps with the insignia of our rank. It was first class, no bugs and shiny new GI shoes.

They fed us very carefully with creamed foods, potatoes, chicken and milk shakes. We had cursory physical exams and they decided we would go home on a troop ship equipped to serve the soft-kinds of food we seemed to be able to eat in our distressed condition. All of this didn't happen overnight, though. It was several days before they had us ready to move out and get aboard.

One thing I remember about Camp Lucky Strike was a guy who seemed always to be just ahead of me when we went for our daily showers. This man, an officer and gentlemen of course, took about four days of showering before his ears finally lost all of the black dirt he had been wearing for so long. I didn't have the heart to say to him, "Hey, fella, you forgot to wash your ears."

What I don't remember about being there was any celebrating of our liberation. Nor was there any marching or close-order drilling. Most of us were just in a daze but happy to be waiting patiently for someone to tell us when we could leave for home.

CHAPTER 27:

OUR SHIP SAILS FOR AMERICA

At last we boarded our ship and were under way. The first stop was Southampton, England. Some of the guys jumped ship there and returned to their Air Groups. That never crossed my mind for even a minute. It took us thirteen days to cross the Atlantic, believe it or not. But, remember, there was still a war going on - with Japan - even though there was no way that a Japanese submarine could have sailed all the way from the Pacific Ocean into the Atlantic without refueling or re-supplying. The ship's captain took no chances. We traveled buttoned up and dark every night at sea.

The ship was jammed full. We ex-prisoners were served four meals a day, all soft foods. Out of all the officers aboard, I was one of 13 who drew duty as "Officer of the Guard" for a day. Why me? Enlisted men were stationed at strategic places around the ship, twenty-four hours a day - two hours on and four hours off. After touring the ship from bow to stern with a sergeant a few times and making sure that the guards were in their proper places, I told him that if anybody was looking for me, I would be in my bunk. I could have caught it for that, but what were they going to do to me? I was still quite benumbed and not highly motivated about much of anything, even fear for disciplinary action.

Sleeping accommodations were extremely tight, with so many passengers. My bed consisted of a folding canvas rack, in a four-high arrangement. There wasn't enough space between bunks to turn over on your side without bumping the guy above you. It took thirteen incredible days and nights but we were headed in the right direction. Returning to active duty was not on my mind yet.

CHAPTER 28:

GREETINGS FROM THE STATUE OF LIBERTY, NEW YORK

Finally, our ship pulled into New York Harbor. The Statue of Liberty never looked better. There were no crowds to greet us, however, and no fireboats spraying water as they do when a really important ship arrives. They dropped us off quietly on the Jersey side at Camp Joyce Kilmer, a place frequently used for embarkation. They fed us well and filled any immediate needs. The news was good. We would be on board trains for home, shortly.

Figure 64. New York Harbor and the Statue of Liberty, June, 1945.

My father called on the telephone. How he found out where I was, I do not know. He was in New York City and asked if I wanted to take the train home with him. Logic didn't enter into my decision. I was still too numb to consider it and declined the offer. I didn't mean to hurt his feelings, but it didn't seem right to disrupt the momentum we now had going for us. It was a mistake, of course, because the train ride took a full day and a night. Troop trains were notoriously slow throughout the war.

CHAPTER 29:

HOME AT LAST

At last I was home in Chicago. The folks were there to meet me and took me straight to their new apartment. They couldn't do enough for me. They were so solicitous for my feelings and waited for me to let them know if I wanted anything. Brother Jim's wedding was in the offing and I had made it home just in time to be his best man. I had no clothes for summer so Dad had one of his old dress uniforms altered for me. I was extremely thin, still, and weighed only 140+ pounds, even after almost six weeks on a very soft diet. (My best estimate is that at the lowest point, I could not have weighed more than 120 lbs.) But I felt all right. Maybe not in the head yet, though.

Getting ready for the wedding had everybody going every which way at once. Jim took me around because I had no urge to try to drive a car as yet. In fact it took a good while for me to get to where I felt comfortable driving. One day, we went out to Hines Veterans' Hospital in West Suburban Maywood, Illinois to visit one of Jim's friends who was a paraplegic due to a war wound. It was very warm that day. As we stood by this poor chap's bed, the heat and the hospital odors suddenly overwhelmed me and I passed out. I remember the nurse putting a cold cloth on my head and saying, "the kid fainted." Yes, the decorated combat veteran home from the war was still just a "kid" after all.

One evening we went to my mother's sister, Aunt Babe Holland's house in Maywood, IL for dinner. All the relatives were there to see me and I gave them a short-long story about the war. They listened intently and in awe trying to understand, but I knew I couldn't explain it all to them that well. It was hard for the people at home to grasp what it was like and it was even harder to describe it for them. I glossed over the worst parts.

Jim and his bride Helen's wedding was a joyous occasion. My nine-year-old brother Johnny was the ring-bearer. They made a lovely couple, as beautiful as one could imagine. Mother and Dad looked great and all the family, too. Two of Dad's army buddies, Colonel Gus Minton and Colonel Larry O'Toole, were there and they talked to me about my going back on active duty. They assured me I would get my captaincy quite soon, although I was still only a 2d Lieutenant, no thanks to my Commanding Officer back at the 379th Bomb Group. The war was still on against Japan with a vengeance and our men were dying every day in the Pacific.

I was having nightmares about that time. It never occurred to me that I had a problem or needed treatment for it or to even admit anything was wrong with me. One dream that seemed to recur had the Germans at the front door to announce that my leave was over and it was time to get back to the POW camp and resume captivity. In another dream I was at the Airbase in England preparing for a combat mission. They made no sense, but most dreams don't. I was trying to adjust to civilization.

My dad just couldn't do enough for me. He took me to get a pair of shoes. I still didn't know that my feet had been damaged as I was growing out of my POW boots. The new shoes felt just like a soft glove when I put them on. It was November 1945 when I finally paid a visit to a Podiatrist for relief from the constant foot pain I experienced while walking. My feet were covered with calluses and bunions. The doctor exclaimed when I took off my shoes and socks: "What the hell have you done to your feet?" For the first time I realized that during those months in prison camp my feet had been growing without my noticing. The Army measured me as five feet nine inches tall in October 1943 when I was commissioned a 2d Lieutenant. My weight then was 160 pounds. By June 1945 I had attained five feet, ten and a half inches and my weight was 140 pounds. I had grown out of the shoes the Germans gave me but still wore them for lack of any other footwear. I felt the pain but without recognizing what was causing it. My feet hurt most in the morning and then I would forget about them. I was advised later that my state of depression had blotted out reality.

The foot doctor did what he could to remove my calluses and prescribed new shoes, at least an extra size wider than what I was wearing. His advice was to let the cramped bones spread back out into their normal position. Lucky for me, they slowly but surely did but it took months. Even the new shoes I obtained at home were too small.

Dad wanted me to play golf with him that first summer of 1945, so I did. But 9 holes out of the traditional 18 was all that I could take at one time. This was another symptom of my mental state. I was feeling "culture shock" coming from behind the barbed wire and living like a starving animal into the luxurious life of the country club where everyone was lolling around or amusing him or herself with a mere game. Didn't they know there was still a War on? Those feelings subsided but it took a while.

My service in combat and as a prisoner of war remain one of the most important parts of my life. This is not to gainsay the happy years with my loving, late first wife who gave me four wonderful sons. At college, I never said anything about my experiences to my classmates but somehow they knew I couldn't talk about them. Nor did I talk about the war for a very long time after that. Once I told a co-worker that I had made a parachute jump but I provided no details. I was amused when he refused to believe my story but said nothing further.

Perhaps my story highlights a truth about being involved in a war to its fullest and living to tell about it. In fact, most combat veterans do not want to talk about what they went through. It is as though (and I heard this on the radio by the son of a WWII Marine officer) "a curtain has come down separating combat veterans permanently from the rest of society." In life we live either in front of the curtain or in back of it. It took time for me to make my way out in front of the curtain and return to a normal life.

There is still nothing like the feelings I have had when getting together with my former combat flying buddies and ex-Pow's from Sagan's South Camp. Being reunited with them, I feel completely comfortable. But when the POW reunions are over and it's time to return home, a strange feeling comes over me. Somehow, I don't want to leave them. This passes when I am back at work. I have kept in touch with my buddies and watched them fade away one by one. Still alive, though, are my last pilot, Col. Steve King (California), fellow navigator Jack Sinise (Illinois) and my prison cellmate Valleau Wilkie (Fort Worth, Texas). We are old men now but still functioning and staying in touch with one another.

On Memorial Days back in the early 1930's, I watched real live Civil War Union Army soldiers and marveled at their ability to march in the parades. They seemed very old to me then. Now, I'm their age and every bit as much a character from the distant past as they were then. It's known as being really old.

No, writing this book did not scare up any Ghosts of the past. They were already there with me. I started putting words down in 1994 and just let them flow. Then, the manuscript sat on a shelf at home for years. I remarried and my wife, Alice, gave me the incentive to organize my war memorabilia and letters or watch her throw them out. Once I got started, it came easily. I had learned touch-typing in college out of the book that came with the machine and, the more I used it, the better and faster I became.

I read a book review in the New York Times some years ago which gave me an idea to use in trying to make my story as interesting as possible. The reviewer said that what was missing in war stories he had read was telling the reader how it felt while placing one's life on the line. If you haven't noticed that, perhaps I was too subtle and did not achieve my goal.

An odd thing about ex prisoners of war is that they get along best among their own kind. At the Veterans Administration, they tell me that ex-POW's from different wars do not mix well at all.

I still hark back to the dark days at Stalag VII-A in Moosburg, Germany. There was nothing good to say about it. And, yet, I recall one time there when I discussed my feelings with my good friend, Fergie Ferguson. I asked him to tell me about his "Early Bird" experience. He was captured in early 1943 - I wondered how he compared our current situation with those early days of his captivity. I was serious and so was he. He said that no matter how much longer he and others had been "in the bag," than I was, the brutal winter march of January 1945, our awful cattle car train ride and now our deadening existence at Stalag VII-A made us all equals regardless of the length of time served behind the wire. This conversation was uplifting to me and gave me a new perspective on the experience.

It's a matter of pride for a war prisoner how long his captivity lasted. Jim Ferguson was the exception among the early birds who still, to this day, seem to have their noses in the air in the presence of a latecomer. They simply can't help themselves.

CHAPTER 30:

BACK TO COLLEGE, GRADUATION

After VJ Day, the war was over for me and it was time to get back into College. Dartmouth College, Hanover, New Hampshire accepted me readily. Actually in the fall of 1945. there were not very many veterans who had been mustered out of service by then. They asked very few questions. The government's GI Bill was going to pay for my tuition and $100 per month. I wrote a letter stating my interest and reasons for wanting to enroll and was admitted without delay.

As it turned out, it was just the right place for me. I was able to finish in a hurry - which I was in - and also to spend some time in the Eastern United States. I was not in any mood for collegiate "Rah-Rah" things so I went straight through for three years, summer and winter without stopping. By June 1948, I was ready to start my new life in the peacetime world.

POST-TRAUMATIC STRESS DISORDER

This is the name psychiatrists came up with after the war to replace "Shell Shock" in World War I and "Combat Fatigue" in World War II. In the 21'st Century, this diagnosis has attained acceptance if not complete understanding of the effects on our service men and women of mortal combat and particularly victims of wartime capture and imprisonment. The author is personally convinced that all prisoners of war have it.

One isolated experience which possibly demonstrates the war's effects on me happened at college on a cold and snowy winter's night in February of 1946. I was walking alone back to my dormitory room from town when a gunshot rang out. Without hesitation, I threw myself headlong into a snow bank and lay there for a minute contemplating the humorous side of the event. In another moment I was back on my feet, a student again. In a book I read recently about symptoms of PTSD, for the first time I learned that my war experiences had instilled in me conditions known as "hypervigilence" and "exaggerated-startle-response." My reaction to the unanticipated gunshot had revealed more than I knew about myself and now at last I finally understood – 60+ years later.

Other symptoms of PTSD I have come to recognize are: "denial" and "emotional detachment." I now recognize that my self-impression of being imperturbable in response to irritations is another kind of reaction. As an example, one morning a few years back on board a Commuter-type prop plane just after taking off on a Midwestern flight, the pilot announced that we were returning to Chicago's O'Hare Field immediately because there had been a failure of the control of the ship's flaps. He advised us passengers to place our foreheads against the seat in front of us and prepare for a hot, flapless landing.

The plane landed safely slowed down only by its brakes and while the other passengers were visibly upset and shaking in their boots, I was relaxed and smiling. A traveling companion commented on my cool and calm demeanor. Of course after flying many hours in combat with people shooting me, perhaps I had become benumbed. I also had travel accident insurance which I recommend to take the fear out of flying.

POST-LOGUE

According to Lieutenant General A.P. Clark, USAF Ret., an early-bird Kriegie himself shot down over France while flying an RAF Spitfire in 1942, the US Army Air Forces lost approximately 10,000 bombers (50-50 B-17's and B-24's) and 8,000 fighters to enemy action over Europe during WWII. These many of our planes were manned by over one hundred thousand stalwart men who did not return from their missions. At war's end, there were approximately 40,000 Army Air Force POW's being held by the Germans for a survival rate of 37%. (The Germans also held another 48,000 captured U.S. ground combatants.)

For many years I denied that the Germans tortured or beat us although some of that actually did happen. (In my case perhaps it was the shoes.) I have changed my mind, now. Our Nazi captors never had the time or personnel to do what the Japanese, North Koreans and the North Vietnamese did to captured Americans because there were too many of us, 88,000 in fact. I don't think the rank and file German soldier thought much about it but his leaders came up with a way to afflict all of us at once by neglect subjecting us to starvation, deprivation, disease and exposure. And it didn't cost them a single "Pfennig" (Nazi penny). However, had the war gone on much longer, a lot of us prisoners would have died. It wasn't "Hogan's Heroes," for sure. It never was.

POSTSCRIPT

In April 2005 at the reunion of the Stalag Luft III "Krie-gies" I took the microphone at the podium and had the full atten-tion of those present, about 300 in number. I announced that after sixty years I wanted to speak briefly about the stratification of the "early bird" prisoners and the "late comers," like myself. I said that as a latecomer I felt an obligation to apologize to the early birds even as long ago as it was. What was I apologizing about? I asked, rhetorically? "For being late getting there," I said. And then I add-ed: "I was busy fighting the damn war." They laughed heartily but the separation was still there. Thanks to the thoughtful advice of my dear friend and fellow combine member, the late Jim Ferguson, I could now laugh along with the best of them about my short time "in the bag" (nearly 11 months) because, in the end, I survived the worst part of our captivity, thank the Lord!

I am honored to wear the Distinguished Flying Cross for "extraordinary achievement in flight", the Air Medal with three Oak Leaf Clusters for repeat awards based on missions flown, the Prisoner of War Medal, the World War II Victory Medal, the European Theater Medal with two battle stars for the campaigns in which I participated (pre-invasion and post-invasion), and the American Theater Medal. I also have the Presidential Unit Citation awarded to everybody in our Bomb Group for its "Grand Slam" performance in the month of May 1944 when we led the entire Eighth Air Force in the five major categories of effective bomb-ing. These awards came at a price which I was always willing to pay and did to the best of my ability. In March 2009, the French government further showed its high regard for American combat veterans who fought in France in WWII by awarding me the Che-valier Legion of Honor. My record of flying six bombing missions against enemy targets in France in war time was accepted as suf-ficient to qualify for this prestigious award. I'm very grateful to receive this honor.

Figure 65. Author's medals bordered by German Officer's Dress Dagger and German Army Bayonet: from the top: Navigator's Wings, Distinguished Flying Cross, Air Medal , POW Medal (post-war) flanked by Presidential Unit Citation and silver parachute, WWII Victory Medal, European Theater Medal with two battle stars and American Theater Medal.

THE STORY BEHIND THE TITLE OF THIS BOOK

One Saturday morning at Advanced Navigation School in the fall of 1943, I and my fellow cadets stood by our bunks at attention for inspection. As the officers went down the line, they stopped in front of me. One of them tauntingly asked: "Casey, why did you join the Army?" The 18 year-old kid in me answered: **"To fight for my country, sir."** My classmates laughed aloud but I let it pass. It was a good answer to a ridiculous question and it still is today.

Donald E. Casey, J.D., DFC.

E-mail: doncasey@mail2world.com
Website: www.doncasey.info

For further information, contact the Air Force Academy Library, P.O. Box 188, Colorado Springs, CO 80840.

ABOUT THE AUTHOR

Donald E. Casey volunteered for the Aviation Cadet program of the U.S. Army Air Corps in December, 1942 at age 18 and was called for active duty in February 1943. On completing aerial navigation school on October 23, 1943 he was commissioned a 2d Lieutenant and was awarded his silver navigator's wings, still age 18 by two weeks.

He flew as a navigator in B-17 bombers on 28 combat missions out of England with the 379th Bomb Group of the 8th Air Force until June 18, 1944 when his aircraft was shot down by anti-aircraft fire and he and four crew members survived while the other four were killed in action that day.

Lt. Casey was captured by German soldiers and spent six months in Stalag Luft III (South Compound) the "Great Escape" prison camp in Zagan, Poland with 10,000 captured Allied flying officers. On January 27, 1945 Russian Army troops approached Zagan and were close enough for him and his fellow prisoners to hear the explosions of the cannons from less than 30 miles away. He and his fellow prisoners were evacuated westward under armed guard on foot in a subzero blizzard and via cattle- car train to Stalag VII-A at Moosburg, Germany in Bavaria. He and 110,000 Allied POW's were finally liberated by General George Patton's 3rd Army on April 29, 1945 and rescued amid starvation, exposure and disease.

On returning to the United States in June of 1945, he was mustered out of the Army in time to enroll in Dartmouth College in New Hampshire in the Fall where he received a Bachelor of Arts degree in Economics in June 1948.

After College he worked briefly in New York as a trainee in the investment banking business after which he was transferred by his company to Denver, Colorado for three years. In 1952 he returned to his home city in Chicago, Illinois where he worked for a large life and health insurance company for three years while attending law school at the University of Loyola graduating in 1957.

Figure 66. The author pictured after receiving the Chevalier of the French Legion of Honor medal from the Republic of France in August 2009.

In 1957, Casey joined the Chicago law firm of Brundage & Short practicing trial law in the civil courts in Cook County, Illinois and was admitted to practice in the U.S. District Court for the Northern District of Illinois and the U.S. Courts of Appeals for the Seventh and Fifth Circuits.

He is still engaged in the active practice of law in his fifty-second year as an attorney in Chicago with the law firm of Springer, Casey & Dienstag, P.C.

After the war, Don married Anne Hollis Casey with whom he had four sons; his wife Anne passed away in 1976 and he is presently married to Alice Rae Casey and has two grandchildren and three step-grandchildren.

Mr. Casey's hobbies are golf, jazz piano, writing, sports and photography. He is 85 years of age and enjoys speaking about his war experiences before high school students and other interested groups.

In 2009, he was awarded the Chevalier of the French Legion of Honor medal for his combat service against Nazi-German Armed Forces in France during the War leading to the liberation of that nation. The U.S. Army has honored him with the Distinguished Flying Cross, the Air Medal with three oak leaf clusters, the Prisoner of War Medal,

The WWII European Theater Medal with two battle stars, the Presidential Unit Citation, the WWII Victory Medal and the American Theater Medal.

This book has earned him the World War II Writer's Award for 2009 by the Sterling Cooper Publishing Division.

INDEX

LaVergne, TN USA
25 October 2010

202198LV00012B/16/P